SHIFTING THE BOUNDARIES

Transformation of the Languages of Public and Private in the Eighteenth Century

SHIFTING THE BOUNDARIES

Transformation of the Languages of
Public and Private in the Eighteenth Century

edited by Dario Castiglione
and Lesley Sharpe

UNIVERSITY
of
EXETER
PRESS

First published in 1995 by
University of Exeter Press
Reed Hall, Streatham Drive
Exeter, Devon EX4 4QR
UK

British Library Cataloguing in Publication Data
A catalogue record of this book is available
from the British Library

ISBN 0 85989 444 4

Typeset in Garamond by
Kestrel Data, Exeter

Printed and bound in Great Britain by
Antony Rowe Ltd, Wiltshire

Contents

List of Contributors

Jonathan Barry (Department of History, University of Exeter). Editor with Joseph Melling of *Culture in History* (1992) and author of other studies on eighteenth-century social and local history.

John Brewer (Department of History, European University Institute, Florence and University of California, Los Angeles). Author of *The Sinews of Power* (1989) and of other studies on seventeenth-century and eighteenth-century European culture.

Dario Castiglione (Department of Politics, University of Exeter). Co-editor of *Political Studies* 1996 Special Issue on 'The Constitution in Transformation' and author of other studies on seventeenth-century and eighteenth-century political thought.

Malcolm Cook (Department of French, University of Exeter). General editor of *Modern Language Review*, and author of *Fictional France: Representations of Social Reality in Fiction 1775–1800* and of other studies on eighteenth-century French literature.

Dena Goodman (Department of History, Louisiana State University). Author of *The Republic of Letters: A Cultural History of the French Enlightenment* (1994) and of other studies on eighteenth-century French culture and society.

Vivien Jones (Department of English, University of Leeds). Editor of *Women in the Eighteenth Century: Constructions of Femininity* (1990) and author of books on Henry James and Jane Austen and of other studies on women and literature.

John Christian Laursen (Department of Political Science, University of California, Riverside). Author of *The Politics of Skepticism in the Ancients, Montaigne, Hume, and Kant* (1992) and of other studies on eighteenth-century political thought.

Maria Luisa Pesante (Department of History, University of Turin). Editor with Marco Geuna of *Passioni, interessi, convenzioni. Discussioni settecentesche su virtù e civiltà* (1992) and author of other studies on the origins of Political Economy.

Mark Salber Phillips (Department of History, Carleton University). Author of a forthcoming book on historical writing in the eighteenth century and of other studies on Renaissance Italy.

Lesley Sharpe (Department of German, University of Exeter). Germanic editor of *Modern Language Review*, and author of *Friedrich Schiller. Drama, Thought and Politics* (1991) and of other studies on eighteenth-century German literature.

Edoardo Tortarolo (Department of History, University of Turin). Editor of *Storia della Storiografia* and author of *La ragione sulla Sprea. Coscienza storica e cultura politica dell'Illuminismo berlinese* (1989).

Ursula Vogel (Department of Government, University of Manchester). Editor with Michael Moran of *The Frontiers of Citizenship* (1991), and of other studies on the history of political thought.

Preface

This is a collection of essays dealing with the problematic boundaries between the public and the private spheres in Europe (Britain, France and Germany in particular) from the late seventeenth to the end of the eighteenth century. The essays arose from a two-year project organized by the Eighteenth-Century Studies Group at the University of Exeter with the aim of examining, in the light of the latest research in diverse fields, the relevance and applicability of this powerful dichotomy.

Scholars of the period generally agree that the public/private distinction is in many ways artificial and misleading. In their more abstract meaning, public and private provide what Heinz Kohut (in *The Analysis of the Self*, New York, 1971) has termed 'experience-distant' (as opposed to 'experience-near') categories, and they seem therefore incapable of shedding light on discourses and self-perceptions which pre-date the modern use of the distinction. Scholars also notice that, although graphically powerful, the association between public and private and physical and social *spaces* is misleading. Other images are often used to make the point that there is no neat separation between the two spheres, while the position of the subject (or the spectator) makes boundary distinctions mostly relative.

Public and private nevertheless provide a starting point from which to explore different kinds of activity in a variety of areas and the development of various social spaces. Moreover, in different ways in different times, the distinction has functioned as one of those 'great dichotomies' which juridical, social and historical sciences have deployed—both descriptively and axiologically—to map their own fields of enquiry (cf. N. Bobbio, *Stato, governo, società*, Turin, 1985). The advantage of such 'great dichotomies' is that on the one hand they are jointly exhaustive of the intellectual universe to which they are meant to be applied and that, on the other, they are mutually exclusive. Both qualities contribute to the totalizing nature of the distinction and to its paradigmatic function, thus subsuming within its own conceptual field other, reputedly less important, dichotomies.

Current notions of public and private broadly reflect the either/or nature of the distinction as theorized in liberal thinking. This is not the only historical form in which the dichotomy has appeared. Its original formulation was in Roman Law, where what pertained to the Roman polity (*ad statum rei romanae*) and what to the utility of single individuals (*ad singulorum utilitatem*) were distinguished under two separate branches of the law, which—in Medieval and Modern times —came progressively to define the mutually exclusive, but sometimes disputed, domains of public and private law. A parallel development is to be found in the civic humanist conceptualization of the distinction between the virtues and types of relationships in the political community and those in the household.

Both conceptions, clearly available in the eighteenth century, are somewhat different from the liberal paradigm which is believed to have developed at that time. This is why the Enlightenment is often seen as the crucial period for the formation of the modern distinction between public and private. But, of course, the exact nature of the liberal conception is contested. It has been suggested that it should be considered as the syncretic product of two different models, the 'individualist' and the 'organic'. The dominant concept in the individualist model is obviously the private, determined by posing the naturality of 'specified persons' at its centre. This model considers things public only residually, as those located beyond the ever increasing circles of 'individuality' and self-realization through the aggregation of separate natural individuals. The organic model regards the public as more than the simple sum of separate individuals, and therefore takes the social group as its primary element, and by drawing ever decreasing circles arrives at its more 'individualized' manifestations.

A different account of the conceptual and ideological strains emerging through the liberal conception is the one that emphasizes the divided nature of the private, which comprises both the intimate sphere of the family and the de-personalized network of social (but non-political) relationships. This apparent distinction within the private sphere has been described as reflecting an ideological split between classical liberalism, which establishes the separation of public and private as a way of delimiting and protecting the 'social' from the 'political', and liberal romanticism, which is deeply concerned about the oppressive force of the 'social' over the more intimate and individualistically-determined sphere of the 'personal'. Safeguarding the 'personal', so it is maintained, may require a stronger right to privacy against the demands of state, public opinion, the traditionalism of community, and also of kin.

More recently, feminist writers have taken a different view, by stressing how these various representations of the public/private distinction miss the fundamental point of the genderedness characterizing the way in which these spheres have been historically constructed. Liberal and romantic aspirations to find a space where the self can recover liberty and find respite from the demands of either strangers or kin (or both) are therefore deemed to be inscribed (in the sense of both being conceivable and being practically realizable) in the subordination of women. Moreover, it is symptomatic, or so they maintain, that the paradigmatic institution of privacy, the family, is either neglected as part of the private sphere—as happens in the dichotomy between the political and the social—or partly idealized, as is the case of the opposition between social and personal.

The contested nature of current conceptions of public and private makes it the more difficult to establish with precision at which point they became available and indeed dominant. The availability, noted above, of alternative conceptions, and their likely contribution to the shaping of modern ideas of public and private, is another reason for looking at the emergence of this distinction as the complex product of diverse discourses and social practices. The title of this volume has thus a double focus. First, it refers to the conscious efforts of men and women in the Enlightenment period to explore and discuss the boundaries in their experience and points to the broader historical changes that led to or militated against consciousness of categories such as public and private. Secondly, it suggests the aim of the volume, which is to bridge different historical traditions and discourses and, by deconstructing accepted notions of the public/private divide, to contribute to a more complex and differentiated view of the Enlightenment period.

The influential studies of Jürgen Habermas (*Strukturwandel der Öffentlichkeit*) and Reinhart Koselleck (*Kritik und Krise: Eine Studie zur Pathogenesis der bürgerlichen Welt*), on the one hand, and Philippe Ariès and Roger Chartier (*Histoire de la vie privée*), on the other, have had a profound influence on our understanding of the complex patterns of formation of the public and private spheres in early modern times. While acknowledging the ground-breaking work of these historians and taking them as a starting point, many of the essays in this volume explore the more subtle pattern of conceptual oppositions emerging from specific circles and relevant in specific contexts. The fruitfulness of the interdisciplinary approach becomes obvious when one is attempting to reconstruct various kinds of publics, in the cultural and social spheres as well as in the political realm. A number of essays deal with the nature of public opinion in relation to state control and with the role of the intelligentsia in creating a scrutinizable politics.

Several essays in the volume continue the debate on the gender bias of the public/private distinction, revealing also the crucial importance of the period in bringing about a new synthesis of the processes of gender discrimination and category formation. The result is a less stark distinction between public and private than is often assumed. A number of essays investigate non-political forms of sociability and the complex relation of various types of writing to the categories of public and private. Though interdisciplinary and varied in approach, the essays are meant to complement one another and have been arranged in such a way as to help the reader make the links between them. The collection is completed by a postscript which unravels the principal lines of the historical interpretation emerging from the essays, relating them back to the sociological scheme found in Habermas and suggesting new perspectives from which to review it.

A number of the essays in this collection are based on or related to papers delivered at two symposia held at the University of Exeter in 1992 and 1993. These were the focal points of the two-year project on public and private. We should like to thank the Nuffield Foundation and the British Academy for the conference grants we received. The Research Committee of the University of Exeter supported the project, and we also received financial help from the Faculties of Social Sciences and Arts, the Departments of Politics and of History and Archaeology and from the Schools of English and American Studies and Modern Languages. We should also like to thank those who contributed to the events by presenting papers or chairing discussions: Ros Ballaster, Thomas Crow, Tia Denora, Iain Hampsher-Monk, Eckhart Hellmuth, Ludmilla Jordanova, Colin Jones, Paul Langford, Günter Lottes, Jo McDonagh, Dorinda Outram, Jean Quéniart, Jane Spencer and Bob Witkin.

Dario Castiglione
Lesley Sharpe

One

This, that and the other: Public, Social and Private in the Seventeenth and Eighteenth Centuries

John Brewer

In this essay I offer an analytical synthesis of the problems that I believe recur in accounts of the categories of public and private in the early modern era.[1] I want to begin my discussion of the public and the private with two different but familiar historical narratives, one German, the other French. The first, that of Jürgen Habermas and Reinhart Koselleck, is concerned with the public; the second, that of Philippe Ariès and Roger Chartier, is concerned with private life. As the American scholar, Dena Goodman, has recently pointed out in an illuminating essay, these two stories, though told from very different perspectives, have much in common.[2] The German works are concerned with politics and the public; the French, though they address the role of the state, are more interested in the intimate world of the family and of forms of sociability.

The two key German texts are Jürgen Habermas's *Strukturwandel der Öffentlichkeit*, published in 1962, translated into French in 1978 and into English in 1989, and Reinhart Koselleck's *Kritik und Krise: Eine Studie zur Pathogenesis der bürgerlichen Welt* (1959), translated into French in 1979 and into English in 1988. Both of these works discuss the emerging distinction between public and private in the late seventeenth and eighteenth centuries, but their perspectives are rather different. Koselleck is concerned to trace the origins of modern, utopian and totalitarian ideologies (of both Left and Right), whose first manifestation he sees in the Jacobinism of the French Revolution. Habermas, on the other hand, is concerned to explain the moment at which a realm of discourse and the institutions that sustained it first emerged in the form of a critical public sphere, one whose rational deliberations, often harshly critical of the state, were not compromised either by their commodification or by political coercion. Koselleck pessimistically pursues the origins of Terror; Habermas, an optimist in the short (though not the long) run, pursues the origins of civil society.[3]

Koselleck argues that the political distinction between public and private emerged in the aftermath of the religious wars of the seventeenth century. The exceptionally divisive conflicts that rent Europe produced a new theory of the state, one that drained it of morality, leaving it with an ideology of *raison d'état* that demanded from its subjects only outward conformity, whilst leaving them private space in which they could realize their faith and exercise their conscience. Out of this private sphere emerged the Republic of Letters, at first concerned to avoid matters of state and politics, to assert its transcendence of the partial, but eventually, especially in its Enlightened forms, claiming critical superiority over the organs and practitioners of politics. This claim to innocence was, in Koselleck's view, the most dangerous feature of this sort of criticism, for it legitimized the rejection of political compromise and blinded its proponents to their own desire for power, creating a utopian intolerance of any constraint on its moral view.

Koselleck links this politics that refused to recognize its political character, what he calls a hypocritical 'politics by indirection', to continental Freemasonry and to the secret order of the Illuminati founded by Adam Weishaupt in that year of liberty 1776. The Masons embodied many of the values of the Republic of Letters, notably an emphasis on brotherhood within the society, a determination to transcend the conditions of inequality and the forms of distinction, political and religious, that obtained in society at large. In this respect they were much like the numerous societies and associations—reading clubs, debating societies and the like—that were part of the sociability of eighteenth-century Europe. But the Masons added a special ingredient—secrecy. Secrecy, according to Koselleck, was justified by the Masons as necessary to protect the morally legitimate activities of such societies; but in practice it served only to encourage a politics without accountability and responsibility, a politics of delusion. It was the obverse of a transcendent, all-embracing moral view that refused to recognize the restraints of politics and which could therefore claim every aspect of social life as its object of scrutiny.[4]

I do not want to pursue this line of inquiry, which obviously links with a large body of work on the French Revolution and which is consonant with, though not the same as, the position adopted by François Furet and others. Nor do I wish to deal with some of the obvious historical objections to a theory that sees the opponents of the state as excluded from it rather than occupying an ambiguous position within it.[5] Rather, I want to point to the interesting way in which Koselleck elaborates 'the private' and 'the public', for in Masonry Koselleck reinscribes private as 'secret', rather than as merely 'particular' or not *res publica*, and delineates the public as a universal category which means that the private as 'particular' is totally erased. It is as if the opportunity of the late seventeenth century, the chance to create politics in the sphere of the private conscience, was lost, being replaced by a hybrid that duplicated both the secrecy of 'mysteries of state' and the claims to universal power of the absolutist state. The covert politics of the Masons undercut their challenge to the absolutist state because their commitment to secrecy presupposed a social order which was otherwise utterly transparent to those who held political power. The opportunity to create an intermediate politics between the state and the private subject was lost. When the assumptions behind the Masonic vision were revealed in the Revolution they produced a limitless politics of Terror.

The sense of a lost opportunity is also present in Habermas's very different account. Habermas's object is to chart the history and explain the consequences of the emergence of what he calls 'the public sphere'. Habermas defines 'public sphere' as 'a forum in which the private people, come together to form a public, readied themselves to compel public authority to legitimate itself before public opinion'.[6] He sees this phenomenon as having a specific site (the term 'forum' is significant here), one that is urban rather than courtly, and which is embodied in a number of institutions, most notably the clubs, salons, coffee-house coteries and tavern societies that flourished in such abundance in European polite society (Habermas, pp. 30–36). These institutions and their activities were sustained, in turn, by the vital institution of the press. The published word, writes Habermas, was 'the decisive mark' of the 'new domain of a public sphere' (Habermas, p. 16).

These institutions, Habermas argues, had a number of distinctive features. First, in contradistinction to the hierarchical polity of which they were a part, they observed within the institution an ethos of equality which self-consciously disregarded or ostensibly elided differences of social status among their members. This did not necessarily entail a commitment to equality in society at large but it did affect the conduct of members within the individual groupings (Habermas,

p. 36). Secondly, though these institutions were not equivalent to or coterminous with the public, they nevertheless claimed to speak for the public and to define who its members were. They saw the body of the public as potentially or in principle inclusive, capable of embracing all members of civil society, though in practice this inclusive view was elided into one that confined membership to the (male) owners of property. Thirdly, members of the public sphere took their brief to be the discussion of the fine arts and literature and of those matters of policy which had formerly been defined as the 'mysteries' of church and state. Fourth, if their brief was culture and politics, their judge was 'reason', the exercise of human deliberation and orderly criticism free from either domination or coercion. And, finally, their court and schoolhouse was the press, notably the periodical press, exemplified in the English case by the greatest of what Habermas erroneously calls 'the moral weeklies', the *Spectator* of Addison and Steele. Such publications Habermas argues, enabled the public to hold 'a mirror to itself; it did not yet come to a self-understanding through the detour of a reflection on works of philosophy and literature, art and science, but through entering itself into "literature as an object"' (Habermas, p. 43). Put another way, the public was enabled through the press to imagine itself.

Habermas attributes these developments to changes in both economy and the state: to the growth of traffic in both commerce and news, and to the increasingly depersonalized character of public authority in a mercantilist state that was more and more interested in the use of news and information as an instrument of diplomatic, commercial and military policy, as a means of controlling the private sphere of commodity production. Taken together these two developments led private individuals in civil society to organize themselves as a public to contest the authority or, at least, to affect state policy and adjudicate its claims to regulate civil society.

Habermas's account isolates three separate but sometimes overlapping spheres. The first is that of public authority and the state, what in the eighteenth century was often referred to as 'police', but which also includes the realm of the court; the second is the 'public sphere' of politics and letters centred on 'the town'; and the third is the private sphere which, in turn, divides into the world of commodity exchange and social labour, on the one hand, and the family's internal space, what is sometimes termed the 'intimate sphere', on the other (Habermas, p. 30).

I want to emphasize certain features of Habermas's argument. First, although he maps the public sphere onto certain spaces—the town, voluntary associations and the like—it is the nature of the activities in these spaces that creates the public sphere. It is their capacity to pursue a public good adjudicated through the procedures of unconstrained reason that creates a public sphere. The abandonment of such rational, universal ends amounts to the dissolution or disintegration of the public sphere into its aggregate parts. Without its object it ceases to be. It follows that the public sphere is an unstable and precarious entity, threatened by the two forces that brought it into being, namely the absolutist state and the sphere of commodity production, and therefore likely either to be absorbed by the sphere of public authority or to disaggregate into the private realm.

The precise significance of this formulation becomes apparent when we consider what Habermas has to say about the conditions that obtained in the eighteenth century and how they changed in the nineteenth. Habermas concedes that the development of a critical public depended in the first instance on the private interests of those who ran the press and sold culture. 'To be sure' he writes, 'at one time the commercialization of cultural goods had been the *precondition* for rational-critical debate' (Habermas, p. 164). But he goes on to argue that such debate was protected from the contaminated forces of the market place: such discussion, he says 'was itself in principle excluded from the exchange relationships of the market and remained the centre of exactly that sphere in which property-owning private people would meet as "human beings" and only as such' (Habermas, p. 164). All this changed, he argues, between about 1830 and the late nineteenth century, a period when the press became primarily a profit-seeking enterprise and was not dedicated to stringent criticism, when the public fractured into fragments, and when culture itself became a matter of leisure and entertainment rather than strenuous debate.

> The public sphere in the world of letters was replaced by the pseudo-public or sham-private world of cultural consumption . . . When leisure was nothing but a complement to time spent on the job, it could be no more than a different arena for the pursuit of private business affairs that were not transformed into a public communication between private people. To be sure, the individuated satisfaction of needs might be achieved in a public fashion, namely, in the company of many others; but a public sphere itself did not emerge from such a situation. When the law of the market governing the sphere of commodity exchange and of social labour also pervaded the sphere reserved for private people as a public, rational-critical debate had a tendency to be replaced by consumption, and the web of public communication unraveled

into acts of individuated reception, however uniform in mode. (Habermas, pp. 160–61)

The public sphere dissolved into the private, removing the critical buffer that opposed the all-powerful state.

The institutions that until the nineteenth century had ensured the coherence of the public as a critically debating entity were weakened. The public divided into 'minorities of specialists who put their reason to use nonpublicly and the great mass of consumers whose receptiveness is public and uncritical' (Habermas, p. 175). This process of fragmentation, Habermas maintains, was largely led by 'upwardly mobile groups whose status was still in need of cultural legitimation' (Habermas, p. 174). What had begun as a culture of criticism became a culture of conformity in which the public sphere was filled with 'exchanges about tastes and preferences' (Habermas, p. 171) and politics became a matter of horsetrading among the elite and of the manipulation of the public. Gone was legitimation before the public; now politics was a matter of special interest groups and political associations, notably parties, seeking to fabricate public support.

So what for Koselleck was the moment at which a benighted, moralizing, totalitarian politics was born is for Habermas the point at which a civilized politics of rational discourse was briefly made. Indeed Habermas wants to argue that the formation of an effective, critical public sphere was the product of a special historical moment— roughly that of the eighteenth-century Enlightenment—during which it became uniquely possible to create an effective and coherent public sphere. There is, as several commentators have pointed out, more than a hint of nostalgia for the Age of Reason in Habermas's account.[7]

The second point that I wish to stress is the close relationship that Habermas posits between the emergence of the public sphere and the development of a sphere of intimacy, one in which a sense of freedom and pure subjectivity can be realized and which he associates with the bourgeois family. For, as Habermas stresses, one of the key issues debated in the public sphere was that of freedom and subjectivity, of what it meant to realize oneself as a person. The forms this discussion took, he emphasizes, were frequently literary and usually rendered through the medium of print. This sense of pure humanness was a public construction which depended both on the representation of the intimate sphere and on the public elaboration of its values. In short, the public sphere produced an unprecedented discussion and unparalleled public exposure of private life (Habermas, pp. 43–51).

The chronology that Koselleck and Habermas adopt is also that to be found in the collaborative third volume of *Histoire de la vie privée*, at least in the view of one of its general editors, Philippe Ariès. In its general conception *Histoire de la vie privée* seeks to chart the process by which a relatively undifferentiated society is distinguished into public and private realms, a process that Ariès attributes to the rise of the state, an increase in literacy and to new forms of religion. Ariès identifies a number of measures of privacy: the zoning of the body and an accompanying modesty; the valorizing of solitude; the development of a private literature of self-reflection and autobiography; the importance attached to close friendship; new ideas about the importance of daily life; and changes in the organization of living space. These developments are seen as both signs and consequences of a process by which individuals came to occupy the social space freed by the rise of the state and the decline of communal forms of sociability. Into that space were inserted new forms of association and conviviality which were made up of individual private persons.[8]

Again, I want to stress certain aspects of this account. First, in a number of obvious respects, Ariès's analysis, especially as it is elaborated by Chartier, bears similarities to and is compatible with the account offered by Habermas. Indeed Chartier explicitly alludes to Habermas's account.[9] The labels attached to certain developments may differ (the institutions and practices of Habermas's public sphere appear in *Histoire de la vie privée* as aspects of privacy) but we recognize them as the same phenomena.

Nevertheless, it is difficult to position *Histoire de la vie privée* in relation to Habermas' formulation because the French text seems to embody more than one view of the subject. Collaborative volumes are always difficult to shape, and one cannot but be struck by how there seem to be at least two books in the third volume of *Histoire de la vie privée*, one that Ariès conceived, whose primary focus is intimacy and individuality and the loss of community restraint, and one that Chartier edited, which is more concerned with the shifting line between the public and the private, more interested in forms of sociability, and more conscious of the fact that activities such as reading can have differing valence and significance. What I am saying is that I detect a persistent tension in *Histoire de la vie privée* between different conceptions of the private and also between different ways of treating it as a subject. One approach, that of Ariès, errs towards an essentialist view of privacy, tending to see it as a thing with specific features, while the other (to which, as we shall see, I am much more sympathetic) regards the line between the public and the private as a matter of spatial and political perspective and as matter for persistent adjustment and dispute.

7

Whether we regard it as a virtue or a failing, it seems that *Histoire de la vie privée* does not adopt a consistent approach to its subject.

Both Habermas's account of a fragile and potentially privatized public sphere and the persistent tension that I detect in *Histoire de la vie privée* around the notion of private as 'social', rather than as 'intimate' or 'personal', point to the difficulties we face when trying to interpret the status of practices that occur in the large grey area between that which was palpably a matter of state and that which was obviously intimate. I want to explore this territory with several objects in mind: I want to try to unpackage the several meanings of the terms public and private as used in the eighteenth century, and I want to show how those meanings could shift in time and space.

Unpackaging Public and Private

Let me begin by examining the usage of the terms 'public' and 'private' in one major English language source, namely the *Eighteenth-Century Short Title Catalogue* which aims to record complete information on every title in English published between 1700 and 1800. There are more than seven thousand items (7,607) in the *ESTC* in which the term 'public' or 'publick' appears on the title page and more than fifteen hundred (1,594 to be exact) which include the term 'private'.[10] I do not want to dwell on the use of the term public(k), except to say that the meanings of the term are fairly predictable, following Dr Johnson's definitions in his Dictionary. They are, as an adjective: 'belonging to a state or nation'; 'open, notorious, generally known'; 'general, done by many'; 'regarding the good of the community', and 'open for general entertainment'. And as a noun: 'the general body of mankind, or a state or nation; the people', and 'open view; general notice'.[11] So all of the larger definitions of public with which Habermas is concerned— publick in the Roman law sense of connected with policy and the state, public as concerned with a general good, and public as 'publicity' —were to be found in eighteenth-century English usage.

But it is on the private that I wish to focus. The disparity between the frequency with which the terms 'public' and 'private' were used, though it may partly be explained by the nature of the source (the character of the title page) nevertheless alerts us to an important feature of the term 'private' in this period, namely its residual character, the degree to which it is what the public is not. Of course, the terms depended symbiotically upon one another for their definition, but the relationship was not symmetrical. The 'private' was 'the other'. This view did not, of course, go unchallenged. Indeed, one might postulate that one of the features of the eighteenth and nineteenth centuries was the repeated attempt to transpose this asymmetry, to treat the private as primary and the public as other. But, as we shall see, this process was repeatedly inhibited by the capacity of the public to absorb and represent the private.

How was the term 'private' used? As in the case of 'public' much of the usage is predictable. Economic activity is characterized as 'private' in two senses, in that it is not the activity of the state but of particular individuals and because it has particular rather than general ends: we have 'private wealth', 'private traders', 'private credit', and 'private contracts'. This is the private realm that Habermas subsumes under the heading of commodity exchange. We have private institutions or practices—a private literary society or private club—whose privacy lies in the fact that they do not afford general access, even though their objects may be general and public. They are the private institutions that help to make up Habermas's public sphere. And there are, as we might expect, the private territories of mind and body. 'Private judgment' is contrasted with 'church authority', construed either pejoratively as 'free thinking' or in a better light as individual conscience or 'private devotion'. Matters corporeal, whether medical or sexual, are repeatedly described as 'private', something that we might best translate as 'intimate'. (It should be added that when private is used as meaning 'secret' or is linked with the adjective 'secret' it is an almost certain indication that the subject-matter will be illicit political or sexual activity, and quite often both. Secrecy is the realm of courts and closets, whether as the 'secret springs' of politics or as the 'secret disease' contracted sexually.)

But the most common usage of private is one in which the term is contrasted with some larger (more public) body: private tuition is contrasted with schools, private devotions and private Christians with the church, private beneficence with public charity, and private individuals with the family. As these examples indicate, the boundary of the private is constantly shifting. When contrasted with the state, the private realm is coextensive with civil society; but it can also be confined to families, though these, in turn, can be viewed as public when contrasted with individuals. The private here is 'the not public'; private is always particular, but some privates are more particular than others, and the most particular is the individual, seen either corporally or mentally. It is as if public and private are shifting territories on a map, means by which social space was defined. This feature of 'public' and 'private' was recognized by eighteenth-century English commentators who spoke of the public and private 'spheres',[12] although interestingly enough, in view of the importance placed on a private domestic sphere in recent feminist analysis of the bourgeois family, it was unusual to equate the private and domestic spheres. Indeed the terms domestic, domestick and domestical appear rarely on title pages and are more likely to refer to native, as opposed to foreign matters, than to the household. There was, however, an increase in the number of titles concerned with the 'domestic' as household in the 1780s and 1790s, though even here there is little evidence to show that what is being discussed is a *space* rather than a value.

What then do we infer from this brief examination of the use and meaning of private? We learn that there is no fixed definition of private but many different definitions, some of which depend upon territories and spaces, others of which depend upon ends. The designation of a practice as private depends in large part upon the position of the viewer. (I use this visual metaphor deliberately to emphasize the importance of position and space.) It is not possible to draw the boundary of the private from within; it has to be envisaged from outside, although the way in which it is imagined or represented will vary. This is true even of the individual, of the self, who engages in 'self-examination', 'self-dedication', 'self-love' or even 'self-defilement' or 'self-abuse'. To put it another way, if there is no outside, nothing is private, for there is nothing private to survey. And it is this that alerts us to two of the most crucial issues in a fruitful analysis of the public and the private, the importance of understanding the processes by which the one is represented in and by the other, and of paying particular attention not to those spaces at the polar ends of public and private but to the spaces in between—those areas, borders or boundaries which repeatedly shift and which are repeatedly crossed.

I can best explain what I mean by these rather abstract remarks by way of an example, that of letter writing and journal keeping. Letter writing, particularly the writing of 'familiar letters' to those who were lovers, family or intimate friends, has long been seen as one of the signs of modern privacy. Expressive of private thoughts or intimacies, written in the private study or closet away from the gaze of others, concerned to reveal the private character of their author as well as the special character of the relationship between the author and his or her correspondent, they embody many of those features identified in *Histoire de la vie privée* as symptomatic of a new sense of individuality and intimacy.[13] Their special status is revealed by the sense conveyed by Samuel Richardson in *Clarissa* that the forcible acquisition of private correspondence is tantamount to the (sexual) violation of the author's body and by Antoine-Joseph-Michel de Servan's analogy between the seal of a private letter and the hymen of a virtuous woman.[14] But, as these two remarks which link corporeal and psychic integrity—one made in a best selling epistolary novel, the other in an attack on the practices of the *cabinet noir*[15]—indicate, it was and is exceptionally difficult to retain the integrity of private correspondence.

It might seem that, in concentrating on the act of creating letters—as opposed to the subsequent history of the letter—we can retain their privacy. Seventeenth- and eighteenth-century letter-writing manuals in England placed great store in the ability of correspondents to express their feelings transparently, naturally and conversationally, an ability that was often seen as especially feminine.[16] Yet, as always, the fabrication of naturalness was an elaborate art, one which depended on acquaintance not only with writing manuals but with exemplary collections of published letters such as those of Madame de Sévigné, which for much of the eighteenth century remained the exemplum of genteel familiar correspondence in both France and England. The skills of private revelation and intimate conversation were learned through the public medium of print. Many correspondents, male and female, shaped their subjectivity through their letter writing, but they were able to do so only because of the models and conventions that were publicly available to them.

Every letter, of course, implies a reader, and correspondents usually gave some indication of the intended ambit and scope of a letter—its degree of privacy and its intended audience. Letters would be endorsed 'for my eyes only', or marked 'destroy this letter' (how often has this instruction prompted the wry smile of the historian?); they were sometimes divided into those parts which might be read to a group or broadcast quite widely and into those for the eyes of a single correspondent. Letters were even shaped for those readers whose uninvited presence intruded upon the addressee of the letter. Correspondents in England and France were aware that their letters might be opened by the authorities; they reacted accordingly. They might use cypher and disguise, offer false trails and information to the authorities, or even address them openly in a letter ostensibly intended for a private correspondent.

In the literature of privacy we privilege certain moments in the life of a letter, especially those of its conception and its first receipt. But letters have a history which, as letter-writing manuals warned and as correspondents often complained, was difficult to control.[17] Even privately preserved correspondence was often annotated, ordered and even subsequently censored; it became a structured collection which bore the stamp of its collector (who may or may not have been the original recipient) as much as of its original author.

Of course, much ostensibly private correspondence had a larger object than that of private transmission. It was a commonplace that one of the most important ways in which knowledge grew was through a *commerce de lettres*.[18] It was the key device of the Republic of Letters, the means by which the London Royal Society expanded its knowledge and influence.[19] When radicals in the 1790s wished to organize a national movement for political change, they set up *corresponding societies*. These networks of letter writers were public, even when their correspondence did not end up in print. The letters were deemed public both because they were written to be read by a body of men engaged in a common pursuit and because that purpose was a public one, concerned either with culture or politics.

Correspondence held the Republic of Letters together. It created spatial links between Lutheran pastors in small towns in Germany, Huguenot publishers in the Low Countries and scientists in Paris. And it shaped the hierarchies of status within the Republic, in which one's prominence as a correspondent was a vital importance. As the classical scholar and politician, Gisbert Cuper boasted: 'I have a hundred or so volumes of letters, with the responses of Scholars, who honour me with their friendship and correspondence.'[20] Quantity, of course, was not all. A famous correspondent—a Bayle, Locke, Voltaire or Diderot—was a major catch. Luminaries of the Republic of Letters and the Enlightenment were notoriously pestered by solicitous correspondents. Such (often unwarranted and unwanted) intrusions were justified by those who perpetrated them on the grounds that the object in writing was public not private. But they would then boast of the intimacy they enjoyed through private correspondence with a great man, often producing the letters as proof of their privileged familiarity. Such stratagems showed how a letter writer could play on that tension between public and private that was so much a part of epistolary relations: the original contact was justified as a public act but then transmuted into a form of intimacy.

The point at which the public and private valences of letter writing were most often manipulated was when private correspondence acquired the public medium of print. Attention to this phenomenon has been largely confined to such famous collections of letters as those of Madame de Sévigné or Lord Chesterfield and to the development of the epistolary novel both in France and England—one thinks immediately of Laclos and Richardson. In both these cases form and content appear private, familiar and intimate, even if they are exposed to the public gaze of the reader of print. But the use of epistolary form in published work was, as Dena Goodman has shown in the case of France, far more widespread.[21] The same was true in England. Periodicals and magazines used letters from readers (original, doctored and fictional) in order to discuss all manner of subjects. The first series of the *Spectator*, which consisted of 555 essays issued between March 1711 and December 1712, included 250 such letters, some of which survive in their original manuscript form.[22] Newspapers relied upon correspondents for material or presented their contents in epistolary form. In the first four months of 1764 *The Gazetteer*, a London paper, received 861 letters, of which 560 were published 'at length'; 262 noticed under the heading 'Observations of our Correspondents'; thirty-nine letters remained to hand.[23] Most of these were not concerned with private matters but with the public issues of the day. Similarly 'Letter to' or 'Letter from' or 'Letters upon' were among the commonest forms taken by polemical works, usually pamphlets, on politics, religion and culture. The *Eighteenth-Century Short Title Catalogue* contains more than 20,000 such items.

Letters, whether on personal and private subjects in such periodicals as John Dunton's *Athenian Mercury* or in newspapers on affairs of state, played on the distinction between public and private. In both instances the letters were anonymous or pseudonymous. They were from 'a gentlewoman of small Fortune', 'a lady in the country' or, when discussing matters of politics, from 'Cato' or 'Junius' or 'An Independent Freeholder'. Correspondents belong in a category; their private identity remains concealed; they have an epistolary persona. (This, of course, was one of the most disconcerting features of the published anonymous letter as opposed to the autographed manuscript letter: it failed to provide the author with a fixed identity, creating a realm of equality in which status and rank could be elided. It seemed, echoing Koselleck, to be secretive and potentially duplicitous.) But those who offered private correspondence up to the public privileged those letters which seemed most private, those which were least altered by their transition into the public sphere. Letters were described as 'compiled for private use', written by 'a private hand' or as 'first collected for private use, now printed for publick benefit'; they were praised when sent between two correspondents 'in their private capacities as friends' or when 'glimmering out of a private heart's epistolary correspondence'. And because it was important to establish that the letters were not originally intended for the public eye, we are sometimes offered an explanation of how they came to be printed: 'the gentleman to whom this letter was written by a private friend . . . was so struck with the arguments it contains . . . that he determined to publish the whole.'[24]

This brief history of the journey taken by a letter from the realm of the private into the territory of the public points to the importance of the figure of the editor, the person who brought the private into the public.[25] On the one hand the editor, both as artificial construct and as person, was a figure of consequence who provided the public text with authority, vouching for its authenticity, explaining how the document or correspondence came to hand and how, if at all, it had been altered for the public gaze. On the other, the editor was a source of anxiety: he or she was not usually the author and often not even the recipient of the correspondence but a third party whose interest and motives might be pecuniary and disreputable and who might not attend to the concerns of the original correspondents.

In the commercialized environment of eighteenth-century London publishing, booksellers advertised for the private letters of notables, and had no compunction about laying private letters, never intended to be seen publicly, before the reading public. This invasion of privacy (if such it was) was justified on the grounds that even the most intimate correspondence of a notable was a matter of public importance. It produced an interesting response, the most famous example of which was that of the poet Alexander Pope. Knowing that his enemy, the bookseller Edmund Curll, was buying up his correspondence, Pope covertly released materials to Curll, hoping not only to shape his reputation but to trick the bookseller into an illegal error. Pope's intrigue, yet another instance of an attempt to manipulate the categories of public and private, misfired.[26] But it is only the most famous of many examples of writers (and not just literary figures) becoming increasingly conscious of how their private correspondence would be read publicly, an awareness which made them willing and eager to manipulate it for posterity.[27] It was the process of making private correspondence a genre of publication, of recognizing that if one's privacy was to be publicly represented, it was better to do it oneself than to rely on (often unreliable) others.

The large increase in the number of private histories and auto-biographies of ordinary people in the second half of the eighteenth century is less an indicator of a greater commitment to or interest in private life than of a consciousness of the degree to which private life, or to be more accurate its representation, could be an object of perusal by those with whom one had no direct acquaintance. These memoirs are repeatedly justified on purely personal grounds or as an act of familial piety, but their form and contents often belie this, indicating quite clearly that a larger public—who may or may not, but who might eventually examine the text—is very much in mind. It is significant here that, at least in the English case, these personal histories are not contemporaneous with but post-date religious and philosophical notions encouraging the examination of the self as a means of achieving moral or religious understanding. Their number or, at least, the number of surviving texts, increases inordinately in the second half of the eighteenth century, in the period of exceptional consciousness of how private life was subject to the public gaze.

I am claiming here that the growing realm of print and of the published word had an important effect on the way in which private communication was conducted and the self presented, a private world which was informed by a consciousness of its being observed or of having the potential to be observed in public. Readers and writers are often seen by modern commentators as more free, less subject to local horizons, and less embedded in community constraints than those who are not literate. But to argue that the loss or weakening of these particular inhibitions was tantamount to the acquisition of freedom is to swallow the ideology of modernity, to accept a Kantian view of subjectivity. Constraints are not removed by the emancipatory culture of the printed or public word; they are changed. They operate more abstractly, but the gaze of the distant reader is every bit as present (and just as constraining) as the look of the inquisitive neighbour and the scrutiny of priest and congregation. It did not have the universal scope of divine scrutiny, which could presumably penetrate all available forms of concealment; but rather it looked no further than representations and appearances.

Indeed, one cannot but be impressed by the remarkable preoccupation in this period with appearances and ways of looking, with actors and spectators. Didactic literature, of which the *Spectator* was the most distinguished but by no means the sole example, was overwhelmingly preoccupied with teaching its readers how to appear and how to look. There is a remarkable consciousness of how all aspects of the self —demeanour and body language, dress and material possessions, conduct and taste—are signs enabling the observer to understand the character and station of the observed.[28] (This is accompanied by the concomitant anxiety that a culture of appearances is easily transmuted into a culture of disguise.)

As the *Spectator* and other instructional literature shows, there is no clearer indication of the power of this sense of being seen than in the enormous proliferation of observation and commentary about the private. The private was something that had to be discussed; it also had to be envisaged. The private had to be argued about, its representation disputed. This was a conversation in which all were interested because all were potentially implicated. Print culture was not important because of the way in which it encouraged solitude or created a private realm; it was important because it established a new framework within which reading and the pursuit of solitude and privacy—activities which after all had a pedigree that dated back at least to classical antiquity—could be understood.

I want to emphasize here that the private consciousness of the public representation of privateness was not merely a consequence of print culture, of the proliferation of mechanically reproduced words. It also depended upon the simultaneous growth in the number of mechanically reproduced images engraved on wood and copper. These, in turn, very often drew on the visual equivalent of the manuscript letter, the uniquely produced painting or drawing. As the numerous images reproduced in *Histoire de la vie privée* attest, there was an enormous proliferation in the number of spatial representations of 'ordinary life', of views into the private realm which posit an 'inside' viewed from without. Again, as in the case of print, it is not the implied presence of the viewer that is novel, but rather the existence of a representation which exemplifies and embodies the capacity of the private subject to be viewed by an abstract and distant beholder. And it is this consciousness that explains the intense debates that developed around the different forms of representation of everyday life.

We can observe this consciousness of being viewed in the configuration of the domestic interior. Domestic space is usually presumed to exemplify the sealed off privateness of the modern, bourgeois household. But, if we look at the representations of seventeenth- and eighteenth-century households examined by Simon Schama,[29] if we look at the language used to describe London burgher households built after the Fire of London and examine their configuration, what we discover are domestic spaces configured to look both out and in. The standardized vertical town house is configured with ground floor rooms called 'convenient' but not apartments 'of most show', while the first floor includes social space intended for different sorts of sociability. Important among such rooms is a public private room 'a drawing room or dressing room for the lady . . . it is a room of consequence, not only for its natural use in being the place of dressing, but for the several persons who are seen there. The morning is the time many choose for despatching business [and so must] admit [people] while they are dressing'.[30] The exterior architecture reinforces this sense of the first social floor as a space to be seen. In the standard façade of the London Georgian house the first floor windows and the first floor elevation is greater than any other. Major entertainments in such space were highly visible, 'every curtain, and every shutter of every window open, shewing apartments all in a blaze of light, with heads innumerable in continual motion.'[31] Here, again, we can see the recognition that, if the private is to be represented, then it should be subject to some control from those who are to be seen, and that a consciousness of the potential representation of the private helps shape the forms of private conduct.

What I hope I have been able to demonstrate is the remarkable interpenetration of public and private in this period. This is partly a matter of for whom and to whom practices were represented. Thus, our discussion is a discussion of spaces, viewers and publics. But it is also a question of who controls the representation of practices and how this is achieved, which, as Habermas recognizes, is a political question. First, it is political in that it asks who claims the authority to interpret what is public (and therefore what is private); secondly, the control of the representation of practices is concerned with a social and moral end, a conception of what is universally (that is, publicly) good.

I have focused in my remarks about the public and the private on the effect of technologies of mechanical reproduction, especially that of print, in bringing about their interpenetration. Obviously this is a far from sufficient account or explanation of the phenomenon, though it certainly was one of its prerequisites. But a full account would have at least to include many of the changes discussed in *Histoire de la vie privée* and much more: an Augustinian sense of the importance of inwardness and self-examination; a notion (normally associated with Descartes) of instrumental reason that sees the self as something that can be shaped and worked on—just as the external world is no longer given but is an artifact of mind; a concern, associated with Montaigne, with the distinctive make-up of particular selves (especially oneself); and above all the notion, particularly but not exclusively associated with Protestantism, that, in the words of John Milton, 'To know/That which before us lies in daily life/Is the prime wisdom.'[32]

The privileging of the ordinary and the consciousness of man's ability to shape himself—of technologies of the self—had the paradoxical effect both of enhancing a sense of privacy—especially of the corporeal and psychic self—and of providing the grounds on which it could be invaded, policed and remade. This process, I want to emphasize, cannot be reduced to the civilizing process as described by Norbert Elias. The sources of the eighteenth-century private self are far more diverse than the (admittedly important) literature derived from courtly civility; the literature of politeness in eighteenth-century Europe, even in France, might embody values that were anti-courtly and even anti-aristocratic.

The point I wish to emphasize here is that the proliferating representation of privateness and the quotidian was not some sort of sociology (though it did produce its sociology in theories of sympathy and of political economy) but that it contained a strong prescriptive element. Representations of the private were not just windows on a private world but some of the most powerful means by which a public conception of the proper ordering of the private might be achieved. We can see this very clearly in the case of the novel and the debate that it engendered. For if, on the one hand, the novel is often seen as a source of 'realism' because of its frequent representation of everyday life, what also stands out is its excruciating consciousness of its status as a form of representation. Novels were frequently about reading and writing and especially about the effect of reading novels. The issue here is one of what justifies the public representation of the private. The answer (at least the answer offered by novelists) is usually that of moral instruction: thus Richardson in his best-selling *Clarissa*, a novel that was translated into German, French, Dutch, Russian, Italian and Portuguese, writes: 'one of the principal views of the publication [is] . . . to caution parents against the undue exertion of their natural authority over their children in the great article of marriage: and children against preferring a man of pleasure to a man of probity, upon the dangerous but too commonly received notion, *that a reformed rake makes the best husband.*' Novels provided patterns by which to live. Of course they were often accused of being prurient and voyeuristic (the fate of Richardson) or of being immoral (the fate of Rousseau) or—the most common accusation—of offering delusive ideas rather than sober instruction. But these accusations indicate how important it was to be able to claim a general public object in order to justify penetrating the veil of privacy. In short, the question of territories and spaces so admirably illuminated in *Histoire de la vie privée* was closely linked to the question about ends which Habermas makes the basis of his discussion.

We are now, I think, in a position to understand rather better the question naturally posed by historians of the French Revolution, namely why did it engender a passion for a seamless and transparent publicness in an age apparently besotted with the invention of intimacy? The answer does not lie, I think, in Koselleck's realm of the secret but rather in Habermas's public sphere. The public sphere had not only placed unprecedented importance on the private but had provided both the grounds and the means by which it could be colonized and invaded. Indeed, to some extent the private sphere was already a hostage to the public. All that was needed were the political circumstances that permitted the multivalent views of the private expressed in the public sphere to be reduced to the single gaze of the revolutionary state. The Pandora's box of private life had already been opened. All that the Committee of Public Safety had to do was look into it.

Notes

1. I should like to acknowledge the help of Michele Cohen, Laurence Fontaine, Eckhart Hellmuth, Ludmilla Jordanova and Stella Tillyard in shaping this essay.
2. 'Public Sphere and Private Life: Toward a Synthesis of Current Historiographical Approaches to the Old Régime' *History and Theory* 31 (1992) pp. 1–20. I want to make clear my very considerable debt to Dena Goodman's work, not only to this essay but to her discussion of the status of letters in 'Epistolary Property: Michel de Servan and the Plight of Letters on the Eve of the French Revolution' in John Brewer and Susan Staves (eds) *Early Modern Conceptions of Property* (London, 1994) pp. 339–364, some of whose themes I discuss below.
3. For an important comparative study of these two texts see Anthony La Vopa, 'Conceiving a Public: Ideas and Society in Eighteenth-Century Europe' *Journal of Modern History* 64 (1992) pp. 79–116.
4. See Keith Michael Baker, 'Politics and Public Opinion under the Old Regime: Some Reflections' in Jack R. Censer and Jeremy D. Popkin (eds) *Press and Politics in Pre-Revolutionary France*, (Berkeley and Los Angeles, 1987) pp. 204–246 (209–10).
5. See La Vopa, 'Conceiving a Public', pp. 89–90 and 92.
6. *The Structural Transformation of the Public Sphere: An Inquiry into a Category of Bourgeois Society* (Cambridge, MA, 1989) pp. 25–26. References to this work will be given as 'Habermas' in the main text.
7. See La Vopa, 'Conceiving a Public', p. 101, but compare J. Habermas 'Further Reflections on the Public Sphere' in C. Calhoun (ed.) *Habermas and the Public Sphere* (Cambridge, MA and London, 1992) pp. 421–60 (p. 430).
8. *Histoire de la vie privée*, III: *De la Renaissance aux Lumières* ed. by Roger Chartier (Paris, 1986) pp. 7–19, translated by Arthur Goldhammer as *A History of Private Life*, III: *Passions of the Renaissance* (Cambridge, MA and London, 1989) pp. 1–11.
9. *Histoire de la vie privée* pp. 23–24; *A History of Private Life* p. 17.
10. These figures were derived from the current CD-ROM version of the *ESTC*.
11. There is no change in the definitions offered in the editions of the Dictionary produced in Johnson's lifetime. They remain those of the first edition of 1755.

12. See, for example, the sermon of 1776 entitled, *The Proper Business of the Ecclesiastic Life, in a Public and a Private Sphere.*
13. This subject has been primarily a literary one (see, for example, Bruce Redford, *The Converse of the Pen. Acts of Intimacy in the Eighteenth-Century Familiar Letter* (Chicago and London, 1986), also *Men/Women of Letters, Yale French Studies* 71 (1986)). I am not here concerned with the question of whether such letters constitute a literary genre and my position in the debate about whether such works are intimate and private or directed towards a public, a debate centred on the writings of Madame de Sévigné (see Bernard Beugnot, 'Débats autour du genre épistolaire: réalité et écriture' *Revue d'Histoire Littéraire de la France* 74 (1974) pp. 195–202 and Louise K. Horowitz, 'The Correspondence of Madame de Sévigné: Letters of Belles-Lettres', *French Forum* 6 (1981) pp.13–27 for summaries of the controversy between Bernard Bray and Roger Duchene), is made clear in the following discussion.
14. See Goodman, 'Epistolary Property'.
15. The *cabinet noir* was the section of the central post office in Paris where post was opened and subject to government scrutiny (see Eugène Vaille, *Le Cabinet noir* (Paris, 1950)). A similar practice obtained in the London post office.
16. For the different situations in England and France see Janet Gurkin Altman, 'The Letter Book as a Literary Institution 1539–1789: Towards a Cultural History of Published Correspondences in France', *Yale French Studies* 71 (1986) pp. 17–62 (pp. 33–35). The issue of epistolarity as a female form is not one I wish to explore here except to assert that the question is one of gender not of sex.
17. See, for instance, the warning offered by, among others, *Every Man His Own Letter-Writer* of 1782: 'It is customary among the polite to sign their names at a considerable distance below the conclusion of the letter, and thereby leave a large vacancy over the name. This, however, should not be practised, for this reason, because tis putting it in the power of an ill-disposed person (should your letter happen to fall into such hands) to take an injudicious advantage, by writing what he pleases over your name, and making you, in all appearances to have signed a writing you would by no means have set your hand to.'
18. See Ann Hartmann Goldgar, 'Gentlemen and Scholars: Conduct and Community in the Republic of Letters, 1680–1750', unpublished PhD, Harvard University.
19. See *Revue de synthèse, Les Correspondances, leur importance pour l'historien des sciences et la philosophie: Problèmes de leur édition*, 3rd series, vols. 81 and 82 (1976).
20. Cited by Goldgar, 'Gentlemen and Scholars'.
21. See Goodman, 'Epistolary Property'.
22. Joseph Addison and Sir Richard Steele, *The Spectator*, ed. by Donald F. Bond, 5 vols (Oxford, 1965) vol. I pp. xxvii–xxxix.

23. See Robert L. Haig, *The Gazetteer 1735–1797. A Study in the Eighteenth-Century English Newspaper* (Carbondale, 1960) p. 71.

24. See, for instance, John Nichols, *Anecdotes, Biographical and Literary, of the Late William Bowyer, Printer. Compiled for Private Use* (London, 1778); *The Divinity of Our Blessed Lord and Saviour Jesus Christ, Fully Proved, both from the Old and New Testament. By a Private Hand* (London, 1719); *The Plain Man's Instructor in the Common Prayer of the Church of England, First Collected for Private Use. Now published for Public Benefit* (London, 1713); *Common Sense: In Nine Conferences, Between a British Merchant and a Candid Merchant of America, in their Private Capacities as Friends* (London: 1775); Francis Okely, *Dawnings of the Everlasting Gospel-Light, Glimmering out of a Private Heart's Epistolary Correspondence. Now Made Public by Francis Okely* (Northampton: 1775); *A Letter to a Country Gentleman. The Gentleman to whom This Letter was Written by a Private Friend, was So Struck with the Arguments it Contains, that He Determined To Publish the Whole* (London, 1784).

25. For an important discussion of the editor see Robert Iliffe, 'Author-Mongering: The "Editor" between Producer and Consumer' in Ann Bermingham and John Brewer (eds) *Image, Word and Object. The Consumption of Culture in the 17th and 18th Centuries* (London, forthcoming))

26. See Maynard Mack, *Alexander Pope: A Life* (London and New Haven, 1985) pp. 653–58.

27. See, for example, J.L. Clifford, 'The Authenticity of Anna Seward's Published Correspondence' *Modern Philology* 39 (1941) pp. 113–22.

28. For an excellent discussion of these themes see Michael Ketcham, *Transparent Designs: Reading, Performance and Form in the Spectator Papers* (Athens, GA, 1985).

29. *The Embarrassment of Riches: An Interpretation of Dutch Culture in the Golden Age* (London, 1987).

30. See Dan Cruickshank and Neil Burton, *Life in the Georgian City* (London, 1990) p. 55.

31. *Life in the Georgian City*, p.46–47.

32. For an important discussion of these themes see Charles Taylor, *The Sources of the Self: The Making of the Modern Identity* (Cambridge, 1989) and Quentin Skinner, 'Who are "We"? Ambiguities of the Modern Self *Inquiry* 34 no. 2, pp. 133–53.

Two

Regendering the Republic of Letters: Private Association in the Public Sphere, 1780–1789*

Dena Goodman

Habermas's *Structural Transformation of the Public Sphere* has opened up a new terrain for eighteenth-century scholars.[1] In attempting to map the public sphere whose borders and topography Habermas only sketched out, historians have begun to look more closely at the discursive practices and institutions by which that sphere—in which, for the first time, private persons came together to use their reason publicly—was constituted. My own work has focused on Parisian salons, while others have looked at theatres, coffee-houses, Masonic lodges, conversation and the press.[2] An institution which has not received any attention in this context is the *musée*, which spread throughout France in the 1780s.

The *musées* figure in the history of education and are often compared to academies. They are usually seen as a development out of Freemasonry and as the precursors of the clubs that would take shape in 1789, when intellectual sociability would be transformed into political sociability.[3] As such, they may well be the key to the transformation of what Habermas calls the literary public sphere into the political public

*This article is substantially drawn from my book, *The Republic of Letters: A Cultural History of the French Enlightenment* (Ithaca, 1994). It is presented in this form with the permission of Cornell University Press.

sphere, a transformation that entailed the exclusion of women.[4] In the eighteenth century, the literary public sphere was known as the Republic of Letters, and in the history of that Republic, the *musées* challenged Enlightenment salons as centres of intellectual sociability and exchange. In so doing, they displaced the female *salonnière* from the centre of the Republic and regendered it masculine. As commercial ventures, these new institutions were more fully public than the salons they replaced; whether or not they were more democratic remains to be seen.

The history of the Parisian *musée* begins in 1777, when an energetic young man named Claude-Mammès Pahin de La Blancherie launched a journal he called *Nouvelles de la République des Lettres et des Arts*. The title of the *Nouvelles* cast it in the tradition of Bayle, and the prospectus gave its purpose in the familiar terms of eighteenth-century literary journalism. 'The work that we offer to our Country and to foreign Nations under a title consecrated long ago in Literature', wrote La Blancherie, 'has as its aim to facilitate the communication of minds, opinions, talents, and research [*travaux*] in all fields.'[5]

The typicality of La Blancherie's project was such that, in a competitive market, he had to explain how it differed from the journals and gazettes it resembled. The innovative move that worked was the offer of his editorial office as a meeting place for contributors and subscribers and a showroom for their work. With this invitation he extended his journalistic enterprise into a project of direct association. Because Paris was by now the centre of a cosmopolitan Republic of Letters that dated from at least the seventeenth century,[6] La Blancherie could expect that many of his contributors and subscribers would come for a visit. When they did, they were invited to meet other visitors and the local citizenry at his office on Thursday afternoons. Within a few months it was clear that the major attraction of La Blancherie's project was the weekly meeting. 'On the first of this month I was sent the prospectus of a journal entitled: *Nouvelles de la république des lettres*', the abbé François-Valentin Mulot wrote in the first entry of his journal for the year 1778. 'What I admire most in his plan is the assembly that he announces of scholars of all countries; there can without doubt be nothing more useful than this communication of minds.'[7]

From Mulot's diary we learn something of what went on at one of the first Thursday meetings. As Mulot described them, all the topics discussed that day revolved around objects: a pair of engravings with accompanying verses, said to be by a sixteen-year-old girl; a marble engraving said to have been found near the city of Catane; a microscope that had just been approved by the Académie; and a translation of a scientific work on 'the inflammable air of swamps', that had just appeared. While the latter two objects provoked interest and admiration, the first two stimulated critical discussion. Could this work have been done by a self-taught young girl? Was the engraving a genuine antiquity or of more recent vintage? Clearly, the pleasure for Mulot and those present lay in discussion itself. By taking the objects of discussion out of the pages of the journal and into a sociable space, La Blancherie had enabled his subscribers to engage in the sort of critical discussion that characterized the salons, rather than simply selling them his own judgments, as other journalists did.

In May 1778, Jacques-Henri Meister, the editor of Grimm's *Correspondance littéraire*, reported on La Blancherie's establishment to his subscribers; by June it had made the *Mémoires secrets*.[8] Meister opened his article with a paean to the entrepreneurial spirit: 'There is nothing that cannot be imagined in Paris for acquiring fortune and fame,' he wrote, 'there is nothing in which one cannot succeed with a little boldness, a lot of persistence [*suite*], and stubborn energy.' With minimal resources and a lot of hard work, he went on, La Blancherie had formed 'quite an interesting establishment for distinguished foreigners, scholars, men of letters, and artists'. Meister went on to describe the distinctive activities of the weekly meetings. There were neither formal readings nor general conversation, he explained. One was free to read whatever one wanted and to talk with whomever one wanted to meet. Writers and artists gathered just as La Blancherie hoped they would; new books and works of art were indeed on display for people to look at. And so many people were turning out that the small apartment where the meetings were held was no longer adequate.

Within a year, La Blancherie issued a new prospectus which elevated the weekly meeting to an 'ordinary assembly of scholars, artists, etc.', and made the *Nouvelles* secondary to it.[9] The prospectus of 1779 marked a definitive shift in the focus of the project from a periodical to an association; it transformed journal subscription into club membership and made La Blancherie, in the eyes of his contemporaries, the founder of the first *musée*.

Further testimony as to the success and popularity of La Blancherie's establishment came after it had been in operation for about a year in a letter from a Richard Derb—dated 8 May 1779, and published in the London-based francophone *Courrier de l'Europe*.[10] At La Blancherie's assembly, Derb—found walls hung with ancient and modern art, works of sculpture, mechanical objects and manufactured goods, books from far and wide and on all subjects, natural history exhibits, engravings interspersed with the objects; and, most exciting of all, 'a crowd of interesting and famous men whom, successively, M. de la Blancherie was receiving, close to whom he conducted us (for several of us were foreigners), and to whom he presented us in making us known by our tastes'.

Was the visitor thrilled? 'In an hour and a half', he wrote, 'we saw pass before our eyes a portion of the most scholarly men of this city. I would note to you Dr Franklin himself, whom I was charmed to see outside his own home. I thought I was seeing again the Portico, the Lyceum! I saw, in fact, more: satisfaction and liberty reigning among this multitude of men who succeeded one another over the course of four hours.' The visitor observed one group watching demonstrations of new machines, while others

> seated in different circles, conversed upon some subject in the sciences or the arts, several making observations on the price and the merit of the paintings; some, grouped apart, read individually or out loud passages from books; here a conversation in German, there one in English, and everywhere great nobles mixed with scholars and artists: a geometer, a lockmaker, a painter, a musician, etc.

Like the *salonnières*, whom he clearly emulated, La Blancherie never rested for a moment. He was everywhere, 'responding to each one's questions, being polite [*faisant politesses*] to everyone'.

The English visitor closed his letter with the information that this magnificent establishment was not without its troubles, beset as it was on all sides by those motivated by envy and jealousy who were trying to close it down. Indeed, even the newspapers, he wrote, were engaging in a conspiracy of silence that was making it difficult for La Blancherie to attract the subscribers he needed to get on a sound financial footing. Mr. Derb—had thus not only taken a few packages from La Blancherie for London delivery, but had promised to publicize the venture in England. 'I promised', he wrote the editor of the *Courrier* in closing, 'to consign to your impartial pages this testimony of the recognition that I owe him, and to which I invite all my compatriots in congratulating them for having so amiable a correspondent that I am perhaps the first to announce to them.'

The virtues of a 'general agent for the Republic of Letters'—as La Blancherie called himself—had more in common with those of the *salonnière* than of the *philosophe*. Meister praised La Blancherie's meetings for precisely their lack of academic formality and suggested that support for the project was based on the novelty of its publicity as well as the nobility of its aims:

> Any free, independent association that can serve to render the communication of enlightenment faster and easier deserves encouragement, and it is undoubtedly from this point of view that the institution of M. de la Blancherie has obtained the consent of the police, the vote of the Academy of Sciences and that of various other literary societies.[11]

Here Meister revealed not only his own support of an establishment that seemed to respond to the desire for a free and open space for discussion as the basis of enlightenment, but also the effective constraints on such an institution. Salons did not need the consent of the police to open their doors, nor did they need a vote of confidence from royal academies. In what sense, then, can La Blancherie's assembly and those establishments that would be modelled on it in the 1780s, be said to have been 'free' associations?

Both the *Correspondance littéraire* and the *Mémoires secrets* reported on La Blancherie's project because the Académie des Sciences had approved it. Franklin and Condorcet, who were later to serve on the commission that would declare Anton Mesmer a charlatan, gave La Blancherie their encouragement and, more important, an official seal of approval.[12] The verdict, which La Blancherie now had the privilege of printing in his many advertisements, had been rendered on 20 May 1778. Meister's report on La Blancherie's project in the *Correspondance littéraire* appeared the same month. The *Mémoires secrets* first reported on it on 19 June.

While the Académie's endorsement was good public relations for La Blancherie, it was also virtually a requirement in eighteenth-century France. There was no freedom of association in the Old Regime: all associations that were not officially authorized were illicit. Since the fourteenth century, the monarchy had consistently issued prohibitions against any assembly not approved by the state. As recently as 1737, the ordinance of the Paris police that had outlawed the Freemasons had been written as a ban on all assemblies; in 1778, the *parlement* of Paris upheld action by the police of Lyon that made it 'unlawful for all persons regardless of standing and rank to assemble or band together in the town, outskirts, or suburbs without being authorized'.[13] As privileged bodies, academies had the right to determine whether or not any new institution was encroaching on their privileged competency. The approval of the Académie des Sciences both legitimated La Blancherie's establishment in the eyes of the public and the police, and guaranteed that the Académie would not interfere with his operation. When the Académie investigated La Blancherie's activities, it acted both in its own interest as a privileged *corps* and in the monarchy's interest as a royal academy with letters patent from the king.

Official approval did not, however, solve La Blancherie's financial problems. While his original prospectus had identified men of letters as his true patrons, the economic precariousness of the project required more substantial financing. By November 1779, the *Mémoires secrets* was reporting that the entrepreneur was forced to subsidize the *Nouvelles* out of his own pocket and had put out a call for more substantial subscriptions. 'He invites scholars to subscribe and to imitate the King and the Queen, Monsieur, Monseigneur the Comte d'Artois, and Madame the King's sister, who have taken several copies of it.'[14] Even so, La Blancherie's enterprise went under within six months.[15]

In 1781, however, La Blancherie was back with 'forty subscribers of the highest quality'.[16] He now had an elaborate financing plan based on three levels of patronage. To stimulate subscriptions at all levels, he also proposed a lottery—'to bait the cupidity of the subscribers', the *Mémoires secrets* explained. 'Beyond the advantage of entering freely into the sanctuary, closed henceforth to the profane,' the article continued, 'they will have the hope of possessing by the luck of the draw some of the precious pieces exposed during the year, which will be acquired with the excess of the funds coming from various subscriptions, after expenses have been met.'[17]

By referring to the 'profane', the *Mémoires secrets* was implicitly comparing La Blancherie's assembly to the Masonic lodges that had become increasingly popular over the course of the eighteenth century.[18] Gone were the free and open meetings of men of letters, artists, and amateurs, of Frenchmen and foreigners equally citizens of a cosmopolitan Republic of Letters. With the loss of self-patronage, the public space for free discussion and the exchange and spreading of enlightenment had become a closed club, entry into which was based on money, and the implication of which was new distinctions: between the 'ins' and the 'outs'; and then among the various classes of subscriber/patrons. Publicity had drawn the attention of the Académie and the police, and new regulations put additional limitations on membership. Like the academies, but unlike the salons, La Blancherie's institution was deemed public and thus needed a set of regulations approved by the police.[19] These had been published in a new prospectus in 1779, which also included both a full copy of the Académie's report and the new system of patronage/subscription.

In the new prospectus, La Blancherie reformulated his statement of purpose: the weekly meeting was no longer an afterthought, but the main focus. Access to the meetings, however, was limited by the new regulations. While La Blancherie had originally invited all subscribers and visiting scholars to gather at his office, he now established rules of entry. 'The purpose of the assembly indicates adequately who the persons are that ought to frequent it,' he wrote. Nevertheless, he went on to spell out who these people were:

> All those men known by their rank, their dignities, and by the public profession of the sciences, letters, and the arts. No other will be received, unless he is presented by the persons designated above, or announced by a letter in their hand, of which he shall be the carrier.

> Foreigners and travellers will be admitted only in as much as they are invested with a public character, or presented, or announced in the manner that has just been designated.[20]

La Blancherie also informed his readers of those who would not be admitted: women. 'Since women will not be admitted at all to the rendez-vous,' he explained, 'they will be received between noon and three o'clock: they will have the time that has been requested by ladies of the highest order to satisfy their curiosity in regards to the objects on display.'[21]

The police had never used their authority to limit access to printed materials on the basis of either status or gender, but the transformation of journal subscription into club membership had raised new issues. Readership was gender-neutral, even if certain genres or periodicals, such as the *Journal des Dames*, for example, were aimed at a single-gender audience, and even if subscription rates could be used to limit potential subscribers by their capacity to pay. Nothing prohibited men and women equally from reading the *Journal des Dames*, or, for that matter, the *Encyclopédie*; and nothing prohibited the sharing of printed works by members of reading clubs to spread out the costs, or the rental of such material, or the printing of cheap editions. Indeed, once the French stopped writing in Latin, they implicitly opened up readership to literate women as well as men. The character of French writing in the eighteenth century reflects the appreciation of this new audience. By the eighteenth century, Roger Chartier points out, the iconography of reading was predominantly female, whereas before it had been exclusively male.[22]

With a publishing project, La Blancherie could appeal to a readership undifferentiated according to either rank or gender; with a project of association, these criteria were put into play. Under the eyes of the police, La Blancherie restricted access to his weekly meetings in much the same way that the academicians did. When the Académie française began holding *séances publiques* in 1673, only men were permitted to watch the academicians perform; women were not allowed to attend until 1702. The exclusion of women from membership of the Académie remained, however, even though it was *de facto* and not *de jure*: nowhere in the regulations of the Académie française were women mentioned at all.[23]

The history of Freemasonry, too, was a history of male sociability. The *Constitutions* upon which Freemasonry was based explicitly excluded women.[24] In France, however, women protested their exclusion and playwrights mocked it. Suspicions were voiced about what men might be doing without respectable women in their company.[25] As a result of pressure from women and capitulation by a significant portion of the brothers, 'lodges of adoption' began to be formed by some French lodges for female associates around 1760, despite continuing opposition from misogynist Masons. In 1774, lodges of adoption were officially authorized by French Masonry's governing body, the Grand Orient.[26]

It has been argued that the admission of women to Freemasonry extended to them the egalitarian ideal that made the lodge an institution of Enlightenment.[27] But even if the practices of Masonic sociability did foster a certain degree of autonomy and a critical spirit among male Masons, the 'sisters' they 'adopted' were excluded from these practices. Not only did the sisters lack all autonomy within the lodge, but the lodges of adoption were themselves, as the name suggests, dependents of masculine lodges. Morally, the virtue preached to Masonic sisters was, in the words of René Le Forestier, 'inactive, verbal, and whimpering'.[28] Adoption was the adaptation of Freemasonry to a new foundation in male dominance to replace the old strategy of female exclusion.

Secrets were fundamental to the self-definition of Freemasonry, and women, in the name of virtue, were not allowed to share them—despite the fact that these 'secrets' were well-known to the literate if profane public by the 1770s and were formal rather than substantive. Indeed, secrecy was definitive of Freemasonry only because of the insistence on it, and thus the continued exclusion of women from the formality of secrecy made all the difference.[29] Even so, the rituals by means of which women passed to higher grades in the lodges of adoption did not initiate them into the 'secrets' of Freemasonry. Instead, the sisters were tested to see if they had the 'virtue' to resist trying to learn them. The woman who passed all the tests, the Grand Mistress, was, according to the words of the ritual, no more than the 'honorable companion of the Grand Master', who could be replaced on her throne by a wax figure if necessary, to fulfill her functions.[30]

In the 1730s, French Freemasonry had excluded women in order to create a social order in opposition to the perceived libertinage of dominant forms of sociability of the day.[31] By the 1770s, Masonic brothers had found a way to include women while maintaining moral and political authority over them. The brothers became the moral judges of their new sisters. Having now proved his virtue through membership and advancement in the fraternity, the male Mason was neither threatened by the seductive power of women nor subject to their authority. He was now qualified and entitled to judge their virtue and their merit. He defined and defended the moral order.[32]

According to Jacques Brengues, the introduction of the Scottish Rite of single-sex sociability into France constituted 'a breach in the salon system of the century instituted, even institutionalized, by women'.[33] When the lodges of adoption were created in the 1770s, they did not assimilate either the personnel or the values of Enlightenment salons that were then in their heyday. They turned rather to the women constructed by the discourse of heterosexual love: of gallantry, seduction, and sex. Their language is at the heart of both the old discourse of gallantry and the new one of conjugal love, wifely submission, and domestic harmony that would be adopted by the fraternal republic of 1792.[34]

In the 1780s, women were invited into institutions of intellectual and Masonic sociability as objects of male desire and learning, and as submissive subjects of male-defined morality. In the 1779 regulations of La Blancherie's *musée*, the exclusion of women from the ranks of the members was made as explicit as it was in the Masonic *Constitutions* promulgated fifty years earlier. Only by protesting this exclusion did women earn the observer status already granted them by the Académie française in that same distant era. They gained access to the display of objects, but they were still excluded from interaction with men. Certain men—those who could demonstrate 'public credit'—were thus granted active citizenship in this configuration of the Republic of Letters, while all women were restricted to the role of passive citizens. While La Blancherie's establishment had room to accommodate more men than did either a salon or an academy, it was still restricted according to criteria that were familiar to the eighteenth-century public. Like the salons, it was the space of a socially defined elite; like the academies and lodges, it was a masculine space.

Not until Jean François Pilâtre de Rozier received permission in 1782 to admit women to his *Musée de Monsieur* and compete directly with La Blancherie was the restriction on female participation in La Blancherie's establishment lifted. Pilâtre was an apothecary who would soon gain fame in balloon experiments and subsequently lose his life attempting a Channel crossing in one.[35] When he first proposed a new *musée* in the fall of 1781, he sought not just member/subscribers, but patrons and protectors, and he named his establishment for the most powerful of them: the Comte de Provence, the King's brother who was known simply as 'Monsieur'. Ensconced already in the Count's entourage and employed in the service of his wife, Pilâtre lined up a group of blue-ribbon backers.[36] By December, a prospectus was circulating, and the *Mémoires secrets* could report that the *Musée*, authorized by the government and under the protection of Monsieur and Madame, threatened to drive La Blancherie out of business. By January, not only had the Académie des Sciences given Pilâtre its encouragement, but other royal academies had signed on as well: the Académie française, the royal observatory, the royal medical society, and the royal veterinary college had all given their endorsements.[37]

What appealed to the *Mémoires secrets* was the pedagogical mission of Pilâtre's *musée*. It had two professed aims: to provide laboratories and scientific equipment for amateurs and professionals; and to instruct beginners in the use of the equipment and to demonstrate its practical applications. Not only would expensive equipment be thus made available to those who could not afford to buy it, but courses would be offered in a variety of subjects.[38] By contrast, the *Mémoires* found La Blancherie's establishment 'so cold, so vague, so monotonous, so deprived of movement, interest and instruction', that it was doomed to fail. Pilâtre's *musée* was so much more 'useful' that it would soon replace and absorb it. Telling in this judgment was the editor's overt disgust for the entrepreneurial spirit for which Meister had praised La Blancherie. 'The motives of cupidity, the mercantile ideas which have been mixed up with this project', he claimed, 'must necessarily turn off people who are experimental [i.e., 'scientific'] and know the manoeuvres of all these literary intriguers'.[39] The *Musée*'s secretary later pointed to the modest price of subscriptions as evidence that its goal was solely the 'propagation of enlightenment'.[40]

In fact, Pilâtre was simply a better entrepreneur than La Blancherie, as his immediate and tremendous success, as well as those who have studied his finances, attest. Not only did he use his position at court to gain government authorization and the endorsements of the official *corps* of the Republic of Letters; he also took advantage of his competitors in the private sector. When a group was expelled from the rival *Musée de Paris* he welcomed them to join him, offering to transfer memberships at no cost; he also offered membership privileges to all the members of the *Société Patriotique de Bretagne*. By the time of Pilâtre's death in 1785, the Académie des Sciences itself had taken out a group subscription, with the name of its perpetual secretary, Condorcet, heading the list.[41]

Pilâtre's second prospectus, probably written in 1783, was followed by the government-approved regulations. It advertised the *Musée* as a place where those who could not get into all the various establishments that made Paris the capital of the Republic of Letters could learn everything they needed to know:

> The Capital possesses many interesting establishments whose details are as unknown to the nationals as to foreigners: the professors of the Musée who have gained an entrée into most of these establishments, will explain here all that would elude the curiosity of travellers.

Why go anywhere else? Pilâtre's establishment was the *musée* of all *musées*.[42]

Moreau de Saint-Méry's '*Discours sur l'utilité du Musée*' reveals not only the purposes and structure of the *Musée de Monsieur*, but also the very specific role that women were asked to play in it. In 1784, Moreau was elected secretary of the *Musée*, the result of a democratizing move on the part of Pilâtre, whose purpose was to draw in the public by giving them responsibility for running the association, while allowing himself to withdraw from administrative work to concentrate on his balloon projects.[43] The subscribers were asked to elect an administrative board and a secretary, and the latter position fell to Moreau.[44] In 1805, Moreau had printed in Parma a deluxe edition of the speech he had delivered as the newly inaugurated secretary of this society full of hope and promise. 'What more certain proof of the utility of this establishment', he asked,

> than the eagerness with which people come from all over to [join] it; than the very objects with which the spaces are decorated and that speak of this utility? In fact, in whatever direction you look around, everything here announces the cult that is rendered to the sciences, everything says how admirable are the secrets of nature, the research into which this temple is consecrated. (pp. 1–2)

Moreau discoursed at some length on the particular services offered to the public by the *Musée* that would justify its claim to utility. These services fell into four categories: association, instruction, exhibition, and decoration. Association and exhibition were already well-established as the functions of La Blancherie's weekly assembly. Moreau, therefore, concentrated on the pedagogical aspect of the new *musée* as the basis of its utility and 'special destiny'.

At the *Musée de Monsieur* not only would scholars and men of letters already dedicated to the exchange and advancement of knowledge gather together, but the 'beacons of light' that their association constituted would attract novices as another means of the expansion of the Republic of Letters through its project of Enlightenment (pp. 8–9). Through the use of modern technologies of publicity, the *Encyclopédie* had sought to surpass even the ancient library of Alexandria, in which all knowledge was gathered only to be lost in a blaze of fire. The model of the *musée* was the ancient museum attached to that library, in which the scholars employed by the Emperor Ptolemy lived and worked, cataloguing and commenting on the books that represented his imperial power. As the library had been made public through print thirty years earlier, so would the *musée* that was its human dimension now become a public association.[45]

The pedagogical aim of the *Musée* was to make available to Parisians of modest means the broad sweep of Enlightenment knowledge. As La Blancherie had translated journal subscription into membership with a weekly meeting, Pilâtre had transformed the subscription project of the *Encyclopédie* itself into a direct pedagogy with courses of instruction modelled on the topoi of the great work of the Enlightenment.

Association and pedagogy were the first two services offered to the public by the *Musée*; the last two were exhibition and decoration. Like La Blancherie's meeting space, the *Musée* would serve as a venue of public display for the works of artists, artisans, and inventors. While La Blancherie's aim was simply to help creative people sell their work, Moreau saw exhibition as a means of attracting the critical attention needed by young artists to develop their talents (pp. 27–29). The utility of exhibition lay in the reciprocal judgment and mutual regard of the public, a peer review that saw the enlightened public as equals in matters of judgment and thus as all contributors to the cultivation of talent. The practice of critical discourse that La Blancherie had brought out of the pages of his journal and into his meetings was thus formalized in the *Musée de Monsieur*.

Decoration, the final service that the *Musée* offered the public, was something else altogether. Women were to fulfil this function, and Moreau offered them to the (male) public as an added incentive to join this *musée* over its rivals. 'I will be reproached perhaps for having waited so long before speaking of an advantage that this *Musée* does not share with any other establishment relative to the sciences', he said, in closing his speech. Members of the *Musée* would have the pleasure of seeing among them

> that adored sex which seems to come here to dispute with the sciences for their admirers. Seduced by superficial men who ... have persuaded them that scholars were sombre and unsociable beings, women have for a long time taken pleasure in their frivolity; but they know at last, from their own experience, that the love of the sciences takes nothing away from the social virtues: they even have the talent to make this love serve to render even more dangerous the seductive art of pleasing. Charming sex, how much your presence adds to the pure pleasures that are tasted in this asylum! Embellish it often, and the sciences will have there an even more assiduous cult. (p. 29)

The seductive role given women in this new establishment was most clearly marked in the differential subscription rates: women subscribed at half-price.[46]

How different this mixed-gender society was from the salon! There the *salonnière* had been at the very centre of conversation, controlling and guiding it within the bounds of politeness.[47] And if some men had written petulantly over the years of their dissatisfaction with having to be judged by women in the salons, with having to work with and through them to attain their goals of literary fame and fortune, men like them had now found a solution to this problem: men would advise and judge each other, and women would embellish the public space in which they did so.

Pilâtre and Moreau were not interested in spreading Enlightenment to women; they simply wanted to make enlightened men more attractive to women, and women more attractive to enlightened men in order to draw in more (male) subscribers. Only for this reason were women invited to take the courses offered by the *Musée*, and to mingle with the real (male) scholars, students, and men of letters in this 'salon' without a *salonnière*.[48]

The founders of the *musées* saw no need for women to act as *salonnières*, but they did recognize a need to offer the enlightened and enlightenable male public the kind of social space that women had been shaping in their Parisian homes for the better part of two centuries. The 1783 regulations of the *Musée de Monsieur*, for example, described the establishment in salon-like terms as 'forming a free society, that has as its basis that precious equality that mixes ranks without confusing them'.[49]

A third and final prospectus, published in 1785, presented the *Musée de Monsieur* as more salon-like than ever. It would still be a meeting place for men of letters where young people could find instruction, encouragement, and advice, but this prospectus pointed out the agreeableness of the company, especially for foreign visitors who, 'enjoying the same advantages as the nationals, will also have an infinitely more precious one, that of finding themselves all of a sudden at the centre of the arts and of *la bonne compagnie*'.[50]

The kind of social space described by the English visitor to La Blancherie's Thursday meeting in 1779 would now be found in the *Musée de Monsieur*: the social space at the centre of the Republic of Letters which was also the centre of *la bonne compagnie*, and that would obviate the need for going to any rival establishment. But unlike La Blancherie, Pilâtre emphasized that the presence —not, however, the activity—of women was key to the success of such a social and intellectual space:

> Women, who by the care they take to cultivate their minds, and by their success in more than one field, prove to us every day the progress of our century, will inspire, by their presence alone at the *Musée,* that urbanity that makes the charm of all society, and which could not exist without them.[51]

When the men of the 1780s designed and marketed new institutions of intellectual sociability for the male citizens of an expanding Republic of Letters, they continued to evoke the salon society that their establishments were meant to displace. But women were not the active centres of these new institutions. In both La Blancherie's establishment and the *Musée de Monsieur*, they were marginalized, and their value to the association marginalized as well. Women could do no more than examine objects of male creation in La Blancherie's establishment; in Pilâtre's they were allowed to associate with the creative males who made those objects, but only to attract more of them to the association and to overcome their own prejudices about the unattractiveness of men and their science.

Unlike the men who wrote *éloges* of the great *salonnières* of the 1770s, the men who founded *musées* in the 1780s did not acknowledge that women played a necessary role in shaping and governing the social and intellectual space of the Republic of Letters.[52] Women were an attraction and an object, but they were no longer an active, ordering force. In defining these new institutions and delimiting the role that women were allowed to play in them, men took their lead not from the salons, but from Masonic lodges. The memberships in *musées* and lodges overlapped significantly, and we can see the similarity between them in how they regulated and circumscribed women's role.

La Blancherie failed in the end, but not without leaving behind a legacy in the form of a new sort of institution of intellectual sociability. He became a model for other young men who would launch projects of association for a Republic of Letters shaped by the project of Enlightenment that had itself been shaped by *salonnières*, but whose champions no longer saw a need for them. The *musées* situated the Republic of Letters squarely in a masculine public sphere that displaced women from its centre. The revolution that transformed the Republic of Letters began not in 1789, but in 1779, when men began to meet without the supervision of women in private associations of their own making. When the literary public sphere was transformed into the political public sphere in 1789, it had already become masculine; the 'democratic' Republic of 1792 reflected the limitations and exclusions of the Republic of Letters of the 1780s.

Notes

1. Jürgen Habermas, *The Structural Transformation of the Public Sphere: An Inquiry into a Category of Bourgeois Society*, trans. by Thomas Burger (Cambridge, MA, 1989).
2. See Habermas, *Structural Transformation*, pp. 31-43 and the following studies: Goodman, *The Republic of Letters*, chapters 3-4; Jeffrey S. Ravel, 'The Police and the Parterre: Cultural Politics in the Paris Public Theatre, 1680–1789' (PhD dissertation, University of California at Berkeley, 1989); Margaret C. Jacob, *Living the Enlightenment: Freemasonry and Politics in Eighteenth-Century Europe* (New York, 1991); Daniel S. Gordon, *Citizens without Sovereignty: Equality and Sociability in French Thought, 1670–1789* (Princeton, 1994); Lawrence Klein, 'Coffee Clashes: The Politics of Conversation in Eighteenth-Century England' (unpublished paper, 1992); Jack R. Censer and Jeremy D. Popkin (eds) *Press and Politics in Pre-Revolutionary France* (Berkeley, 1987); Jeremy D. Popkin, *News and Politics in the Age of Revolution: Jean Luzac's 'Gazette de Leyde'* (Ithaca, 1989); Roger Chartier, *The Cultural Origins of the French Revolution*, trans. by Lydia Cochrane (Durham, NC, 1991).
3. Hervé Guénot, 'Musées et lycées Parisiens (1780–1830)' *Dix-Huitième Siècle* 18 (1986) pp. 249–50; Johel Coutura, 'Le Musée de Bordeaux' *Dix-Huitième Siècle* 19 (1987) p. 162; Louis Amiable, 'Les Origines maçonniques du Musée de Paris et du Lycée' *La Révolution Française* 30 (1896) pp. 484–500; Daniel Roche, *Le Siècle des lumières en province* 2 vols. (Paris and The Hague, 1978), vol. 1 p. 66; Patrice Gueniffey and Ran

Halévi, 'Clubs and Popular Societies' in *A Critical Dictionary of the French Revolution* ed. by François Furet and Mona Ozouf, trans. by Arthur Goldhammer (Cambridge, MA, 1989) p. 460; Michael L. Kennedy, *The Jacobin Clubs in the French Revolution: The First Years* (Princeton, 1982).

4. Habermas, *Structural Transformation*, pp. 51–56.

5. [Claude-Mammès Pahin de La Blancherie], *Prospectus* for *Les Nouvelles de la République des Lettres et des Arts* (Paris, 1777), pp. 3–4.

6. See Françoise Waquet, 'Qu'est-ce que la République des Lettres? Essai de sémantique historique', *Bibliothèque de l'Ecole des Chartes* 147 (1989) pp. 473–502.

7. Maurice Tourneux (ed.) 'Journal intime de l'abbé Mulot (1777–82)' *Mémoires de la Société de l'Histoire de Paris et de l'Ile-de-France* 29 (1902) p. 38.

8. Friedrich-Melchior Grimm, et al., *Correspondance littéraire, philosophique et critique*, ed. by Maurice Tourneux (Paris, 1877–1882); *Mémoires secrets pour servir à l'histoire de la République des lettres en France* . . . (London, 1780–1789).

9. Claude-Mammès Pahin de la Blancherie, *Correspondance générale sur les sciences et les arts* (1779) p. 8.

10. Richard Derb—to the Editor of the *Courrier de l'Europe*, 8 May 1779. Reprinted in F. Rabbe, 'Pahin de La Blancherie et la salon de la correspondance (1)' *Bulletin de la Société Historique du VIe Arrondissement de Paris* 2 (1899) pp. 40–43.

11. *Correspondance littéraire*, May, 1778.

12. 'Extrait des Registres de l'Académie Royale des Sciences de Paris du 20 mai 1778' in La Blancherie, *Correspondance générale* pp. 28–30. On Mesmer see Robert Darnton, *Mesmerism and the End of the Enlightenment in France* (Cambridge, MA, 1968) pp. 62–64.

13. Gordon, *Citizens without Sovereignty*, p. 37; Jean Morange, *La Liberté d'association en droit public français* (Paris, 1977) pp. 29–30; William H. Sewell, Jr., *Work and Revolution in France: The Language of Labor from the Old Regime to 1848* (Cambridge, 1980) p. 41; Maurice Agulhon, 'Vers une histoire des associations' *Esprit* n.s. (June 1978) pp. 13–14.

14. *Mémoires secrets* 26 November 1779.

15. *Mémoires secrets* 8 May 1780.

16. *Mémoires secrets* 28 June 1781.

17. *Mémoires secrets* 1 July 1781. A 1784 proposal for a *musée* in Toulouse included a lottery whereby subscribers would be reimbursed for their subscriptions 'successively'. See Baron de Desazars de Montgaillard, *Histoire de l'Académie des Sciences de Toulouse. Le Musée. Le Lycée. L'Athenée, 1784–1807* (Toulouse, 1908) p. 20.

18. Margaret C. Jacob, *Living the Enlightenment* (Oxford, 1991); Reinhart Koselleck, *Critique and Crisis: Enlightenment and the Pathogenesis of Modern Society* (Cambridge, MA, 1988) pp. 62–97.

19. Jean-Louis Harouel et al., *Histoire des institutions de l'époque franque à la Révolution* (Paris, 1987) pp. 465–66.

20. La Blancherie, *Correspondance générale* pp. 9–10. 'There is a shift in meaning', writes Habermas of the term 'public', when 'we say that someone has made a name for himself, has a public reputation. The notion of such personal prestige or renown originated in epochs other than that of "polite society" '. (*Structural Transformation* p. 2). If polite society was institutionalized in the salon, then La Blancherie's requirement that members of his assembly have a 'public character' marks the shift to a new order.
21. La Blancherie, *Correspondance générale* p. 12.
22. 'The Practical Impact of Writing' in *A History of Private Life* vol. III: *Passions of the Renaissance*, ed. by Roger Chartier, trans. by Arthur Goldhammer (Cambridge, MA, 1989) p. 147.
23. *Les Femmes et l'Académie française.* (Paris, 1981) pp. 9–1.
24. René Le Forestier, *Maçonnerie féminine et loges académiques* (Milan, 1979) p. 37; Margaret C. Jacob, 'Freemasonry, Women, and the Paradox of the Enlightenment' in Margaret Hunt et al. (eds) *Women and the Enlightenment* (New York, 1984) p. 69; Jacques Brengues, 'La Guerre des sexes et l'amour-maçon dans la poésie' *Dix-Huitième Siècle* 19 (1987) p. 105.
25. Le Forestier, *Maçonnerie féminine* chapter 2.
26. Le Forestier, *Maçonnerie féminine* pp. 26, 39, 57–58; Collette Bertrand, 'Comment la franc-maçonnerie vient aux femmes' *Dix-Huitième Siècle* 19 (1987) p. 208.
27. This is the main argument in Jacob, 'Freemasonry, Women, and the Paradox of the Enlightenment', and two articles by Janet M. Burke: 'Freemasonry, Friendship, and Noblewomen: The Role of the Secret Society in Bringing Enlightenment Thought to Pre-Revolutionary Women Elites' *History of European Ideas* 10 (1989) pp. 283–293; and 'Through Friendship to Feminism: The Growth in Self-Awareness among Eighteenth-Century Women Freemasons' *Proceedings of the Western Society for French History* 14 (1978) pp. 187–96. See also Bertrand, 'Comment la franc-maçonnerie vient aux femmes' pp. 208–09. The case for Free-masonry as an institution of democratic sociability is made by Ran Halévi, *Les Loges maçonniques dans la France d'Ancien Régime: aux origines de la sociabilité démocratique* (Paris, 1984); and by Jacob in *Living the Enlightenment*. For a critique of the latter argument see Chartier, *Cultural Origins*, p. 165.
28. Le Forestier, *Maçonnerie féminine* p. 64.
29. Le Forestier, *Maçonnerie féminine* p. 32. Louis-Sébastien Mercier included a chapter on Freemasons in the *Tableau de Paris*. In it he noted that the police left them alone, but that the more rigorous Masons were upset at the looseness of Parisian Freemasonry, signified by the lodges of adoption. (*Tableau de Paris* (Amsterdam, 1783–88) vol. VII pp. 194–96). Thierry's *Almanach du voyageur à Paris* for 1786 listed both lodges and *musées*.
30. Le Forestier, *Maçonnerie féminine* p. 60.
31. Mme de Lambert and Mme de Tencin had responded to the same problem

by forming salons that were the precursors of Enlightenment salons. See Goodman, 'Enlightenment Salons' p. 333.

32. Brengues, 'La Guerre des sexes' pp. 112–13.
33. Brengues, 'La Guerre des sexes' p. 116.
34. Lynn Hunt, *The Family Romance of the French Revolution* (Berkeley, 1992).
35. On Pilâtre and the *Musée de Monsieur* see René Taton, 'Condorcet et Sylvestre-François Lacroix (1)', *Revue d'Histoire des Sciences et de leurs Applications* 12 (April–June 1959) pp. 130–38; Charles Dejob, 'De l'établissement connu sous le nom de Lycée et d'Athénée et de quelques établissements analogues' *Revue Internationale de l'Enseignement* 18 (1889) pp. 4–38; William A. Smeaton, 'The Early Years of the Lycée and the Lycée des Arts. A Chapter in the Lives of A.L. Lavoisier and A.F. de Fourcroy' *Annals of Science* 11 (1955) pp. 257–67; Charles Cabanes, 'Histoire du premier musée autorisé par le gouvernement' *La Nature* (1937) pp. 577–83.
36. Amiable, 'Origines maçonniques' p. 492.
37. *Mémoires secrets* 3 January 1782; Cabanes, 'Histoire du premier musée' pp. 577–78.
38. *Mémoires secrets* 3 December 1781.
39. *Mémoires secrets* 10 December 1781.
40. M[édéric].L[ouis].E[lie]. Moreau de Saint-Méry, *Discours sur l'utilité du musée établi à Paris prononcé dans la séance publique du 1er Décembre 1784* (Parma, 1805) n.p.
41. Cabanes, 'Histoire du premier musée'; Taton, 'Condorcet et Sylvestre-François Lacroix' pp. 131–32; Dejob, 'De l'établissement connu sous le nom de Lycée' p. 10.
42. Quoted in Cabanes, 'Histoire du premier musée' p. 579.
43. Taton, 'Condorcet et Sylvestre-François Lacroix' p. 133.
44. Moreau de Saint-Méry, *Discours* n.p. (All subsequent page references will be placed parenthetically in the text.)
45. Diderot, 'Encyclopédie' in Denis Diderot and Jean le Rond d'Alembert (eds) *Encyclopédie, ou Dictionnaire raisonné des sciences, des arts et des métiers* (Paris, 1751–1765) vol. V p. 637. On the library and museum at Alexandria, see Mostafa El-Abbadi, *The Life and Fate of the Ancient Library of Alexandria* (Paris, 1990) pp. 84–90; Luciano Canfora, *The Vanished Library* trans. by Martin Ryle (London, 1989); and Diana Delia, 'From Romance to Rhetoric: The Alexandrian Library in Classical and Islamic Tradition' *American Historical Review* 97 (December 1992) pp. 1449–67.
46. Moreau de Saint-Méry, *Discours* n.p.
47. Goodman, *The Republic of Letters*, chap. 3.
48. Cabanes, who studied the list of patrons and subscribers, found Pilâtre's appeal to women particularly successful. All the women he lists, like the overwhelming majority of the men, were aristocratic. Some joined with their husbands, some, such as the comtesse de Buffon and the princesse d'Hénin, joined as individuals, ('Histoire du premier musée' pp. 578–79).
49. Quoted in Cabanes, 'Histoire du premier musée' p. 580.

50. *Musée de Monsieur et de Mgr. le Comte d'Artois* [Prospectus] (Paris, 1785) p. 3.
51. *Musée de Monsieur* p. 3.
52. See André Morellet (ed.) *Eloges de Mme. Geoffrin* (Paris, 1812) and my discussion in *The Republic of Letters*, pp. 100–10.

Three

Addressing the Public in Eighteenth-Century French Fiction

Malcolm Cook

As novel forms developed and as the genre increased in popularity, so the relationship between writer and reader was transformed and a dialogue developed. A recent study of pornographic fiction suggests that every fiction involves the reader as a kind of voyeur who looks into people's lives and who delves into the intimacy of their personal relationships.[1] Clearly, in fiction, and perhaps more precisely in fiction of the eighteenth century, the world of the private becomes public as intimate accounts are published and divulged. Certainly, novels in the eighteenth century, practically without exception, will tell the tale of love. In France, as the century passes, so the status of the reader is developed and the reader starts to acquire a mentality and an existence of his or her own. If it is rare in the seventeenth century to find prefatorial comment from 'narrator' or 'editor' (never 'writer') to the reader, the very opposite is true of the late eighteenth century. Hardly a novel published between 1780 and the end of the century will fail to include a preface, an 'avant-propos' or something equivalent. As the example on page 42 shows, not all have much to say.

Novelists are ever aware of the need to attract their readers and various strategies will be used. The most obvious is the straight address, such as the one found in Lesage's *Gil Blas*, the first part of which appeared in 1715.[2] The reader is the great unknown—male or female, old or young, he or she has no physical reality. All we know is that to exist he or she has to be able to read. The process of being read to by a third

PRÉFACE.

; ! * * * (. . . . .) = — ? , .
, . , . , . , [! . ! ! ! ! ! — a
y. —] * * * * : : : : : — ;
; — ? ? ? ? ? R ! E ! Q : » » »
» » — ; ; ; ; ; Ç , , (—)
. . . . M. J. = — — - Æ
Œ Æ . . . .
- ! : Æ æ w é ê Œ ! : w D ,
Ç K Æ ç w W ê É È ; , N q
ɪ e , k æ É Œ w æ Ç œ M
ɪ ! ! ! ! ! ! ! ! ! ! ! ! ! ! ! ! !

Gorjy, *'Ann'Quin Bredouille*, 1792.

person will change the intimacy of the dialogue between author and reader and will falsify the relationship. Moreover, the contract which is established is a strange one since rarely will the author identify him- or herself. In his correspondence with one of the most popular novelists of his day, Madame Riccoboni, Laclos will suggest that men and women write different kinds of fiction, but I suspect that without prior knowledge, readers will rarely be able to identify the gender of the writer. There is more than a hint of flattery when Laclos writes: 'No doubt a women, born with a fine soul, a sensitive heart and a delicate wit, can give the portraits she traces part of the charm which she herself possesses.'[3] In fact, as I shall show in this article, rarely are distinctions made between men and women as readers. While Darnton and his followers have done much to identify the conditions of publishing in eighteenth-century France and we now have a much better idea of the book trade, it is practically impossible to identify readers of fiction and we are no closer to the truth now than we were twenty years ago. It is possible to show, as Labrousse has done for Rousseau's novel *La Nouvelle Héloïse*, what the response of different readers was to the novel, but it becomes a complex sociological problem if we try to establish types of readers for different kinds of texts. The traditional view that women read novels while men read manly things like history or law cannot be sustained. The reader who is addressed in eighteenth-century novels normally has no body and no identity. The dialogue which takes place between writer and reader is eerie and mysterious. If the reader is anonymous, so too, usually, is the author. If the reader is spoken to, he or she rarely has the right of reply. There are, as we shall see, some notable exceptions to this.

In this article I trace the evolution of the ways in which readers are addressed by concentrating on a small number of well-known examples. Then I show how writers of the period 1780–1800 use a particular device which is at once inside and outside the text. If we take Lesage's novel as a starting point we find a device which will be imitated throughout the century: a double preface in which the author addresses the reader as well as the narrator/hero. The author claims that the characters sketched in the text have no actual reality and that they do not represent real people (which will make the reader suspicious); the narrator asks the reader for indulgence. He uses the popular 'tu' form since the reader is thought to be a friend, not a stern critic. The account will contain a moral message that the judicious reader will identify. Utility will be mixed with amusement in the traditional manner.

Indeed, it may be true that the first-person narrator will, generally, identify the reader as a friend who suffers from the same defects as him-

or herself. In a novel which female readers might well find offensive, Jacob, the manly peasant hero of Marivaux's *Le Paysan parvenu* (1734–35), delights in recounting his seductive prowess and also takes for granted that the reader is a friend; he does not assume for a moment that his reader might be a woman but, presumably, a good number will be. He says on the first page of his account: 'The account of my adventures will not be without value for those who like to educate themselves.'[4]

There is, nevertheless, a constant irony in the novel, protected by what is now known as a double register. The peasant hero is not aware of his failure to attract the kind of woman he really desires—the implication that he succeeds in life because of his looks and panache is found, eventually, to be quite wrong. Jacob is lucky but fails to realize it. We, the readers, do—indeed, that is part of the charm of the text.

With the appearance of Rousseau's *La Nouvelle Héloïse* in 1761 we find, perhaps for the first time in France, the novel itself accompanied by an important theoretical statement. It is difficult for the modern reader to comprehend the excitement caused by Rousseau's fiction. It was one of the bestsellers of the century, full of moral sentiment and lavish in its descriptions of the Swiss countryside. It is also immensely long. It pays little attention to verisimilitude and yet, constantly, Rousseau shows his awareness of the kind of reader he wants to attract. In the 'Entretiens sur les romans' which follow the novel, the author tries to distinguish reality from the presentation of reality: the artistic representation of passion will be quite different from the expression of passion in reality. Without realizing it, Rousseau was addressing one reader who took to heart what he was saying. In Laclos's *Liaisons dangereuses*, Mme Merteuil, mocking Valmont for his love for the Présidente, repeats almost verbatim, what Rousseau said in the 'Entretien'. Rousseau writes:

> Read a love letter written by an author in his study . . . You will be enchanted, even excited perhaps. But the excitement will be transient and without depth . . . On the other hand a letter which love has really dictated from a lover full of passion will be sluggish, diffuse, full of lengthy passages, disordered and full of repetition.[5]

But what Rousseau says in the second preface seems to contradict what he said in the first. There he said that reading the letters required much patience and that this collection with its 'gothic' tone was more suited to women readers than a book of philosophy. If it was suitable for women with experience of the world, it was dangerous for innocent girls. Chaste girls do not read novels, he says. If they open this one, forewarned as they are by the title, they are lost for ever.

While it will be apparent to modern readers who are familiar with Rousseau's works that he is trying here, as elsewhere, to get the best of both worlds, we must not forget that a novel which most modern readers find long and difficult was read with speed and enthusiasm in the eighteenth century. Difficult though it may be for us to believe, Rousseau was accused of writing a licentious novel by contemporary critics. Rousseau identifies his readers and writes for them. His novel, he claims, will not have any effect on readers living in towns who know the ways of the world. But it might encourage those who live in the country to appreciate the value of the lives they lead.

After the appearance of *La Nouvelle Héloïse* the debate about the nature of fiction intensified. The novel, seen as a dangerous genre by its critics, was now recognized as a literary form which, by its very popularity, could influence the way people led their lives. The 1760s in France saw the success of writers like Marmontel, Mercier and Madame Riccoboni. The novel had become the instrument of moral propaganda in which a constant dialogue was taking place between writer and reader. Reviewing his work in 1786, Marmontel claimed that he wrote to convey to his readers the fruits of his long experience. If young people could enjoy the vicarious experience of a wise author, they, presumably, would not make the same mistakes.[6] If the readers of his *Contes moraux* were identified as young people, one can only say that young people of the eighteenth century were more tolerant than those of today. Marmontel and his contemporaries clearly believed that reading could replace experience. Ideally, fiction teaches people how to lead their lives. Would readers (of whom, of course, there were not many) therefore be better people than non-readers? Obviously not. For it must be apparent to us, even if the view was not shared by all writers of the period, that people do not normally read novels because they want to learn how to behave. As the more perceptive writers realized, it was impossible to identify your reader in advance.

There is no doubt that some novels were written with particular readers in mind, even if one could not be sure that others would not also participate. One of the great successes of the 1780s was a novel by Mme de Genlis entitled, *Adèle et Théodore ou lettres sur l'éducation of 1782.* Mme de Genlis was, by profession, a governess and one reason for the novel's spectacular success was the fact that she had just been appointed as 'gouverneur' (sic) of the sons of the duc de Chartres. Hitherto it had been unthinkable that a woman could be appointed to educate male princes. As the critic of the *Correspondance littéraire* suggested: 'How could one not be curious to see if her book would justify such an extraordinary event?'[7] Such notoriety was not, of course, likely to explain other best-selling fiction of the period. The point which needs to be stressed is that texts were popular for different reasons. Some survive, others do not. Mme de Genlis's novel is long and didactic, has very little suspense and is, on the whole, dull. It appealed no doubt to parents wishing to find fiction they judged suitable for their children. As I have already suggested, Laclos might well have had *Adèle et Théodore* in mind when he addressed the reader in his only novel, now much more familiar to the modern reader than that of Mme de Genlis.[8]

Madame de Genlis is totally aware of the reader she is addressing. Her novel is a treatise on education. It is designed for parents and children. It will provide sustenance for those wishing to partake of the meal of moral didacticism that is her speciality. She says, curiously, that in her novel she often refers to other works on education in the hope that 'pères de famille' (fathers) will be encouraged to read them. She warns her readers of the dangers of reading Rousseau—'what disgusting details there are in the *Nouvelle Héloïse*'.[9] In the 'Reading Plan' which she devises for the young Adèle, she points out that the mother is always on hand to make sure that the pupil interprets correctly what she reads and that any dangerous passages are avoided. Mme de Genlis says that there are no exceptions to the rule that there is not a single work that a child aged between 7 and 15 can read without danger. She suggests that 'children' should not read a book by themselves until they are aged between 18 and 19 or even later. It is difficult to believe that the advice given by Mme de Genlis gained universal approval. The writer of a novel does not expect to be confronted by an intermediary between him- or herself and the reader. The relationship which develops is one of intimacy: the reader is a friend who has made a commitment to the text. So it is that in the 1780s and especially in novels which might be loosely defined as licentious, a dialogue between reader and writer becomes part of a pattern.

Diderot's novels, not published until 1796 but written between 1760 and 1770, are excellent examples of the close relationship which is developing. The text is no longer simply a detached account in which the reader is a passive listener to a fascinating tale. In Diderot's fiction the reader is constantly engaged—sometimes, as in *Jacques le fataliste*, he or she has to make a judgment about a preferred ending. The author taunts the reader to find a conclusion which will be suitable. Elements which are commonplace in other novels are not provided in

Jacques le fataliste. For example, when the two interlocutors refer to a letter, the reader expects to see a copy of it. But the narrator intervenes: 'Reader, you've stopped reading. What's up? Ah, I think I know. You'd like to see that letter. Mme Riccoboni would certainly have let you see it.'[10] Diderot knows that readers of his fiction will also be readers of other fiction. He can allude to Sterne, to Richardson to Don Quixote, to *Pantagruel* and to the *Compère Mathieu* knowing that his allusions will be understood by the majority of his readers. As Diderot knows, readers of fiction will be familiar with texts which might be called essential. Addressing the reader in fiction entails knowing what readers will have read: the irony which develops from shared knowledge will add to the reader's pleasure and will also invite comment on the nature of the illusion which is being produced. In this, as in other works, Diderot is the master. In *La Religieuse* (called by the author the counterpart of *Jacques le fataliste*), the young *narratrice* is a nun who has been forced into a convent against her will. Her eloquent appeal for freedom is addressed to a real man, a friend of Diderot's, le marquis de Croixmare. In the memoir/novel the narrator (the author?) occasionally seems to forget whom she/he is addressing. The reader is totally involved in the moving account to the point of overlooking errors of fact, errors of verisimilitude and, eventually, even the deliberate breaking of the illusion. Diderot, at least, recognized that the reader is willingly compliant. He/she will play the role of reader as long as the author plays his or her role as writer.

This takes us to a particular phenomenon which has not, as far as I know, ever been studied in detail. We have seen discussions taking place outside the body of fiction, in prefaces, postfaces, epilogues and so on.[11] Fiction of the 1780s and 1790s regularly includes an address to the reader, not through the text itself nor through its traditional means of preface/*avant-propos* but through the accumulation of footnotes. This is not to say that such a device has not been used before, but I suspect that only at this point is it becoming systematic. The proliferation of what might be judged to be licentious novels of the 1780s might explain the incidence of this technique. For it does not, I think, survive in any significant way into the nineteenth century. I will look at examples from three authors: Rétif de la Bretonne, Laclos and the marquis de Sade.

If we look first of all at Rétif's *La Paysanne pervertie* of 1784–5 we will notice that there is a proliferation of footnotes. These are the author's own notes which, often, guide the reader towards the complementary work, *Le Paysan perverti*. Rétif writes two novels with interrelating themes and events and, eventually, brings them together.

The footnotes are intended to save the reader time by sending him or her in the right direction for supplementary information. But the footnotes have other purposes: they suggest to the reader that the letters which make up the story actually exist, that they have a concrete reality; the editor/author has them in front of him and is making the necessary correlation. But the notes have another more important function. They guarantee that the text can be assessed as a moral text by introducing critical comments and by offering supplementary information about the characters. For example, in Letter XV from Gaudet to Edmond, we find a footnote which refers to the marquis who has not yet been introduced: 'It was the marquis who is going to play such an important part.'[12] Other notes have a more obvious impact on the meaning of the text. For example, in the letter from Gaudet to Ursule found in Letter CXII, the 'editor' intervenes constantly, addressing the reader with an accumulation of short phrases designed to ram home the moral message: 'He's using the "tu" form already with you'; 'There she goes, selling herself shamelessly'; 'Oh wretched children, so good in the past.'[13] On other occasions the footnotes, apparently from the editor, occupy half a page. They disrupt the reading process by breaking into the narrative —the reader has little choice but to read them, highlighted as they are typographically and emphasized as they seem to be. A good example in the *Paysanne pervertie* is to be found in Letter CXIX. Here the 'editeur' starts commenting on the content of the letter, showing the extent to which Ursule, the heroine, has been corrupted and pointing out that her eventual penitence will force the reader to feel compassion. He particularly addresses the 'young readers' and claims that this work, by showing corruption in all its ugliness, will teach the reader how to recognize the real thing when confronted by it in the world (p.399).

When a novel is composed of letters the author has no voice, except, of course, through commentary outside the text. This may explain the incidence of prefatory remarks and footnotes in the two examples we are looking at for the moment. It must be said, however, that not all writers of epistolary novels feel the need to address the reader. In *Les Liaisons dangereures* Laclos uses every device at his disposal to talk to the reader and to enhance the complexity of his creation. Laclos is a master of irony and the external voice will be used to strengthen this aspect of the text. For example, the novel begins with a contradictory series of prefaces (in a fashion which is not dissimilar to that used by Rousseau). The 'publisher' opens the novel by suggesting that the events described could certainly not have happened in recent times and by refusing to guarantee that the letters are authentic. This is the very opposite of the norm and the reader will be surprised. It did not convince con- temporaries who immediately suspected that there was a key to all the characters and who sought to identify them. The 'editor' who collected the letters and reproduced them tells the reader a number of things: that the collection he/she is about to read is not the complete correspondence; that permission to correct stylistic errors was not granted (although the reader looks for them in vain); and that he himself was told not to tamper with the letters since it would endanger the credibility of the novel if all the correspondents wrote in the same style (a common failing in other novels of this type). The most important aspect of this long address to the reader is the offer of a guarantee of moral utility. Two truths emerge: any woman who accepts into her society a man without morals ends up being his victim; any mother who allows another woman to receive the confidences of her daughter is guilty of imprudence. Young readers will learn that the friendship offered by older people is often no more than a dangerous trap. The 'editor' quotes a mother who, after reading the manuscript, said she believed she would be rendering her daughter a great service if she gave her a copy of this text on her wedding day. However, what her daughter might have thought of such a gift is not recorded. The preface, in effect, offers something for everybody. The novel is authentic, it will please some but not others and it will teach everyone something. The preface is unusually long and defensive and barely prepares one for what is to follow, for the opening letter itself is dull in the extreme. It is the rather silly letter of a young woman who has just left her convent. It does not suggest to the reader the complexity of the events which will unfold, nor the study of psychology which is one of the novel's great strengths.

What interests us, for the moment at least, is the way in which Laclos prepares a dialogue with the reader—he provides footnotes which give factual information of a very simple kind: references for quotations, information about missing letters, explanations that certain letters have been suppressed and so on. There are approximately fifty footnotes (and 175 letters) which seems a particularly large number but, as I suggested previously, this device is particularly useful in epistolary novels. The author is able to withdraw from a position of guilt, emphasizing the moral position and highlighting the 'guilty' conduct of certain individuals. For example, for Letter LI we find the following footnote: 'The reader must have guessed some while ago from Mme de Merteuil's morals how little she respected religion. We would have suppressed this whole paragraph but we felt that in showing effects we ought also to make the causes known.'[14] Occasionally, and interestingly, the editor intervenes to say that he/she does not know where a particular quotation comes from. To this day, it is not known whether these are taken from a well-known author or whether they are, in fact, the invention of the character in the novel. (See, for example, Letter LXXXI). The last footnote of all deserves our attention too. There is nothing in normal editions to distinguish it from other similiar footnotes, but in the manuscript of the novel (as the Versini edition makes clear) the note is in a quite different hand. We are told that, one day, it may be possible to complete the work by showing how all the characters finished up. This may well be the publisher leaving the door open for a possible sequel—which, for reasons I cannot explain, never appeared.

Laclos's novel is, of course, exceptional in every way. But there can be little doubt that what he was doing was also part of a literary fashion. The marquis de Sade, himself a great reader of novels, is not blind to the opportunities offered by footnotes, as we can see, for example, by a brief study of a late work, the *Crimes de l'amour*. Sade revels in the innocence of the narrative position, claiming a moral utility for his most obscene texts and delighting in the ironical potential of an omniscient narrator. While many of the foonotes in Sade's texts have a similar function to those of the *Liaisons dangereuses*. I suspect that of all the writers of the period, Sade is the master of the long footnote. One example will suffice. In 'Faxelange ou les torts de l'ambition' the heroine has a dream which, in the event, prefigures the reality which she is to experience. Sade launches into a footnote which occupies nearly half a page, pointing out the significance of dreams: 'Dreams are secret movements which are not given their rightful place; half of us laugh at them, the other half believes them.'[15] Sade's intervention guarantees that the episode in this story will be given due attention and, eventually, the events unfold in the manner which the dream predicted. This collection of 'nouvelles' is not in letter form of course. What Sade maintains here and elsewhere is that the details which he delights in recounting have their own moral purpose: the reader is addressed in every sense—he or she will be shocked, perhaps disgusted by the manner of the account. But the 'editor' figure whose rôle is to guarantee the truth, will engage the reader in a constant dialogue, excusing the lavish detail in the expressed hope that the reader will benefit from the story. The conclusion to 'Faxelange' reads: 'May the story of this event make some readers more just, others more wise. We will not then regret the trouble we will have taken to convey to posterity an incident which, however awful, might serve for the good of man.'[16] Readers will, no doubt, accuse Sade of bad faith. However, he is perhaps no more guilty than any of the authors of novels which might loosely be called licentious, who feel that by engaging the reader in dialogue, they might be forgiven for certain aspects of their accounts.

A number of conclusions must be drawn: what I am suggesting here is that the process of reading certain kinds of novels is more complex than it might seem at first sight. The use of the footnote and other forms of what seem to be editorial intervention represent an important aspect in the development of fiction. For twenty years in the history of the novel, footnotes became part of the fictional fabric. Then, quite suddenly, they seemed to die out. Are there any similar examples of such use in the nineteenth century? Is the novel at the end of the eighteenth century going through a phenomenon which, for the first time, recognizes the importance of the reader and identifies him (or her) as a client? Most writers do not distinguish between their male or female readers. One English novelist, Charlotte Smith, does so in *The Old Manor House* of 1793. In a footnote about the American Revolution, the author addresses the reader saying: 'Of the tragical scenes it occasioned, the reader, if he or she delight in studying circumstances in this war ... is referred to the Annual Register for 1779.'[17] The reader, it is admitted, might be a woman. The reader, in French, will always be a man, if only for reasons of grammar, 'lecteur' always taking the masculine pronoun.

Addressing the reader in fiction will always be a delicate operation. The author is talking constantly to an imaginary reader whose tastes he or she is trying to gauge and whose responses are felt to be known and predictable. If Diderot's *Jacques le fataliste* works as an experimental novel it is because the author knows only too well that the novel will have to appeal to different readers of different sexes and with different expectations. But the reader of the eighteenth century novel wants to be recognized, wants his or her existence to be admitted and expects somes kind of status. The author of fiction must be aware of the effect the novel might produce. Mme de Staël, discussing Rousseau's *La Nouvelle Heloïse* in her *Lettre sur les écrits de Rousseau* suggests that the same novel will have a quite different impact on different readers: 'His novel is for women; he wrote it for them. Women can be harmed or helped by it.'[18] If Rousseau can be criticized it is because he was not sufficiently aware of the influence which might have been exerted by his description of the passion of Saint-Preux. He was too concerned to paint a picture of a woman who returns to the path of virtue and unaware that his picture of Saint-Preux was an exciting and dangerous one.

Addressing the reader in eighteenth-century fiction is a serious occupation. In an age where the influence of fiction was seen to be enormous, the author who remained blissfully unaware of his social responsibility would be criticized and condemned. In fiction the public and the private spheres merge. The intimate relationship which exists between writer and reader is the one which, through various technical devices, is going to modify the course of fiction. Private lives, intimate relationships which are the very stuff of fiction need some introduction. By talking to the reader, by establishing a relationship, a dialogue can emerge. But it is a dialogue where identities remain secret and where interpretation is of paramount importance.

Notes

1. See Jean Marie Goulemot, *Ces livres qu'on ne lit que d'une main. Lecture et lecteurs de livres pornographiques au XVIIIe siècle* (Aix-en-Provence, 1991).
2. In *Gil Blas* we find both a 'Déclaration de l'Auteur' in which the author denies that the portraits in his novel are those of any real people, but in so doing he immediately initiates a dialogue with the reader; and a section called 'Gil Blas au Lecteur' which provides the reader with a strategy for appreciating this particular text. See Lesage, *Gil Blas* (Paris, 1977), pp. 19–21.
3. 'Sans doute une femme, née avec une belle âme, un cœur sensible et un esprit délicat, peut répandre sur les portraits qu'elle trace, une partie du charme qu'elle possède'. Choderlos de Laclos, *Œuvres complètes*, ed. by L. Versini (Paris, 1979) p.765 (my translation).
4. We read in the original: 'Le récit de mes aventures ne sera pas inutile à ceux qui aiment à s'instruire'. Marivaux, *Le Paysan parvenu* (Paris, 1965) pp. 25–26.
5. We read in the original: 'Lisez une lettre d'amour faite par un auteur dans son cabinet . . . Vous serez enchanté, même agité peut-être, mais d'une agitation passagère et sèche . . . Au contraire, une lettre que l'amour a réellement dictée, une lettre d'un amant vraiment passionné, sera lâche, diffuse, toute en longueurs, en désordre, en répétitions.' Rousseau, *La Nouvelle Héloïse* (Paris, 1967) p. 574 (my translation).
6. In the 'Avertissement de l'Auteur' dated 1768, Marmontel wrote: 'Ma poétique était le fruit de mes études particulières: je les communiquais aux jeunes gens, dans l'intention de leur épargner le long travail que j'avais fait pour moi' (*Œuvres complètes* (Paris, 1818) III p. vii).
7. For a detailed discussion of this novel, see my article '*Adèle et Théodore* ou les liaisons dangereuses', *Studies on Voltaire and the Eighteenth Century* 284 (1991) pp. 371–83. The *Correspondance littéraire* article reads: '. . . la singularité, peut-être unique, du choix qui venait de nommer Mme de Genlis gouverneur des fils de M. le duc de Chartres, avait fixé, pour ainsi dire, tous les yeux sur elle' (Janvier 1782, p. 55)

8. For a full discussion of this point, see my article cited in note 7 above.
9. In a long preface, Mme de Genlis defends her novel and attacks Rousseau. This particular phrase reads: 'Que de détails révoltans dans la nouvelle Héloïse' (*Adèle et Théodore ou lettres sur l'éducation* (Paris, 1827) p. viii).
10. 'Lecteur, vous suspendez ici votre lecture: qu'est-ce qu'il y a? Ah! je crois vous comprendre, vous voudriez voir cette lettre. Mme Riccoboni n'aurait pas manqué de vous la montrer' (*Jacques le fataliste* (Paris, 1973) p. 286).
11. For example, in Cazotte's *Le Diable amoureux* (1772), the second edition includes an epilogue in which the author explains why certain changes have been incorporated.
12. 'C'était le marquis qui va jouer un si grand role' (*La Paysanne pervertie* (Paris, 1976) p. 109).
13. We read in the original: 'Tu! Infortunée! Il te tutoie déjà!'; 'La voilà qui se vend effrontément! 'O misérables enfants, autrefois honnêtes!' (pp. 372–73)
14. The French reads: 'Le Lecteur a dû deviner depuis longtemps par les mœurs de Mme de Merteuil, combien peu elle respectait la Religion. On aurait supprimé tout cet alinéa; mais on a cru qu'en montrant les effets, on ne devait pas négliger d'en faire connaître les causes.' (Laclos, *Œuvres complètes* p. 106).
15. 'Les rêves sont des mouvements secrets qu'on ne met pas assez à leur vraie place; la moitié des hommes s'en moque, l'autre portion y ajoute foi.' Sade, *Œuvres complètes* (Paris, 1973) vols IX–X p. 187.
16. 'Puisse le récit de cette histoire rendre les uns plus justes et les autres plus sages. Nous ne regretterons pas alors la peine que nous aurons prise de transmettre à la postérité un événement qui, tout affreux qu'il est, pourrait alors servir au bien des hommes' (*Œuvres complètes*, IX–X p. 208).
17. World's Classics, ed. by Anne Henry Ehrenpreis (Oxford, 1989) p. 360.
18. We read: 'Son ouvrage est pour les femmes; c'est pour elles qu'il est fait; c'est à elles qu'il peut nuire ou servir' (*Œuvres complètes*, I pp. 28–29).

Four

Scandalous Femininity: Prostitution and Eighteenth-Century Narrative

Vivien Jones

I

Two of the most successful eighteenth-century narratives were Hogarth's print series *A Harlot's Progress* of 1732 and Samuel Richardson's novel *Pamela*, published in 1740. In both cases, the original publication spawned an industry of popular imitations and reproductions, both written and visual, and representations of Hogarth's Harlot and of Pamela Andrews appeared on the stage, on china and in popular ballads.[1] These two texts are variants on the story of threatened female innocence. They exemplify the tragic and the triumphalist versions of the classic seduction plot, in which vulnerable femininity is betrayed into ruin by predatory, and usually socially superior, masculinity—or, in the case of *Pamela*, withstands that threat to achieve spectacular social success. The popularity of this narrative suggests its mythic power: it is one of the sites through which an emergent middle class provided itself, as Foucault puts it, with 'a body and a sexuality', through which it 'converted the blue blood of the nobles into a sound body and a healthy sexuality'.[2] At the same time, through its focus on, primarily female, sexual transgression the seduction narrative powerfully articulates the anxieties raised by new and shifting class alliances. The woman whose (inappropriate?) social aspirations are punished by public ruin and/or prostitution stands as the threatening other to the emergent ideal of the 'proper lady', the domestic female whose modest feminine qualities are nevertheless designed to achieve social success by attracting a socially desirable partner.[3]

In this essay, I shall be focusing on versions of this narrative in which the protagonist falls into prostitution, and in which—in rather different ways—telling the story of ruin becomes a means of seeking social rehabilitation. Thomas Laqueur's recent characterization of the novel as a form of 'humanitarian narrative' seems particularly useful here. Laqueur places the novel under this heading alongside 'the autopsy, the clinical report, and the social inquiry':

> Beginning in the eighteenth century, a new cluster of narratives came to speak in extraordinarily detailed fashion about the pains and deaths of ordinary people in such a way as to make apparent the causal chains that might connect the actions of its readers with the suffering of its subjects.

And he goes on to pose the question of 'why the moral franchise is extended at any given time to one group but not another'.[4] I shall be focusing here on that moment in mid-eighteenth-century England when, as various commentators have suggested, the 'moral franchise' was extended to prostitutes, when 'audacious Harlots' became 'fallen Angels', the subjects of popular sentimental narrative and the objects of charitable intervention.[5] At that same moment, verbal, legal and physical attacks on London brothels, which had been recurrent since the setting up of the Societies for the Reformation of Manners in the 1690s, were intensified and fiercely debated.[6] Popular sentimental narrative is clearly inseparable here from a public politics of reform and regulation.

Because she inhabits the boundary between public and private, the economic and the erotic, the prostitute is always a potentially disruptive figure. In its classic sentimental form, the seduction narrative discovers, and seeks to contain, the prostitute as redeemable victim. That redemption might involve actual social intervention, through such institutions as the Magdalen House for Penitent Prostitutes, established in London in 1758. It might, on the other hand, be an imaginative version of that intervention through the feeling response of the sentimental observer or sensitive reader—as in Mackenzie's classic representation of Harley's encounter with Miss Atkins in *The Man of Feeling* (1771), where Harley's compassion is instrumental in reconciling Miss Atkins with her father, returning her to patriarchy. In these particular 'humanitarian narratives', then, issues of state power and responsibility are mediated through the gender and class preoccupations of popular fictions; as so often in the literature of sensibility, stories about penitent prostitutes disturb strategic attempts to separate 'public' from 'private'.

II

I want to explore this particular narrative extension of Lacqueur's 'moral franchise' more closely by suggesting a view of the century framed by two reforming texts: at one end by Wollstonecraft's novel, *Wrongs of Woman* (published posthumously in 1798), in which Jemima, the working-class prison warder and ex-prostitute, tells her own story; and at the other by Defoe's pamphlet of 1726, *Some Considerations upon Streetwalkers*, 'to which is added', as the title-page announces, 'A Letter from One of those unhappy Persons, when in *Newgate*, and who was afterwards executed, for picking a Gentleman's Pocket'. Defoe appends this brief first-person testimony to a pamphlet which is dedicated to 'lessen[ing] the Number of [streetwalkers] as are to be miserable hereafter'; the 'living Set' of prostitutes are considered 'past Redemption'.[7] The letter describes the unrelieved fall of a gentleman's daughter, educated 'suitable to that Rank', but left without provision at her father's death, and so susceptible to 'the Sollicitations of Sir James—'. Having seduced her, Sir James refuses the maintenance he had promised and arranges for her to be taken in by the bawd to whom the letter is addressed. 'The necessitous Condition which I found myself reduc'd to by this new Villany of his, soon made me compliant with [the Bawd's] Requests', until disease makes her 'unfit for [her] Purpose' and the bawd throws her out onto the street and into casual prostitution, drinking, theft, imprisonment and, ultimately, execution (pp. 16–18).

As I have already suggested, Defoe's nameless prostitute anticipates many other versions of her story throughout the century. Wollstonecraft's Jemima thus speaks out of a long tradition of similar narratives, though with a rather different audience. In *Wrongs of Woman*, Jemima tells her story to Maria, the middle-class heroine who has herself been sexually abused by her husband. By drawing attention to the similarities between speaker and listener, Wollstonecraft's feminism disturbs the instrumental power of the classic humanitarian audience.

I shall be coming back to Wollstonecraft's critique at the end of the essay, but I want now to look more closely at Defoe's pamphlet, and its juxtaposition of the streetwalker's letter with a polemic urging social reform. Defoe offers the letter as an example, 'by which the miserable Condition of these Creatures will more fully appear, and consequently, the great Necessity there is to suppress them' (p.16). The pity invited by the first-person narrative contradicts Defoe's explicit argument that existing prostitutes are beyond redemption: the reader's sympathetic involvement extends 'the moral franchise' to the prostitute, suggesting that 'suppression' might actually involve a form of redemptive transformation. This would be a private, moral version of that more efficient redirection of sexual resources which Defoe advocates elsewhere in the pamphlet:

> The great Use of Women in a Community, is to supply it with Members which may be serviceable, and keep up a Succession. They are also useful in another Degree, to wit, in the Labour they may take for themselves, or the Assistance which they may afford their Husbands or Parents. It will be readily allowed, that a Street-walking Whore can never answer either of these Ends; Riot and Diseases prevent one, and the Idleness which directs her to this Course of Life incapacitates her for the other. (p. 6)

Suggested ways of remedying this waste of productive and reproductive labour include tax exemptions to encourage earlier marriage, so that young women, 'prompted by Nature . . . are not forced to become the Instruments of satisfying those Desires in Men which were given for a better Use' (p. 7). The social and physiological model implicit here is still mechanistic, a respectable bourgeois version of the libertine and misogynist discourse in a text like Mandeville's *A Modest Defence of Public Stews*, 1724. There, licensed brothels are recommended as 'a Kind of legal Evacuative', necessary to the health of the body politic.[8] Mandeville's ironic libertinism in turn recalls such anti-female satires as Robert Gould's *Love Given O're*:

> But if the Tyde of Nature boist'rous grow
> And would Rebelliously its Banks o'erflow,
> Then chuse a Wench, who (full of lewd desires)
> Can meet your flouds of Love with equal fires;
> And will, when e're you let the Deluge flie,
> Through an extended Sluce strait drain it dry . . .[9]

Within this tradition, the prostitute is justified as a function of male sexuality: a necessary, and therefore potentially powerful, figure, she is vilified but also celebrated.[10] In 1723, for example, Captain Charles Walker published his *Authentick Memoirs of the Life Intrigues and Adventures of the Celebrated Sally Salisbury*, a prostitute who had recently been tried at the Old Bailey for stabbing a client. The 'Epistle

Dedicatory' makes a joke out of Sally's power over reputation as it stresses the impossibility of finding a suitable patron for the text:

> I was hot upon begging the Protection of some *powerful Man* in Your Interest, famed for Wit and Love, but I foresaw what Envy it would create to the Person, placed, in a manner, at the *Head* of your *Affections* by such a DEDICATION: Besides, I was fearful of giving you a very sensible Disgust, in making *You* seem the *Propriety* of *one Man*, when You know Yourself *ordained* for the Comfort and Refreshment of *Multitudes*.[11]

Defoe's *Moll Flanders* and *Roxana* are much closer to this tradition, but his streetwalker introduces an altogether different representation and reception of the prostitute, as the seduction narrative is harnessed to an emergent middle-class programme of sexual regulation. Walker's satiric text struggles to contain Sally Salisbury's power to disrupt social divisions; Defoe's representation effects a very different kind of containment, drawing the prostitute back into the social body through the mechanism of pity.

In doing so, it anticipates the sympathetic discourse of sentimentalism, with its implicit model of the social body as a nervous system rather than a machine.[12] Thus a reforming pamphlet of 1752 justifies concern for the 'melancholy, grievous, and much-to-be-pitied Situation' of 'the Ladies of the Town' on the grounds that:

> As when any one Member of the Natural Body is aggrieved, all the other Members are sympathetically affected therewith; even so in the Political Body, when any Sect or Denomination thereof are mal-treated or persecuted by uncharitable and partial Men, it is a Duty incumbent upon all those who are Friends to Liberty and Property, these great, happy and advantageous Priviledges, to rouze themselves up in Defence of these most valuable Jewels, and never give over the generous Undertaking, until they have stifled in the Embrio such unjustifiable Attempts.[13]

Social regulation has here explicitly become a function of feeling. Prostitutes are the victims of 'uncharitable' men; to rehabilitate them is a 'generous Undertaking'. The reader is inspired to support change through an extension of sympathy rather than because of the outrage invoked by satire. And it was that 'generosity'—in financial as well as simply moral terms—which the campaigns for a Magdalen House, which followed during the 1750s, sought to mobilize.

III

I want at this point to introduce an analogous group of texts by women writers who were explicitly excluded from that humanitarian project of redemption. I shall be focusing particularly on the reception of *An Apology for the Conduct of Mrs. Teresia Constantia Phillips*, which uses but refuses to sustain the standard seduction narrative. Published serially and then in three volumes in 1748–49, Phillips's *Apology* is one of the 'scandalous memoirs', vindications of their sexual conduct by women who, far from being objects of sympathy, became at the time a byword for unacceptable femininity. Richardson, famously, dismissed Teresia Constantia Phillips, Laetitia Pilkington and Frances Anne, Viscountess Vane as 'a Set of Wretches, wishing to perpetuate their Infamy'; and in John Duncombe's poem *The Feminiad* in praise of women writers, their writings are condemned as 'the dang'rous sallies of a wanton Muse'.[14]

Recent feminist criticism has begun to recover these texts for serious critical attention. Janet Todd deals with them briefly in *The Sign of Angellica*, as victims of the 'pressure towards respectability' which 'prevented them from creating a culturally potent image'. In her work on women's 'self-biography', Felicity Nussbaum explores that ideological belatedness more extensively and examines various ways in which the scandalous memoirs both confirm and contest 'authorized versions of "woman"'; more recently Clare Brant, in a very good essay, has queried the validity of aligning them with autobiography, and locates their concern with identity much more specifically in terms of the gendered discourses of gossip, scandal and the law on which reputation depended.[15] By looking at Phillips's *Apology* in the slightly different context of the prostitution narratives and reform debates which surround it, I hope to help define more precisely why the scandalous memoirs were culturally unacceptable and why they remained outside the newly-extended moral franchise. Their status as outsiders, their failure to activate a humanitarian reading, helps in turn point up the narrow limits of class and gender on which the sentimental reading contract depends.

> The Point you have laboured, and which you would have the World implicitly believe, because you are pleased to say so, is only this, That you was first debauched by Promises, Entreaties, and down-right Violence, by the Honourable Person whose Name you have given us under that of Mr. *Grimes*; that he abandoned you soon after, without Performance of those Promises which partly seduced you, or making the smallest Provision for your Maintenance, which

obliged you to fall into the Course of Life you have since led: And, consequently, you infer, that all the Misery you have since underwent, and all the Follies and Enormities you have been guilty of since that Time, are chargeable to his Account, as the first Betrayer of your Innocence.[16]

This is by an anonymous defender of the Earl of Chesterfield ('Mr Grimes'), replying in 1748 to the 'scandalous aspersions' made in the first volume of Phillips's *Apology*. At issue is the question of sexual responsibility, much debated at the time, and resonant with class antagonisms. To her contemporaries, Phillips, a well-known courtesan, was primarily associated with bigamy: at the age of fifteen, in order to avoid her creditors, she had undergone a Fleet marriage to an already-married man called Delafield who specialized in the service and who then conveniently disappeared.[17] Phillips later married Henry Muilman, a Dutch merchant, whose family, when they found out about her reputation and previous marriage, urged their son to save *his* 'Reputation and Credit' by seeking an annulment on grounds of bigamy.[18] Phillips used the bigamous—and therefore invalid—status of her first marriage to argue that her second remained legal, and that Muilman's children by his second marriage were therefore illegitimate. The *Apology* is mainly concerned, then, with details—including copies of legal documents, letters, and interviews with lawyers—of the labyrinthine lawsuit, lasting eighteen years, through which Con Phillips tried to recover her married status, financial security and public name.

But Phillips provides a narrative origin for her case in her early ruin by 'Mr Grimes' (then Philip Stanhope, later the Earl of Chesterfield). In the first number of the *Apology*, she tells the story of how he raped her at the age of thirteen when she was alone and friendless in London, having left home to avoid the cruelty of her stepmother (formerly her father's maidservant). With the connivance of a bawd figure, in the form of a 'hoop-petticoat maker', Grimes plays on her vulnerability: he woos her with letters, which she quotes, and with promises of financial support, which come to nothing, and eventually achieves his 'dishonourable Ends' by getting her drunk, and stripping and raping her in his lodgings during a public celebration. Thereafter, Grimes's responsibility as 'the Spring from whence have flowed all my other Misfortunes' (I, p. 47) is a recurrent theme in the text:

If any thing can be said to extenuate the Misconduct of a Girl, hurried into the Love of these delusive Pleasures before she had

Reason, or Judgment, to distinguish Right from Wrong, I think some Allowance may be made *for her*, whose first setting out in the World portended nothing but inevitable Ruin and Destruction, to the eternal Shame and Infamy of him who brought it upon her. (I, p. 270)

Not surprisingly, perhaps, it is this reading of her career that Chesterfield's defender finds particularly unacceptable. But there are more public issues at stake here, I think, than just competing and unverifiable versions of what happened in a private relationship almost thirty years earlier—or even than the embarrassment of threatened reputation. Phillips is attacked in the *Defence . . . of a Noble Lord* for her narrative skill, for using 'all possible Art to give [her] Story an Air of Truth' and self-consciously adopting the 'pathetic Disguise' of sentimental fiction as a way of claiming moral authenticity. In other words, for mobilizing on her own behalf (her worst sin, perhaps) the mitigating moral and social excuses provided by a powerful cultural narrative to which she is felt to have no right.[19] In response, the *Defence* pits the 'truths' of circumstantial detail and already established reputation against Phillips's claim to representative status as the victim of gender and class inequalities.

At the beginning of her *Apology*, then, Phillips presents herself as a version of Defoe's condemned streetwalker. At the end of her third volume, she draws on a different tradition in order to give similar representative status to the three men who have figured most prominently in her text. Thus her husband becomes 'The MERCHANT' who 'may find that other Qualities besides Wealth, are necessary to constitute him (in the Trading Phrase) *a good Man*'; an ex-lover, who refused to help her out when she was in financial difficulty, is 'the BEAU ADVENTURER' whom 'her Story will most effectually prevent . . . being hereafter mistaken for a *Man of Honour*' (III, pp. 314–15). And this is her final comment on Chesterfield:

The Publication of her Injuries, may perhaps, for the future, prevent the *high-born* DEBAUCHEE from presuming so far upon the Privilege of Quality, as to think he has a Right to triumph in the Virgin Spoils of a tender Infant, and then abandon her to the almost inevitable Consequence of her lost Innocence, *Shame* and *Misery*. (III, p. 314)

Sentimental narrative is subsumed here into the more old-fashioned mode of prose satire. As Clare Brant has pointed out, in cases of sexual transgression 'reputation turns male agency into female responsibility'.[20] In order to reverse that process and re-attach responsibility to agency, Phillips has to transgress again, breaking out of her sentimental role as victim in order to activate satiric tradition.

Nevertheless, her turning back of responsibility onto men, and onto upper-class men in particular, would seem to be very much in line with immediately contemporary reformist discourse. 'Ludovicus', in the pamphlet of 1752 already quoted, might be describing her case when he cites 'dishonourable men' as responsible for the plight of London prostitutes:

> There are many of those Women, who are at present drove up and down this City and Suburbs, who have just Cause to set up such a Lamentation, who have been betrayed of their Virtue by dishonourable Men, who have swore and vow'd eternal Love; but immediately, upon Enjoyment, eternal Hatred took Place, and villainously deserted them, without making the least Restitution for the irreparable Injury done: Then what must such unfortunate Women do, when thus plunged into an Abyss of Sorrow and Misery . . . ?[21]

A few years later, 'A Reformed Rake' responded to John Fielding's plan for a public laundry which would provide work for reformed prostitutes: an idea which developed into the Magdalen House Charity. With, it must be said, circumspect irony, he took particular exception to Fielding having published prostitutes' names in the newspaper:

> I should be curious to know, Sir, what End could be answered by any such Publications, . . . ? If indeed you were to publish with it a List of the Names of those Persons who *really* debauched these Girls, this might be a Means of having such Men held in Detestation, at least by the *honest* Part of Mankind, and detering others from rendering themselves equally scandalous; or if the Conditions of Concealment of these Male Names, were the Subscription of a Sum sufficient for the support of those Girls they had debauched; this might facilitate the raising a Capital for carrying your Plan into Execution.[22]

In order to read Phillips's *Apology* more precisely against these pamphlets, it is important to understand something of their role within a developing public debate about the policing and suppression of prostitution in London, and to examine the representation of the prostitutes themselves within that debate.

IV

In 1749, the year in which Phillips published the third volume of her *Apology*, a series of riots against London brothels, and the ensuing controversy about how they were policed, refocused attention on prostitution as a problem of public order. Known as the 'Penlez Riots', after Bosavern Penlez, a young peruke-maker who was hanged for taking part, they began when a sailor claimed to have been robbed in a brothel on the Strand and brought his mates back to sack the place. Henry Fielding, the presiding magistrate, was fiercely criticized for over-reacting and for, in effect, defending the property of brothel-keepers against the liberty of citizens.[23] John Cleland, for example, wrote a pamphlet condemning Penlez's execution in which he characterizes the English mob as 'one of the best Proofs of the peculiar Power of Liberty, to inspire gentle and governable Sentiments': 'there is . . . such a Bottom of natural good Sense diffus'd through the common People of *England*, that the least Exertion of legal Authority will serve to check their Fury.'[24] In the Penlez riot, he claims, this 'natural good Sense' was evident in the mob's treatment of the prostitutes:

> acting like true brave Fellows, [they] suffer'd no Injury to be done to the poor Damsels, who got off safe and unhurt; but levell'd all their Rage against the House and Goods of the Caitif, whom they look'd on as the Author of the Villainy exercis'd on their Brother Tar. (p. 18)

'The Caitif' here is the 'Cock-Bawd', responsible for exposing innocent 'fallen Angels' to 'the Seduction of Men superior to them at least in Experience' and of denying prostitutes the right of property: 'nothing, no, not her own Person, is her own Property, or at her own Disposal' (pp. 13, 9). And Cleland sets up an implicit parallel between the cock-bawd's treatment of the prostitute on the one hand; and the magistrates' condemnation of Penlez, representing the benevolent mob, on the other. Both exploitative bawds and draconian magistrates are seen as symptomatic of 'the Spirit of the *English* . . . already too much broke, sunk, and declin'd from its antient Manliness' (p. 46).

It might be argued that in using the prostitute as innocent victim here, deprived of her property rights, Cleland's text is itself collusive with that deprivation. In displacing gender responsibility onto the figure of the cock-bawd, it portrays the prostitute as passive, almost desexualised—very far from the threatening, or at least necessary, figures in Mandeville and Gould. Attention to the politics of gender reveals humanitarian concern as a form of containment; a mechanism which,

I want to argue, is characteristic of the reform movement and which is underwritten in the reading politics of sentimental fiction.

Fielding was particularly sensitive to the accusation that he had inappropriately defended the property rights of brothels, and the Penlez riots led in 1751 to the passing of the Disorderly Houses Act.[25] Applicable to London only, this gave the constable the power to prosecute 'persons keeping bawdy-houses . . . on notice given him in writing by any two inhabitants of the parish paying scot and lot'.[26] The various inadequacies of this Act produced a flurry of pamphlets: some, like Saunders Welch's *Proposal . . . to remove the Nuisance of Common Prostitutes from the Streets of this Metropolis*, wanted more efficient and punitive powers. Others, like that by 'Ludovicus', to which I have already referred, wanted to facilitate an efficient return of prostitutes to productive labour by providing them with humanitarian support. Together, they illustrate the disciplinary collusion of humanitarian and regulatory discourses within the reform project.

In *A Particular but Melancholy Account of the Great Hardships, Difficulties, and Miseries, That Those Unhappy and Much-to-be-Pitied Creatures, the Common Women of the Town Are plung'd into at this Juncture*, Ludovicus claims that the effect of the 'late severe Edict' has been to turn 'these despised Women' onto the street, driving many of them to suicide:

> but, [if] after all that I have advanc'd, nothing is to be done towards the Support of those unfortunate Women, nor no Redress of their Grievances, then I shall wash my Hands clean from being concern'd in the Guilt that so much Severity must at length bring upon the Oppressors, and of which I have given them timely and publick Notice; driving them from House to House, from Court to Court, from Parish to Parish, and at length forcing them to hang and drown themselves, to be free of their Persecutors, is a most cruel and intolerable Imposition in a Land that bears the Name of Freedom.[27]

The failure of the Act, then, has been in enforcing punishment without providing for redemption: reproducing, in effect, the prostitute's treatment by the bawd when she becomes too diseased to be economically useful. As in Cleland, Ludovicus's fiercest attack is reserved for the bawds, those monstrous parodies of the entrepreneur, who 'force the [Whores] to prostitute their delicate Bodies to the Embraces of every Scoundrel', and whom he wants 'either hang'd or transported for Life', as 'the most effectual Means towards paving the Way for a Reformation of Manners amongst these loose disorderly Women' (p. 15). Alongside the bawds, and with almost as much venom, Ludovicus attacks 'private

W—s' as being 'above the Censor, or at least independent of the Calumnies of the World'.[28] To be 'above the Censor', beyond the power of reproach and guilt, is to be beyond the reach of redemption. Their only hope of expiation is in offering financial support to the charitable institution which Ludovicus wants set up as a haven for penitent, penniless prostitutes.

From this middle-class reformist perspective, Teresia Constantia Phillips represents aristocratic licence and precisely fits that category of the 'private W[hore]', in spite of her sense of marginalization and her struggle to re-establish her reputation and credit within the institutions of law and marriage. And her text exacerbates that class position—in its very existence as a female-authored text—so that she refuses to maintain the attitude of penitent passivity, the role of seduced victim that was becoming necessary to the (male) reformist project:

> But as Misfortunes seldom operate upon the Human Mind in a moderate Degree, the Effects they produce being either a total Deprivation of Reason, or else the Spirits are so sunk and broken by them, that the unhappy Sufferer, worn into a stupid State of Insensibility, unresisting, bends under every new Oppression; yet, happy for our Apologist, she is formed with a Disposition very opposite to this *Female Supineness*. Her Misfortunes have shewn her the Necessity of becoming superior to them, and every new Oppression she meets with, adds fresh Vigor to her Fortitude . . .
> (III, p. 34)

The 'unhappy Sufferer, worn into a stupid State of Insensibility' is, of course, precisely what the middle-class reformist version of the seduction narrative both demands and denies. Humanitarian intervention—as opposed to punitive discipline—justifies itself by constructing the prostitute as both passively available for reform and tremblingly sensible of her own undeserving condition.

It also, in spite of claims to give true-life narratives, depends on the effective fictionality, the anonymity, of its subjects. And here again, Phillips fails to conform in her embarrassing assertion of a particular individual identity, her adherence to the old mode of satiric scandal-writing as opposed to the newer, generalized stories of 'nobody' which made sympathy and responsibility less uncomfortably specific.[29] Laqueur suggests that in the ideal humanitarian narrative, the subject is dead and thus available for control by the reader: 'Humanitarianism, while devoted to saving human lives, focusses its attention most powerfully on the dead and becomes a guide to the mastery of death.'[30] Phillips goes as far as acknowledging that 'the Reader has a Right to be superior to a Writer' (III, p. 32), but she refuses to lie down and be dead. In the narratives attached to the Magdalen House project, in contrast, the women are either already dead or they are effectively so, made the property of the reader by means of the sentimental fictional contract.

In his book *Sentiment and Sociability*, John Mullan argues that:

> The language in which the body and the 'theory of sensibility' is produced is also a language which tells of disorder and ambiguous susceptibility ... the elevation of sensibility is not a clear indication of ideological confidence ... at the heart of such 'theory' is distur- bance and hesitation.[31]

Mullan's characterization of sensibility as unstable is useful, and his analysis accurately describes *The Man of Feeling* or *A Sentimental Journey* where the presence of the feeling observer within the text exposes the moral ambivalence and the susceptibility of that position. But the gender politics of the popular sentimental narratives associated with the Magdalen House allow for a greater degree of 'ideological confidence'. There, the feeling reader is outside the text, and the figure of the prostitute provides a vicarious means of control by embodying that unstable susceptibility. In *Histories of Some of the Penitents in the Magdalen-House* (1760), now generally believed to be by Sarah Fielding, four women tell their, supposedly true, stories:

> Tho' the profession of a prostitute is the most despicable and hateful that imagination can form; yet the individuals are frequently worthy objects of compassion; and I am willing to believe, that if people did but reflect on the various stratagems used at first to corrupt them, while poverty often, and still oftener vanity, is on the side of the corruptor, they would smooth the stern brow of rigid virtue, and turn the contemptuous frown into tears of pity.[32]

The narratives are compelling versions of the familiar paradigm. The experienced reader is therefore well able to recognize moments of danger: in one story, for example, the heroine fails to recognize a bawd figure; in another, she confuses social with moral authority by accepting the corrupt sexual mores of her upper-class employer.[33] Through a recognition of the prostitute's misguided susceptibility, the reader is absolved from similar excess. They exert only right-minded sympathy, an expression of superior knowledge rather than simple identification, and, ideally, made publicly evident by subscription to the institution. Thus the bourgeois humanitarian reader reproduces, albeit in moral and financial terms, the sexual power relations of the upper-class men who are so often held responsible for the fate of the women in the stories.

V

In *Wrongs of Woman*, Wollstonecraft's reworking of the humanitarian narrative exposes the inequalities masked by the sentimental contract. As in most classic seduction narratives, the prostitutes in *The Histories of the Penitents* are either 'genteel' by birth, or they attain that status through their capacity for passive sensibility. Wollstonecraft's Jemima —working-class, resourceful and, initially at least, insensitive—thus immediately suggests a radical intervention in the tradition. Jemima's story is surrounded in the novel by other women's testimonies to financial and physical abuse, including of course that of Maria herself. Thus, as Laurie Langbauer points out, Jemima, the prostitute, becomes the type of all women's experience under patriarchy.[34] And that gender identity is reinforced as she and Maria, the working-class prostitute and the middle-class consumer of her narrative, offer each other mutual, rather than one-sided, redemption:

> Jemima, more overcome by kindness than she had ever been by cruelty, hastened out of the room to conceal her emotions . . .

> Active as love was in the heart of Maria, the story she had just heard made her thoughts take a wider range. . . . she was led to consider the oppressed state of women, and to lament that she had given birth to a daughter.[35]

The novel cannot wholly escape the class-based mechanisms of sentimentalism: Jemima's redemption is, after all, primarily signalled by the return of her natural capacity for feeling. Like the Magdalen penitents, she is thus recuperable for a middle-class ideal. But Jemima's narrative also changes middle-class femininity: Maria's immediate response is to write her own testimony and to plead her own cause. Like Constantia Phillips, Wollstonecraft's text refuses to lie down and be dead.

Notes

1. See R. Paulson, *Hogarth: His Life, Art, and Times* 2 vols (New Haven and London, 1971) I pp. 284–91; T.C. D. Eaves and B.D. Kimpel, *Samuel Richardson: A Biography* (Oxford, 1971) pp. 119–53.
2. M. Foucault, *The History of Sexuality. Vol. I: An Introduction* trans. by R. Hurley (Harmondsworth, 1981) pp. 125–26.
3. On the dominant ideal of the 'proper lady', see M. Poovey, *The Proper Lady and the Woman Writer: Ideology as Style in the Works of Mary Wollstonecraft, Mary Shelley, and Jane Austen* (Chicago and London, 1984) pp. 3–8. On the ideological deployment of that ideal in fiction, see N. Armstrong, *Desire and Domestic Fiction: A Political History of the Novel* (New York and Oxford, 1987). On the socio-political significance of the seduction narrative generally, see S. Staves, 'British Seduced Maidens' *Eighteenth-Century Studies* 14 (1980–81) pp. 109–34. In two recent articles, I have explored specific manifestations of this fictional paradigm: see V. Jones, ' "The Coquetry of Nature": Politics and the Picturesque in Women's Fiction' in S. Copley and P. Garside (eds) *The Politics of the Picturesque* (Cambridge, 1994) pp. 120–44; and ' "The Tyranny of the Passions": Feminism and Heterosexuality in the Fiction of Wollstonecraft and Hays', in S. Ledger, J. McDonagh and J. Spencer (eds) *Political Gender: Texts and Contexts* (London, 1994) pp. 173–88.
4. T. Laqueur, 'Bodies, Details and the Humanitarian Narrative' in L. Hunt (ed.) *The New Cultural History* (Berkeley and Los Angeles, 1989) pp. 176–77, and 204.
5. 'audacious Harlots': [Daniel Defoe], *Some Considerations upon Streetwalkers. With A Proposal for lessening the present Number of them. In Two Letters to a Member of Parliament* (London, 1726) p. 2; 'fallen Angels': [John Cleland], *The Case of the Unfortunate Bosavern Penlez* (London, 1749) p.13. On the shift in attitudes to prostitutes and 'seduced maidens' see: W.A. Speck, 'The Harlot's Progress in Eighteenth-Century England' *British Journal for Eighteenth-Century Studies* 3 (1980) pp. 127–39; R. Trumbach, 'Modern Prostitution and Gender in Fanny Hill' in G.S. Rousseau and R. Porter (eds) *Sexual Underworlds of the Enlightenment* (Manchester, 1987) pp. 69–85.
6. See T.C. Curtis and W.A. Speck, 'The Societies for the Reformation of Manners: A Case Study in the Theory and Practice of Moral Reform' *Literature and History* 3 (1976) pp. 45–64.
7. Defoe, *Some Considerations* p. 5.
8. 'Colonel Harry Mordaunt' [Bernard Mandeville], *A Modest Defence of Public Stews:, or, an Essay upon Whoring. As it is now practis'd in these Kingdoms* (London, [1724] 1740) p. 40.
9. R. Gould, *Love Given O're: or, a Satyr against the Pride, Lust, and Inconstancy, &c. of Woman* [1682] in *Satires on Women*, Augustan Reprint Society, 180 (1976) p. 3.
10. On ambivalent representations of prostitutes in the early part of the

century, see T.G.A. Nelson, 'Women of Pleasure' *Eighteenth-Century Life* 11 (1987) pp. 181–98.

11. Captain Charles Walker, *Authentick Memoirs of the Life Intrigues and Adventures of the Celebrated Sally Salisbury* (London, 2nd edition, 1723) fol. A3r.

12. See J. Mullan, *Sentiment and Sociability: The Language of Feeling in the Eighteenth Century* (Oxford, 1988) pp. 231–32.

13. M. Ludovicus, *A Particular but Melancholy Account of the Great Hardships, Difficulties, and Miseries, that those Unhappy and Much-to-be-Pitied Creatures, The Common Women of the Town, Are plung'd into at this Juncture* (London, 1752) pp. 2, 11.

14. Richardson, quoted in J. Todd, *The Sign of Angellica: Women, Writing and Fiction, 1660–1800* (London, 1989) p. 131; J. Duncombe, *The Feminiad. A Poem* [1754], Augustan Reprint Society, 207 (1981) p. 15.

15. Todd, *Sign of Angellica* p.128; F. Nussbaum, 'Heteroclites: The Gender of Character in the Scandalous Memoirs' in F. Nussbaum and L. Brown (eds) *The New Eighteenth Century: Theory Politics Literature* (New York and London, 1987) pp. 144–68 (p.151); rpt. in F. Nussbaum, *The Autobiographical Subject: Gender and Ideology in Eighteenth-Century England* (Baltimore & London, 1989); C. Brant, 'Speaking of Women: Scandal and Law in the Mid-Eighteenth Century' in C. Brant and D. Purkis (eds) *Women, Texts and Histories 1575–1760* (London & New York, 1992) pp. 242–70. See also J. Todd, 'Marketing the Self: Mary Carleton, Miss F and Susannah Gunning', in *Gender, Art and Death* (Cambridge, 1993) pp. 81–95.

16. *A Defence of the Character of a Noble Lord, from the Scandalous Aspersions Contained in a Malicious Apology. In a Letter to the supposed Authoress* (London, 1748) pp. 23–24.

17. For a detailed account of the case, see L. Stone, *Uncertain Unions: Marriage in England 1660–1753* (Oxford, 1992) pp. 236–74.

18. *An Apology for the Conduct of Mrs. Teresia Constantia Phillips, More Particularly That Part of it which relates to her Marriage with an eminent Dutch Merchant*, 3 vols (London, 1748–49) I p. 97. Further page references are included in the text.

19. *A Defence of the Character*, pp. 7, 9. *The Apology* is, of course, ostensibly written in the third person, by someone who has 'known Mrs. Muilman about these twenty Years, which means no more, than that I was once in a Room with her' (I p. 13), and Phillips's amanuensis has long been identified as Paul Whitehead (see Stone, p. 246). It is nevertheless acceptable, I think, to see Phillips as the primary interpreter of her own career.

20. Brant, 'Speaking of Women' p. 247.

21. Ludovicus, *A Particular* p. 8.

22. *A Congratulatory Epistle From a Reformed Rake to John F—G, Esq., upon the New Scheme of reclaiming Prostitutes* (London, n.d.) pp. 39–40.

23. See P. Linebaugh, 'The Tyburn Riot Against the Surgeons' in D. Hay,

P. Linebaugh, J.G. Rule, E.P. Thompson and C. Winslow, *Albion's Fatal Tree: Crime and Society in Eighteenth-Century England* (London, 1975) pp. 89–102.

24. [Cleland], *The Case* p. 19.

25. Fielding's *A Charge Delivered to the Grand Jury, at the Sessions of the Peace held for the City and Liberty of Westminster* (London, 1749) immediately preceded the Penlez Riots. In it, he urges action against brothels, which are described as having become 'in a Manner the Seminaries of Education, and that especially of those Youths, whose Birth makes their right Institution of the utmost Consequence to the future Well-being of the Public' (pp. 49–50).

26. Saunders Welch, *A Proposal to Render Effectual a Plan To remove the Nuisance of Common Prostitutes from the Streets of this Metropolis* (London, 1758) pp. 8–9; and see V.L. Bullough, 'Prostitution and Reform in Eighteenth-Century England' in R.P. Macubbin (ed) *'Tis Nature's Fault: Unauthorized Sexuality during the Enlightenment* (Cambridge, 1987) pp. 61–74 (pp. 66-67).

27. Ludovicus, *A Particular* p. 26.

28. Ludovicus, *A Particular* p. 10; and cf. p. 22: 'if all the private Wh—s and Adul—es [sic] that are in the Land were to be mustred upon Salisbury Plain, the Common Ladies would appear no bigger than the Army of the Israelites, when they went to engage a great Host of their Enemies . . .'.

29. Cf. C. Gallagher, *Nobody's Story: Vanishing Acts of Women Writers in the Marketplace, 1670–1820* (Oxford, 1995).

30. Laqueur, 'Bodies, Details' p. 182.

31. Mullan, *Sentiment and Sociability* p. 237.

32. *Histories of Some of the Penitents in the Magdalen-House, as Supposed to be related by Themselves* 2 vols (London, 1760) I p. v.

33. *Histories of the Penitents* II p. 5; I pp. 35–36.

34. L. Langbauer, *Women and Romance: The Consolations of Gender in the English Novel* (Ithaca and London, 1990) p. 120.

35. Mary Wollstonecraft, *Mary and The Wrongs of Woman* ed. by G. Kelly (Oxford, 1980) pp. 119, 120.

Five

The Fear of Public Disorder: Marriage between Revolution and Reaction

Ursula Vogel

In the preface to the *Vindication of the Rights of Woman* Mary Wollstonecraft confronted the legislators of Revolutionary France with a claim of compelling logic: given that the new constitutional order grounded its legitimacy upon the universal rights of man, the exclusion of 'one-half of the human race'[1] from the entitlements of citizenship stood exposed as a blatant abuse of principle. The withholding of those rights from beings who shared the common attributes of humanity could have no reference point other than the arbitrary ploys of tyrannical government.[2] How would the makers of the constitution have responded to the charge of despotic design? How would they have answered an accusation that tarred them with the intention to 'force all women, by denying them civil and political rights, to remain immured in their families groping in the dark'?[3] They would probably not have accepted or even understood the terms in which they were called to account. 'Women' as such did not exist in the eyes of the law. And in this respect the dominant legal discourses of the Revolutionary period remained firmly within the mould of a long-established tradition. To consider the place of women in the political order was to speak a language that was from the outset predicated upon, and bounded by, assumptions about the natural order of marriage and the family. In breaking down these boundaries the very title of Wollstonecraft's treatise, and similarly of Olympe de Gouges's 'Declaration of the Rights of Woman and of Citizen',[4] express a radical vision that, in their time, lay outside the intentions and goals even of a political revolution.

Given the momentous political and constitutional changes of this period —the abolition of 'feudalism', the separation of state and church, the execution of the king and the demise of monarchical government —it is easy to overlook the pivotal role that the institution of marriage played in the transition from the hierarchical order of the *ancien régime* to the bourgeois society of the nineteenth century. If in the earlier liberal phase of the Revolution the law of marriage served as the spearhead of a radical break with the past we will find that for the framers of the *Code Napoléon* it had become the major vehicle for curbing the dynamic of boundless revolutionary liberty. The introduction of the obligatory civil marriage in 1792, followed by the legalization of divorce, consolidated both the individualist foundations of the new constitutional order and the exclusive sovereignty of the secular state over a terrain that had hitherto been governed by the authority of the church. In the words of the classic text on the civil legislation of the Revolution: 'Le moyen âge disparaîssait. La raison triomphait.'[5] However, as regards the internal order of marriage it was tradition that had the last word of triumph over reason. In the *royautée domestique* the legacies of the Middle Ages were to survive well into the twentieth century.

This chapter will consider the ambivalent meanings which came to define marriage in modern European law as both a constitutive realm of private freedom and as the inner citadel of the public order. Marriage, it seems, was a terrain for which the demarcations between private and public spheres and thus the fundamental guarantees of individual liberty and equality had no force. The absence or weakness of those boundaries might, at first sight, signify nothing more than the entrenched historical backwardness of an institution which for most of the nineteenth century remained insulated against the ascendancy of bourgeois individualism. The antiquated forms and languages of the marriage law would no doubt lend support to explanations which merely record the surface phenomena of unbroken historical continuity and present modernization as simply delayed. However, what such an approach fails to reveal is the underlying dynamic of political processes, in the course of which those traditions came to be challenged, disrupted, and re-made. I shall argue that the intrusion of political notions of order, rule and subordination into the space of private freedom was a distinctive characteristic of the modern legal construction of marriage and, in a period of revolution and reaction, intimately bound up with the perceived erosion of fixed gender boundaries. My analysis will focus on the case of the *Code Napoléon* because in this first and exemplary enactment of a modern system of private law those contradictions are most clearly evident and condensed, as it were, into a single historic moment: 'In the hour of birth of modern bourgeois society the civil law of that society divides along gender lines.'[6]

I shall begin with a brief sketch of those principles and formal classifications that supplied the basic architectonic design to the civil law codifications of the nineteenth century.[7] The point to be stressed here is that within this context of systematic legal reasoning the distinction between public and private had specific meanings which did not coincide with the, to us, more familiar contrast between a political domain, on the one hand, and a site of domestic relations, on the other. Rather, the private law was understood to encompass the whole terrain of civil society, the whole sphere constituted by the uncoerced relations and associations among individuals as private persons. Marriage was part of this universe of private autonomy and contractual freedom and, yet, stood apart from it as an enclave built upon altogether different norms. A closer look at the marriage law of the *Code Napoléon* will allow us to identify the strategic points at which the relations between husband and wife are disconnected from the principles that govern the private relations between legal subjects in the modern state. The main question is how did the jurists and legislators who drafted the *Code* vindicate marriage as a separate normative domain? Strategies of legitimation, as we shall see, appealed both to the immutable dictates of sexual nature and to the unconditional imperatives of the public order. In the domain of normative legal reasoning, and set against the universalist logic of modern conceptions of subjective right, neither appeal could carry conviction; neither could consistently claim the legitimacy of political dominance in the private sphere. Viewed purely from the standpoint of moral and political principle—that is, from the standpoint that informed the emancipatory critique of the early feminists—the division of marriage into two incommensurable spheres of private and public concern was arbitrary, a reflection not of demonstrable truths but of entrenched interests. If, on the other hand, we judge this division from the concrete contexts of social experience and as a political response to the collective anxieties released by the revolutionary leap into an uncertain future, we gain a different perspective. The latter would seem to endorse at least the psychological veracity of arguments that rested the artefact of a new political order upon the 'natural' order of gender.[8] We get a glimpse of the immense difficulties that confronted the modern experiment of deriving the conditions of political cohesion solely from the principle of individual autonomy. We get a clearer sense, too, of how much the success of this experiment has in the past been mediated through the enforced boundaries of gender; how much, that is, the precarious balance between private liberty and public order has depended upon a pattern of dominance and submission that was already securely anchored in the private sphere of marriage.

Private Autonomy, Private Property and Contractual Freedom: The Foundations of Modern Private Law

Legal historians have conveyed the salient characteristics of the emerging bourgeois society of the late eighteenth and early nineteenth centuries in the term *Privatrechtsgesellschaft* (society of private law).[9] The phrase contains not only the technical distinction between private and public law but also an evaluative contrast between the principles of liberty and subordination. While public law addresses those relations in which the sovereign state makes authoritative demands upon individuals as subjects, the private law watches over a realm of voluntary dealings among individuals as private persons. The status of the legal person (*Rechtsperson*) guarantees personal mobility and freedom from ascriptive obligations (such as those inherent in the status of servitude), choice of occupation, rights of private property and contract, direct and equal access to the courts. This is, in the language of contemporary liberal aspirations, a sphere free from domination. Not, of course, a sphere altogether free from legal regulation. Indeed, it is all too often overlooked that the outer boundaries of this space of private freedom are themselves created by the will of the sovereign—a point of particular relevance for the understanding of the marriage law. But inside the realm thus given over to the will and interests of autonomous agents the power of the law does not extend beyond the function of prescribing the formal, validating conditions of voluntary transactions. It defines, for example, the procedures for the acquisition, use and transfer of goods, sets out the framework of obligations between buyers and sellers, creditors and debtors, and accredits the modes of legitimate bequest and inheritance. In short, the nature and scope of private autonomy and the functions of the private law derive from the central right of property: 'car le corps entier du Code civil est consacré a définir tout ce qui peut tenir a l'exercice du droit de propriété, droit fondamental, sur lequel toutes les institutions sociales reposent.'[10]

Yet in post-Revolutionary France, as everywhere else in Europe, the internal order of the marriage association remained exempt from the logic of private autonomy and the 'fundamental right' of private property. True, like other 'societies' under the private law the conjugal society was understood to originate in a valid contract between two autonomous agents. The Napoleonic Code went furthest in defining marriage in purely procedural terms as that 'union between two persons of different sex which, on the basis of a civil act performed by an official of the *état civil*, is declared a legitimate sexual community'.[11] Unlike ordinary civil contracts, however, marriage enveloped the contracting parties in ascriptive, non-negotiable relations of rule and subordination. And it was in virtue of this bond of personal *Herrschaft* that the jurists of this time attributed to marriage a status of distinctly public relevance. Principles more akin to public than to private law bore upon marriage in two important respects. First, it was the public power of the state that determined—authoritatively and in exhaustive detail—the status of husband and wife. Secondly, the powers of command, protection and representation that the law bestowed upon the husband were not unlike those by which we commonly identify the characteristic attributes of political rule. As wives, women ceased to stand in a direct relationship to the state and its law. As long as the marriage lasted their legal agency was either altogether suspended (as under the English Common law) or reduced to that of children or minors under guardianship. The concepts and analogies in which European marriage laws defined this relationship embodied a plurality of institutional and intellectual traditions. But the latter converged in the peculiar, quasi-political meanings which they conferred on the husband's rule over the wife and which harked back to a time when the head of the household or kinship system performed the 'public' functions later assumed by the state. Thus the *puissance maritale* of the *Code Napoléon* recalled elements of the Roman *patria potestas* while the *eheliche Herrschaft* or *Ehevogtschaft* of German law blended vestiges of the Germanic *mundium* (the absolute power of the houselord) with medieval notions of trusteeship and with the *imperium maritale* of natural law. The nexus of 'baron and feme' in the English Common law was situated in a different legal culture, but it, too, echoed the legacies of vassalage, guardianship and of an authority typically held by a ruler over his subject.

The Marriage Law of the Code Napoléon

From the time of its enactment in 1804 the *Code civil* (*Code Napoléon* from 1805 to 1814) enjoyed unrivalled admiration as the exemplary formulation of a modern system of private law. A uniform status of citizenship, manifest in the formal equality of all Frenchmen as legal subjects, cemented both the expanded space of individual liberty and the unity and cohesion of the nation state. In this respect the *Code* consolidated the achievements of a successful bourgeois revolution and the demise of those institutions that revolutionary rhetoric had attributed to the anachronistic legacies of 'feudalism'. The dynamic of formal equality was aimed, on the one hand, at the liberation of property rights from any constraints of corporate and collective ownership and, on the other, at the release of the individual from all relations of personal subjugation The law, that is, left no legitimate space for a private person to rule over another. It recognized neither the condition of perpetual obedience that had once linked a subordinate to his *seigneur* or *maître* nor, conversely, any duties of protection and provision that had marked positions of superior status.[12]

There is only one place in the *Code* (if, that is, we exclude the domain of paternal power, with which I shall not be concerned here) where reminiscences of 'feudal' rule have survived intact—the law of marriage. The *Code* introduces the status of husband and wife in a definition that enjoins both spouses to equal duties of fidelity, assistance and succour.[13] But the asymmetrical dimensions of that mutuality of obligation are clearly spelt out in the next article: 'The husband owes his wife protection; the wife owes her husband obedience.'[14] The connotations of feudal vassalage are reinforced in the exposé of the *Code*'s leading draughtsman who refers to the wife's duty of obedience as 'homage rendered to the power that protects her'.[15] The whole ensemble of differential rights and obligations that marriage imposes on the two spouses follows logically from the key presumption of the husband's *puissance maritale* and its corollary, the wife's legal incapacity (*incapacité de la femme*): a wife is deemed incapable of any valid legal action unless she obtains the explicit authorization of her husband. She cannot, in her own right, enter into binding contractual commitments, make use of her property, set up a business or engage in work outside the home. Under the *puissance maritale* her freedom is circumscribed and controlled in the most tangible physical manner and in the minute details of daily life. A husband's extensive powers of command and surveillance, on the other hand, entail similarly extensive obligations towards his wife, such as to provide her with domicile and subsistence, to represent her financial interests in relation to third parties and to act on her behalf in the public domain of courts and magistrates.

The *Code*'s stipulations with regard to matrimonial property exhibit a similar pattern of asymmetrical mutuality.[16] It is not the case, and it is important to remember this, that marriage annihilates a woman's right to property. Rather, it takes away the capacity independently to acquire and administer property of her own. Thus, the standard regime prescribed by the law combines the separate possessions that the partners bring into marriage into a single mass or 'community' (*communauté des biens*). While in formal terms the wife is co-owner of the community, her equal entitlements will convert into the rights and powers of individual ownership only at the point of divorce, separation or the husband's death. As long as the marriage lasts the jointly owned goods fall under the control and administration of the husband, who 'is entitled to dispose of them—to sell, lease and mortgage them as he sees fit, without the consent of the wife'.[17] The salient point for the purpose of our argument lies in the general maxim that determines the distribution of power over 'property': 'because the husband is the master of the wife, he is the exclusive master over the common property just as if the latter were part of his own.'[18]

It is difficult to identify the appropriate categories in which to conceptualize this relationship and its peculiar standing among the institutions of modern private law. A term like 'oppression', with its connotations of one-sided power, does not accord with what is clearly a bond of mutual if unequal rights and obligations. It would be equally misleading to describe the pattern of marriage as a purely spatial distinction between separate spheres and their differential functions for the common affairs of the household. To suggest that the law does nothing more than to keep women within the boundaries of a private, domestic sphere is to lose sight of the crucial point—namely, that it is left to the will and power of the husband to determine that sphere. Whether it be one of relative freedom (with his authorization the wife can perform all the actions that are otherwise blocked by her 'incapacity') or of virtual imprisonment lies in the discretion of her ruler. It is this pattern of political right and submission that the law enforces as the non-contractual and unnegotiable core of every marriage.

To interpret the *puissance maritale* by analogy with the purposes of benevolent guardianship, with which at first sight it may seem to have much in common, would also lead us to misunderstand the unique features of the husband's prerogative. The latter has no equivalent in other relations of rule and dependence, first of all because women do not share the natural disabilities of minors and, more pertinently, because in the case of marriage the 'guardian's' power includes a proprietory claim to the dependent person's body (more precisely, to her sexual and reproductive capacities). Indeed, that the whole order of marriage is ultimately staked upon the protection of this property right is clear from the *Code*'s definition of adultery which holds the wife, but not her husband, to the most stringent obligations of marital fidelity. The divorce law of 1792 had equalised the conditions on which women and men were entitled to seek the termination of marriage; the 'notorious decline of morals' as one of recognized instances of breach of contract applied equally to both sexes. Against this truly revolutionary break with a long and near-universal legal tradition the *Code* reinstated the double moral standard of the past: 'The husband can demand a divorce on the ground of his wife's adultery. The wife can demand a divorce on the ground of the husband's adultery if he has lived with his concubine under the roof of the matrimonial home.'[19] The criminal law, that law which takes account of the public nature of individual offences, complemented this division of the civil code. It consigned the adulterous wife to a house of correction for up to two years but did no more than exact a fine from the husband guilty of notorious acts of infidelity.

Nowhere, as we shall see in the next section, are the political origins of sexual difference in modern law more clearly evident than in the justifications that targeted women's adultery not only as a pathological state of the private relations of marriage but, at the same time, as a direct threat to the public order as a whole.

Strategies of Legitimation: Nature and Public Order

How did the framers of the *Code* perceive the, for us, so conspicuous contradiction between contractual freedom and pre-established hierarchy? Which concepts and argumentative strategies were available to those who sought to insulate the order of marriage against the postulate of formal equality and thus against the very principle that ensured the unity and cohesion of this modern system of private law? In pursuing these questions I shall draw on the arguments and controversies of the jurists to whom the task of drafting the *Code* was entrusted. The speeches of Portalis, the rapporteur of the Commission and its brilliant strategist, will provide the main focus of analysis. Familiar with the immense detail of French legal practice, equally at home in the philosophical tradition of European jurisprudence and profoundly influenced by Rousseau's political and educational theories, Portalis was well equipped to meet the challenge at hand. The traditional order of marriage had to be presented as uniquely suited to the needs of a modern nation; it had to be shown why practices rooted in the pre-Revolutionary past could answer the most pressing demands of the present. What was needed was a justificatory strategy capable of asserting the permanence of the institution against the corrosive forces of individual liberty and equality. However, to reinvest marriage with the attributes of a 'perpetual contract' could not mean a return to the doctrinal authority and the disciplinary sanctions by which the church had once guarded the sacramental status of the matrimonial bond. Tradition had to be reinvented from a distinctly 'political viewpoint'.[20]

In the guise of a new language of political morality the customary pattern of marital rule stands vindicated by the authority of two axiomatic principles—sexual nature and the public interest. Both principles, that is the salient point, 'trump' considerations of justice. They are constructed in such a way as to bar any comparison with the guarantees of equal status protected in other contractual associations under the civil law. As regards the 'invention of sex'[21] as a category of normative force Portalis's argument is largely indebted to Rousseau and his influential formulation of natural sexual difference.[22] In the legal doctrines derived from the natural jurisprudence of Pufendorf and his school, the terms 'husband' and 'wife' referred to a hierarchy of differential social status (negotiated through a contract of voluntary subordination on the part of the wife).[23] Rousseau erased the social origins and the political 'nature' of this difference by rooting it in the incommensurable yet complementary attributes of male and female sexual biology. This language of natural complementarity was ideally suited to serve the 'reactionary' intentions of the *Code* because it did not need to align itself with anachronistic notions of superiority and inferiority. Instead, it allowed the speaker to portray the ideal marriage as a union capable of fusing the unique capabilities and incommensurable character attributes of both sexes into a life-long commitment sustained by intimate love and destined to secure the happiness and fulfilment of both. In the light of nature's benign prescriptions the appeal to considerations of justice and abstract equality was bound to appear woefully inadequate.[24] Add to this a powerful imagery of difference as a source of personal identity and self-realization which detracted attention from the all-important fact that in both Rousseau's and Portalis's account the felicitous design of sexual difference was cemented by a law that defined male nature by the right of mastery, female nature by the duty of subservience.[25]

Whatever the emotive appeal of these arguments (evident in the immense popularity of Rousseau's ideas at that time)[26] they clearly fail to establish the foundations upon which to build a consistent system of legal rights and obligations. Men and women may be considered different by any number of identifiable biological and psychological traits. But these alone cannot explain why 'the natural vocation of their sex' should impose on wives 'more austere duties', why they should willingly submit to the will and perpetual surveillance of men.[27] Indeed, the text of the *Code* itself contains sufficient evidence, in the form of exemptions and exceptions, to fracture the alleged homogeneity and normative force of the facts of natural difference. We have already observed that the law considers a wife perfectly capable of independent action if she obtains the authorization of her husband. Into the same category of legally recognized capacity belong the traditional privileges of the woman engaged in public trade (whose special status and independent access to the sphere of commercial dealings had been a feature of European legal systems since the Middle Ages). In relation to the affairs of her business, Portalis confirms, 'the husband ceases to be the wife's *maître*'.[28] However, the most effective case against the claimed symmetry of female nature and subordination lies hidden in a simple yet categorical legal distinction that has received far too little attention in the historical reconstruction of gender. All European legal traditions concurred in treating the status of the married woman differently from that of the single woman (spinster, widow, divorcee) and in according to the latter most of the rights of civil independence that they denied to the former. Pothier, the eminent jurist of an earlier generation, was in no doubt that the normative foundations of the law ruled out any attempt to explain the subordination of the wife from the natural incapacities of the female sex. No other legitimating reason was available or, indeed, needed than the 'nature' of marriage itself.[29]

What, then, is the 'nature' of marriage? If sexual difference cannot securely establish a special terrain of justifiable private *Herrschaft*, what can? The deliberations on the draft versions of the *Code* reveal that at strategic points in the debate the draughtsmen took recourse to the demands of the 'public order' as the ultimate arbiter on the constitution of marriage. Consider the one area in which the *Code* seems to make considerable concessions to the contractual freedom of the spouses: it gives them the right to contract property arrangements other than the standard regime of the *communauté*, including options such as the Roman dotal regime, which would leave some powers of management in the hand of the wife. But the space of contractual freedom is bounded by an absolute prohibition. No agreement is held to be valid that would affect the husband's personal rule over the wife by, for example, stipulating joint control over the common property or—the paradigmatic case of an illicit contract—making the wife head of the conjugal society.[30] In order to justify the boundaries guarding this inner sanctuary of marital power the jurists distinguish between the different normative qualities that pertain to the personal relations of marriage, on the one hand, and to the affairs of matrimonial property, on the other. The latter, it is argued, are legitimately the object of individual will and choice because, like all property, they belong to a sphere of merely particular, private interests. A husband's legal powers as *maître* and *chef*, by contrast, stand in a direct relation to the immutable foundations of the public order and are for that very reason withdrawn from the disposal of individual agents.[31]

The independent interests of the public as a 'party to every marriage'[32] are similarly brought into play in the justifications of the double legal standard of adultery. Portalis's endeavour to derive this 'useful and honourable distinction' from the authority of nature alone does not get beyond the assertion wrapped in vacuous if elegant rhetoric that 'the more amiable sex must also be the more virtuous'.[33] The juridical defence takes a different route. It must be seen to connect with a long tradition of legal thought and exegesis which goes back, on the one hand, to the definition of adultery in classical Roman law and, on the other, to the construction of marriage in the development of natural jurisprudence since Grotius and Pufendorf. In this latter context the obligations that the law is to impose on husband and wife are deduced from the double purpose of marriage, namely to ensure the continuation of the human species (through procreation) and, at the same time, to protect the social order against the subversive force of individual sexual passion and promiscuity. Only a detailed investigation of this tradition and of the deep-seated distrust of sexuality that ran through it would reveal why marriage, more than any other social arrangement, exemplified the disquieting proximity of order and disorder and why women's sexual nature, more than men's, was seen to tend towards transgression. Immense weight in this respect falls upon the asymmetry in the constitution of motherhood and fatherhood (an unquestionable fact in the one case, a mere presumption in the other). Like the natural lawyers before them the draughtsmen of the *Code* postulate a chain of absolute obligations which connects the inviolability of the sexual bond of marriage with the very survival and identity of the political order as a whole. Since the state of 'public tranquillity' depends upon the legitimate transmission of family name and property, it rests crucially on the certainty of biological fatherhood, which in turn requires that the husband's exclusive access to the wife's body be never in doubt. Judged by a nexus of iron imperatives, the wife's adultery implies an assault not only on the honour of an individual man but on the interests of society itself. Because it involves the possibility of substituting an 'alien child' for the husband's legitimate heir, women's infidelity threatens to disrupt the chain of certainty that holds society together.[34]

Whose interest is the 'public' interest? At first sight it might appear as if the husband merely exercises his rights on behalf of a higher authority and that the latter, that is the state, has an independent and prior claim on the chastity of the wife. But if marital fidelity is to sustain the foundations of civil society, why would the husband's adultery not endanger that order just as much as the wife's? A comparison with those sections of the *Code* that define the status of children born out of wedlock reveals that the alleged difference in obligation owes nothing to the natural facts that are said to distinguish motherhood and fatherhood and everything to the partiality of the law. It is the law that absolves men's adultery from the charge of a public offence by putting the full burden of legal stigma upon the unwed mother and by making the 'bastard' an outsider of society. With regard to the latter the *Code* affirms the partisanship of the public interest in the most transparent manner. It revokes most of the rights that the *Droit intermédiaire* had conceded to the illegitimate child and categorically proscribes any attempt to identify its father.[35]

In both these examples the public order serves as a tribunal of last resort. The appeal aims to ensure the special status of marriage which would settle it in a normative sphere of its own. And this would, indeed, be the necessary condition for justifying a relationship of personal rule and subordination that can have no legitimate standing in a legal order constituted by private autonomy. We have seen, however, that where the public interest is invoked for this purpose it is virtually indistinguishable from the interests of the husband. It is impossible to define the one without assuming the other. For what is appealed to as an independent source of legitimation—the order and well-being of society as a whole—already presupposes the structures of the patriarchal marriage. To put it differently, the state of public disorder is that imagined state in which the traditional boundaries of gender could no longer be taken for granted.

Conclusion

This chapter has portrayed the ambivalent status of marriage in the construction of the modern legal order. The introduction of the civil marriage in the French Revolution simply spearheaded a long process of transformation and intense ideological struggle, in the course of which the modern state in Western Europe was to establish its exclusive jurisdictional power over the whole terrain of the civil law. In vindicating the secular foundations of the political order against the competing claims of the church nineteenth-century jurisprudence insisted on the private nature of the marriage bond. Not the sanctity of a divinely ordained institution, but the contractual freedom of the individual citizen was to provide the guiding norm for the law. As regards the internal relationships between husband and wife, however, legislators and jurists endorsed the civil sanctity of marriage as an institution of primarily public relevance. How are we to assess this ambivalence? One way of telling the story, and for the political theorist the most obvious one, is to take one's stance with the avowed universalist principles in the name of which both the political doctrines of liberalism and the legal doctrines of natural jurisprudence (the *Vernunftrecht* of the Enlightenment period) had successfully challenged the idea of natural or divinely sanctioned hierarchy. One would, that is, treat the rights and obligations of the marriage partners by the very same moral and epistemological standards that hold good for all relations between autonomous agents. It was this insistence on the indivisibility of universal norms that gave force to the emancipatory demands of Condorcet, Mary Wollstonecraft and Olympe de Gouges. The early feminists—and similarly the legislators who at various stages of the Revolution enacted or envisaged measures aimed at the equality of husband and wife[36]—may have spoken only for a small minority of men and women in their time. But those arguments, debates and political initiatives prove beyond doubt that women's independent agency was not unthinkable in this period, that it did not lie beyond the horizons of what could possibly be imagined by the contemporaries of the Revolution. The language of universal natural right contained egalitarian resources of a kind that could be used to subvert traditional notions of gender hierarchy.[37] Indeed, the profound contradictions that, as we have seen, marked the ideological defence of the patriarchal marriage would suggest that the bonds of rule and subordination had to be asserted in the most rigid form precisely because equality was imaginable and, on the plane of rational discourse, irrefutable. It is true, none of the claims made on behalf of women's full membership of the political community in this time went as far as to question their primary commitment to the sphere of domestic duties. However, although the acknowledgement of sexual difference played its part in the feminist versions of 'republican motherhood'[38] it did not form a barrier against women's entitlement to equal rights or against the vision of marriage as a 'rational fellowship'. Far from conjuring up images of public disorder, equality of the marriage partners was seen to hold out the prospect that a free society would find the strongest guarantee of stability and permanence in a regenerated private sphere.[39]

There was, then, no compelling reason why the general principle of individual agency should not hold good for the relationship between husband and wife. It cannot be emphasized too strongly that neither the epistemological foundations of liberal political theory nor the abstract rationalism that guaranteed the formal unity of a modern legal system could accommodate relationships of incommensurate quality.[40] Judged by the demands of doctrinal consistency the claimed incompatibility between the idea of gender equality and the imperatives of an ordered society would stand exposed as but a ploy of ideological reasoning, of special pleading on behalf of particular interests and established powers.

A different story-line might, however, emerge were we to shift the focus of attention from the normative postulates of legal and political doctrine to the concrete contexts of political experience to which the marriage law of the *Code Napoléon* was meant to respond. Emphasis on the 'reactive' dimensions of the law would give us a different perspective on the dichotomy of private freedom and public order that we have found entrenched in the hierarchical conceptions of the conjugal relationship. And on this reading the 'fear of public disorder' could not so easily be dismissed as merely a construction of patriarchal ideology. It might claim veracity at least in the sense of faithfully representing a mentality for which reflections on the order of the family and the endeavour to consolidate the as yet uncertain boundaries of a new political order were inextricably connected. The 'family romance' of the Revolution, Lynn Hunt has argued, must be understood as encapsulating the collective anxieties of a nation which had killed the father and destroyed the bonds of public patriarchy.[41] In a situation devoid of identifiable authority the perceived corrosion of gender boundaries seems to have given rise to particular and heightened fears. Women's intrusion into the public sphere and their claim to a role other than that of the good wife and mother appeared to revolutionaries and anti-revolutionaries alike as the harbinger of a future for ever vulnerable to the dangers of excessive liberty. In reinstating the unquestionable rule of the husband and father at the centre of the family the draughtsmen of the *Code* would have addressed what was widely and genuinely perceived as a vital problem of politics.

Similar claims about the essentially political nature of gender boundaries figured prominently in nineteenth-century debates on marriage. This is not the place to take up comparative lines of inquiry which would have to situate these debates in varying contexts of European legal and intellectual traditions.[42] But we can say that wherever the legal foundations of marital rule came under threat the challenge sparked apprehensions, genuine or manipulated, about the cohesion of a society in which the aggressive pursuit of private liberty seemed to have eroded the stabilizing power of traditional institutions. The other point to be stressed in this respect is that those concerns were by no means the preserve of 'reactionary' or conservative political forces. On the contrary, it was in the terrain of nineteenth-century liberalism that the public-order argument in support of the hierarchical marriage emerged in its distinctly modern, paradoxical form. Unlike conservatives, liberals required an argumentative strategy that would shelter the husband's prerogatives against the logic of equal liberty without, however, jeopardizing the credibility of liberal principles in general. In pressing for the liberalization of the divorce laws liberals claimed marriage for the domain of private freedom and contractual relations. In stating the case for the continued legal subordination of the wife they appealed to the intrinsically public purposes of this institution. One may blame this paradoxical stance simply upon hypocrisy or, more serious in its implications, upon the irremediably male bias at the heart of liberal principles. Alternatively, we can seek to identify the specific historical manifestation of a dilemma that seems inherent in the liberal project of deriving the conditions of an ordered society from nothing but the resources of individual autonomy:

> we might think that social life is not as stable and self-adjusting as liberals suppose. For example, we might think that individuals will not, by themselves, maintain the web of social relations passed down to them. They will opt in and out of all social ties with such dizzying rapidity that society will disintegrate unless the state actively intervenes . . . , and we may want government to encourage the maintenance of certain social ties, including familial ones, and make exit from these ties more difficult.'[43]

As far as the law is concerned, marriage has by the end of the twentieth century become a contractual partnership. Its internal unity and order, once imposed by the state in the name of public imperatives, is today left largely to the private arrangements between two individuals.[44] What two hundred years ago was but a feared possibility is now recognized as the guiding norm of the marriage law: gender no longer supplies a principle of 'natural' order. At the very time, however, that the rights and obligations of 'husband' and 'wife' have finally shed the connotations of enforced difference the quest for a 'return to family values' has, once again, moved into the centre of public debate. Although many different and diffuse intentions are enveloped in this phrase it is not difficult to discern vestiges of the old assumption that the stability and well-being of a liberal, individualist society depends upon the communal, non-individualistic qualities of the marriage bond. Such demands can today not be met by a 'return' to those certainties that were once given by the hierarchy of gender. To lament the fact that marriage has degenerated into a 'mere contract' bereft of any social and communal obligations[45] is to speak the language of nostalgia unless it is also made clear which kind of relationship has in the past been sanctioned by the appeal to the so-called interests of community. Rethinking public and private spheres today must begin, as it were, at the other end—by conceptualizing a public sphere that accords with the idea of marriage as a union of two autonomous individuals, two equal partners in a common enterprise.

Notes

1. M. Wollstonecraft, *A Vindication of the Rights of Woman* (1792) (Harmondsworth, 1975) p. 89.
2. Wollstonecraft, *Vindication* p. 88.
3. Wollstonecraft, *Vindication* p. 87.
4. O. de Gouges, 'Declaration of the Rights of Woman and of Citizen' (1791) in A.-J. Arnaud and E. Kingdom (eds) *Women's Rights and the Rights of Man* (Aberdeen, 1990) pp. 105, 107.
5. Ph. Sagnac, *La Législation Civile de la Révolution Française (1789–1804)* (Paris, 1898) p. 275; cf. E. Holthofer, 'Frankreich' in H. Coing (ed.) *Handbuch der Quellen und Literatur der Neueren Europäischen Privatrechtsgeschichte*, 3 (2) (Munich, 1982) pp. 883–960.
6. D. Blasius, 'Bürgerliche Rechtsgleichheit und die Ungleichheit der Geschlechter' in U. Frevert (ed.) *Bürgerinnen und Bürger. Geschlechterverhältnisse im 19. Jahrhundert* (Göttingen, 1988) p. 70.
7. Cf. F. Wieacker, *Privatrechtsgeschichte der Neuzeit* (Göttingen, 2nd edition, 1967) parts 4 and 5.
8. Cf. L. Hunt, *The Family Romance of the French Revolution* (Berkeley and Los Angeles, 1992) ch. 4.
9. Cf. D. Grimm, 'Bürgerlichkeit im Recht' in Grimm, *Recht und Staat der bürgerlichen Gesellschaft* (Frankfurt a.M., 1987) pp. 11–52.
10. J.-E.-M. Portalis, 'Exposé des motifs du projet de loi sur la propriété' in Portalis, *Écrits et Discours Juridiques et Politiques* (Aix-Marseilles, 1988) p.126.
11. *Code Civil*, Art. 384.
12. Cf. Sagnac, *Législation Civile* pp. 190–240.
13. *Code Civil*, Art. 212.
14. *Code Civil*, Art. 213.

THE FEAR OF PUBLIC DISORDER

15. Portalis, 'Exposé des motifs du projet de loi sur le mariage' in Portalis, *Écrits et Discours* p. 108.
16. Cf. *Code Civil*, Arts. 1387–98: 'Dispositions generales'; 1399–1539: 'Du Regime en communauté'; 1540–81: 'Du Regime dotal'.
17. *Code Civil*, Art. 1421.
18. K.S. Zachariae, *Handbuch des Französischen Civilrechts* (Heidelberg, 1811) III p. 214.
19. *Code Civil*, Arts. 229, 230; cf. U. Vogel, 'Whose Property? The Double Standard of Adultery in Nineteenth-Century Law' in C. Smart (ed.) *Regulating Womanhood. Historical Essays on Marriage, Motherhood, and Sexuality* (London, 1991) pp. 147–65.
20. Portalis, *Écrits et Discours* p. 39.
21. Cf. T. Laqueur, *Making Sex. Body and Gender from the Greeks to Freud* (Cambridge, MA and London, 1990) chs. 5 and 6.
22. Cf. Portalis, *Écrits et Discours* pp. 106 ff; cf. J.-J. Rousseau, *Politics and The Arts: A Letter to M. D'Alembert on the Theatre*, A. Bloom (ed) (Ithaca, NY, 1968) pp. 47–57, 81–9, 100–13; Rousseau, *Emile : or, On Education* (London, 1911) Book 5.
23. Cf. Samuel Pufendorf, *Herrn Samuel Pufendorfs acht Bücher vom Natur- und Völkerrechte* (Frankfurt a.M., 1711) Book VI, ch. I, 12.
24. Some feminist interpretations have credited Rousseau with a deeper understanding of the multi-layered texture of gender relations compared to the superficial diagnosis of the early liberal feminists which based itself upon a single, uniform principle of justice. Notwithstanding the patriarchal/reactionary thrust of his texts, Rousseau's insight that the bonds of abstract equality which constitute individuals as citizens in the public sphere do not hold for relations based upon sexual love is said to provide a better guide to what is implied in the recognition of women as women : Cf. C. Pateman, ' "The Disorder of Women": Women, Love and the Sense of Justice', in Pateman, *The Disorder of Women. Democracy, Feminism and Political Theory* (Cambridge, 1989) pp. 17–32; M. Gatens, *Feminism and Philosophy. Perspectives on Differerence and Equality* (Cambridge, 1991) pp. 9–28. It should, however, be stressed that the suspension of abstract universalism in favour of difference entails considerable risks of misunderstanding where we are concerned with women's legal agency. Given the historical entanglement of 'difference' with *Herrschaft* it is difficult to see how anything but the insistence on the abstract principle of equality of women and men as individuals could have broken this nexus. It is a difficulty which in many respects still envelops the attempts by feminist legal theory today to replace the dominant liberal discourses by an alternative language that could assert both women's difference and their entitlement to autonomy: Cf. W.W. Williams, 'The Equality Crisis: Some Reflections on Culture, Courts, and Feminism' in K.T. Bartlett and R. Kennedy (eds) *Feminist Legal Theory*, (Boulder/San Francisco/ Oxford, 1991) pp. 15–34; D.L. Rhode, 'Feminist Critical Theories' in ibid. pp. 333–50.

25. Cf. Rousseau, *Emile*, Book 5; Portalis, *Écrits et Discours*, pp. 106–108.
26. Cf. C. Honegger, *Die Ordnung der Geschlechter. Die Wissenschaften vom Menschen und das Weib 1760–1850* (Frankfurt/New York, 1991) ch. 2; J. Landes, *Women and the Public Sphere in the Age of the French Revolution* (Ithaca and London, 1988) ch.3.
27. Portalis, *Écrits et Discours* p. 108.
28. Portalis, *Écrits et Discours* p. 109.
29. Cf. Pothier, *Traité du Contrat du Mariage* (Paris, 1772) pp. 122–27.
30. *Code Civil*, Art. 1388: 'Les époux ne peuvent deroger ni aux droits resultant de la puissance maritale sur la personne de la femme et des enfants, ou qui appartiennent au mari comme chef . . .'
31. Cf. *Conférence du Code Civil* (Paris, 1805) vol. 5, pp. 211–24.
32. Portalis, *Écrits et Discours* p. 92.
33. Portalis, *Écrits et Discours* p. 108.
34. Cf. *Conférence du Code Civil* II pp. 122, 180; for the arguments of the natural jurists, cf. A. Dufour, *Le Mariage dans l'École Allemande du Droit Naturel* (Paris, 1971) Part 2, *passim*; U. Vogel, 'Political Philosophers and the Trouble with Polygamy: Patriarchal Reasoning in Modern Natural Law' *History of Political Thought* 12 (1991) pp. 230–51.
35. *Code Civil*, Art. 340: 'La recherche de la paternité est interdite.' Cf. also C. Brinton, *French Revolutionary Legislation on Illegitimacy 1789–1804* (Cambridge, MA, 1936).
36. These measures include the reform of the divorce law mentioned above and proposals submitted to (and rejected by) the Convention of 1793 to abolish the legal incapacity of the married woman and to give both spouses equal rights of control over the community of goods.
37. Cf. Hunt, *Family Romance* pp. 201–02 for a critique of Pateman's claim that the principles of liberal theory are irremediably biased against women.
38. Cf. Landes, *Women and the Public Sphere* pp. 129–38.
39. Cf. U. Vogel, 'Rationalism and Romanticism: Two Strategies for Women's Liberation' in J. Evans et al. (eds) *Feminism and Political Theory* (London, 198) pp. 21–34.
40. Cf. Max Weber, *Wirtschaft und Gesellschaft*, ed. by J. Winckelmann (Tübingen, 5th edition, 1972) pp. 401–40.
41. Cf. Hunt, *Family Romance* ch.6.
42. U. Gerhard, 'Die Rechtsstellung der Frau in der bürgerlichen Gesellschaft des 19. Jahrhunderts' in J. Kocka (ed.) *Bürgertum im 19. Jahrhundert* (Munchen, 1988) I pp. 439–68.
43. W. Kymlicka, *Contemporary Political Philosophy. An Introduction* (Oxford, 1990) p. 256.
44. Cf. J. Gernhuber, *Lehrbuch des Familienrechts* (Munich, 3rd edition, 1980) pp. 25–27, and 148–65.
45. T. Halsey, *The Independent on Sunday*, 14 November 1993.

Six

Theodor Gottlieb von Hippel: Argumentative Strategies in the Debate on the Rights of Women

Lesley Sharpe

In his famous article *Beantwortung der Frage: Was ist Aufklärung?* (An Answer to the Question: What is Enlightenment?) published in 1784 in the *Berlinische Monatsschrift* Kant distinguishes between the public and the private uses of reason:

> I understand by the public use of one's own reason that use that someone makes of reason as a *scholar* addressing the whole of the reading public. I mean by private use that use that someone is permitted to make of his reason in a particular post or office in society that has been entrusted to him.[1]

Thus, in Kant's view the army officer or the clergyman is not entitled in the course of his duties to disobey orders or refuse to officiate at services. As 'scholars', however, rather than as functionaries, they may expatiate on the issues raised by their work and place them before the public for discussion. This is, for Kant, the public use of reason and the means of bringing about enlightenment. The Prussian jurist Theodor Gottlieb von Hippel, associate of Kant and mayor of Königsberg, seems to have taken a leaf out of Kant's book in publishing his treatise *Über die bürgerliche Verbesserung der Weiber* (On the Civil Improvement of Women) in 1792. Though he lived in a state whose laws he upheld and had helped to revise in his professional capacity, he laid before the public, under cover of anonymity, a profound challenge to the accepted notions of women's legal status, of the married state and of woman's nature and alleged unfittedness for public office. In doing so, he shows he is aware of and intends to demolish the prejudices that united even the most disparate of eighteenth-century political thinkers against the notion of citizenship rights for women.

Theodor Gottlieb Hippel was born in 1741 in East Prussia to parents of very modest means.[2] The 'von' was added to his name in 1791, when he successfully petitioned the King of Prussia, Frederick William II, for elevation to the nobility on the basis of the family ancestry. For one so concerned with the modernization of the state and the extension of the rights of citizenship, this striving to be ennobled seems at first a curious contradiction, but is in fact characteristic of a secretive and ambitious man: a lively advocate of marriage who remained a bachelor: a poverty-stricken student whose enormous wealth on his death in 1796 baffled even close friends: a prolific writer who had an almost pathological fear of being identified as the author of his works. He studied first theology and then law at the University of Königsberg. This study, in the late 1750s, was at a time when Kant was just beginning to lecture there. He gradually specialized in his legal career as a criminal lawyer and made a contribution to the formation of the Prussian legal code, the *Allgemeine Preussische Landrecht*, for which he was honoured by Frederick the Great. While enjoying a successful career in public life (he became mayor of Königsberg in 1780), he published anonymously a series of literary works—poems, plays and two novels—which, until the recent revival in interest in his work on women, have been his chief claim to fame.

Hippel's treatise appeared in the same year as Mary Wollstonecraft's much more famous *Vindication of the Rights of Woman* and a year after a significant though neglected treatise by Emilie von Berlepsch (1749–1818), *Über einige zum Glück der Ehe nothwendige Eigenschaften und Grundsätze* (On Some Characteristics and Principles Necessary to Happiness in Marriage).[3] It is highly unlikely both from the point of view of timing and circumstances that Hippel read Wollstonecraft. He may, however, have read Berlepsch, as she published her essay in two parts in Christoph Martin Wieland's well-established journal the *Neue Teutsche Merkur*. Though her ideas seem unlikely to have influenced him, it is nevertheless useful to survey what more outspoken German women were writing on the question of their status at the time. Berlepsch's essay is more remarkable if, as is likely, she wrote it some ten years before it was finally published. She writes from a lively consciousness of the discrepancy between the married woman's legal position and the socially more demanding role being placed on her as companion to her husband and early educator of their children. Berlepsch longs for women to develop greater self-reliance and independence of judgment so that they do not value themselves exclusively in terms of their ability to please men. She stresses the need for the moral reform of marriage rather than arguing for a change in the legal status of women. Friendship involving mutual respect (as in Wollstonecraft) should be the basis for marriage. Claudia Honegger argues that Berlepsch was moving towards claiming a distinctive feminine culture, an area of cultural autonomy for women—an idea fostered by her visit to Scotland (of which she wrote a lengthy account entitled *Caledonia*) and her awareness of the activity of women writers in Britain (Honegger p.18). Alongside Berlepsch one should also mention Marianne Ehrmann, editor of two women's journals in the early 1790s, *Amaliens Erholungsstunden*, published by Cotta, and *Die Einsiedlerin in den Alpen*. These journals contain numerous and varied articles by Ehrmann herself, including a number on aspects of the condition of (middle-class) women. Ehrmann similarly advocates the cultivation of greater powers of rational judgment on the part of women so that they can resist the moral debility caused by the enforced triviality of their lives. While never questioning woman's calling to be a wife and mother (though Ehrmann's insistence on this begins to suggest the need to pacify either her more conservative readers or her publisher) she argues for better education for women on the grounds that, through their influence on children, they are vital to the state: 'The welfare of the individual family depends to a great extent on a woman's fulfilling her proper duties, and this is the basis of the prosperity of the state.'[4]

By comparison with that of his female compatriots, Hippel's approach stands out by its radicality, because it takes as its starting point the question of natural justice rather than that of happy marriage. The women argue from the assumption that marriage is the destiny of women. Both advocate that women try to accommodate themselves to men while also thinking for themselves. Hippel's argument is distinguished by an avoidance of prescriptions for happy marriage. This would seem at first to conflict with the fact that about two decades earlier he had written an entirely separate treatise on marriage called *Über die Ehe* (On Marriage) first published in 1774, though later quite extensively revised.[5] This strongly conservative work is an encouragement to marriage for young men in particular, as a way of counteracting the trend towards illicit sexual relationships and the production of illegitimate children. Though there are hints of a more forward-looking view of marriage (he suggests that marriage should be regarded as a contract based on love and designed for the economic wellbeing of the couple rather than primarily as an institution for the procreation of children) it is very conventional and presupposes the subordinate position of women and certainly never questions their lack of legal standing. Along with Goethe's first novel *Die Leiden des jungen Werther* (The Sufferings of Young Werther), *Über die Ehe* was the German bestseller of 1774 and went into several more editions, thus far exceeding the popularity of *Über die bürgerliche Verbesserung der Weiber*, the more radical stance of which was reflected to a limited extent in the later editions of *Über die Ehe*. While Hippel may have wished to avoid contradicting his earlier views by advancing a new view of marriage in his treatise on women, his depiction of marriage in *Über die bürgerliche Verbesserung der Weiber* is, as we shall see, so negative, that he may have found it advisable simply to rely on the anonymous authorship of both works and let the apparently conflicting views stand.

Comparisons with Wollstonecraft further underline the radicality of Hippel's approach, even though he shares many of her assumptions. Both writers, like Condorcet, recognize and accept the public/private divide but wish to dissociate it from the male/female polarity.[6] Both adhere to the view that the mind has no sex and that physical differences between the sexes and in particular the inferior strength of women do not justify any conclusions about moral or intellectual inferiority. Both suggest that upbringing, environment and restricted opportunities are far more important than physical differences in creating and widening the gulf between the sexes. Both writers were motivated in part by the denial to French women of the right of citizenship, though Hippel's overall political standpoint is much harder to discern than Wollstonecraft's. Certainly he does not discuss overtly the necessity for a complete revolution in social and economic relations to underpin the new deal for women. In that sense he is less radical than she. But in other respects he is more, claiming not only the right and potential fittedness of women to be teachers, administrators, doctors and judges, but asserting that only if this occurs can the public sphere be regenerated in such a way as to create a humane civil society, worthy of the respect and participation of its citizens. In approaching the matter of women's participation in the public sphere he anticipates some of the problems of our own day on the question of marriage and its relation to the broader social and political aims of the state (lucidly set out by Ursula Vogel in her essay in this volume). Though in pressing his argument he appeals, like many commentators, to the benefit of the state, his underlying position suggests that the question of rights for women should not be subordinated to any idea of what the state needs or of the public good or of the purpose of marriage. Rather, the rights must be granted and the ensuing transformation of the state, of society, and of marriage itself accepted as necessary and beneficial. Admittedly this would seem to be an unthinkable prospect to a Prussian jurist, however liberally inclined. But Hippel shrouds himself in anonymity, separating himself from his public office, and leaves his readers to draw the most radical conclusions rather than stating them himself. Arguably his approach in this matter is the consequence of his being a man. Unlike Wollstonecraft, he simply ignores the practical problems arising from his call to give women access to the workplace and to the professions. He is uninterested in motherhood, for which Wollstonecraft had a passionate concern. Yet Wollstonecraft had an arguably over-optimistic confidence in the effectiveness of political change to bring about enlightenment with regard to the position of women. For her it is 'an obvious inference, that as sound politics diffuse liberty, mankind, including woman, will become more wise and virtuous'.[7] Hippel draws a much bleaker lesson from the French Revolution. The refusal of the National Assembly in France to respond to the call for citizenship rights to be extended to women is the proof that change of this kind will not follow as a natural progression. Although he sees the roots of the subjection of women in mankind's earliest development, he sees its continuance as being essentially the result of an irrational impulse—men's fear.

Argumentative Strategies

Unlike Wollstonecraft, who was writing avowedly for middle-class women, though presumably hoping for a sympathetic response from rational and liberal-minded men, Hippel directs his treatise at educated men, identifying himself constantly with his readers in 'our' treatment of the female sex. Unlike her, he writes under the cover of anonymity. So despite similarities in their basic standpoint, stylistically and tactically they conduct their arguments quite differently. Wollstonecraft writes with zeal and directness, her impatience surfacing again and again. Though she takes to task many traditionalist male writers, beginning with Rousseau, women themselves are often the target of her criticisms for their frivolity and vanity, even though social con-ditioning and male attitudes are in her view largely to blame for this. Hippel's style is playful, deliberately unzealous, often oblique. He uses satire, irony and near-parody. His object is to make his fellow men, men of the Enlightenment, look ridiculous to themselves by exposing not simply the arguments by which women were excluded from the public sphere but the underlying motives for that exclusion, motives which are very unflattering to men. As well, therefore, as arguing for the rationality of women, he points out the irrationality of men. The exclusion of women is thus exposed as an abuse of reason and an exploitation of privilege comparable to the worst kind of despotism. Hippel applies the language of politics to the realm of marriage and denounces it as an unnatural despotism based on fear. His readers, men of the Enlightenment, conscious of their participation in debates on such issues as slavery and the reform of the criminal code, are shown up as perpetrators of a domestic despotism. Yet these unsettling and radical assertions are made with a playful irony and an allusiveness that make Hippel far less immediately accessible than Wollstonecraft and his targets less obvious.

In his introduction to *Über die bürgerliche Verbesserung der Weiber* Hippel links his subject to the wider Enlightenment debate on emancipation. His title is an echo of an influential treatise, *Über die bürgerliche Verbesserung der Juden* (On the Civil Improvement of the Jews), by Christian Dohm and published in 1781. This echo also gives us a clue about the intended readership of Hippel's treatise, namely the same group of reform-minded professional men who would have read Dohm and similar works of reform literature in the 1780s and 1790s. In his four main chapters he discusses and dismisses the arguments justifying the inferior position of women. He then explains how and why men have achieved their dominance, his specialist knowledge of European legal history being skilfully deployed, and finally suggests what steps might be taken to remedy the situation. These steps, apart from the granting of citizenship and equal legal status, are to admit women to the professions as a means of transforming the public sphere.

Hippel aims his barbs at three main targets: Kant and Rousseau as one, anthropology as the second, and male psychology as the third. He begins with an attack on the widely held idea that women are incapable of abstract thought and therefore disqualified from participation in the process of enlightenment. His target is more distantly Rousseau, but much more immediately Kant. In ironic style he reinterprets the fall of man in the Garden of Eden to give credit to Eve for breaking the fetters of instinct and setting mankind off in its progress towards a higher perfection. Hippel therefore makes Eve the mother of the Enlightenment:

> When God, having taken counsel about the work of creation, determined that this plan should be carried out, He created the

first and best pair of human beings right away at an adult and
marriageable age with the result that their wedding could not be
put off for a single hour. They came into the world with the
requisite number of years, just as ruling princes bestow ancestors
on their newly-created nobles. Although the male, Adam, had the
privilege of being the first-born, the Lady Eve was fully com-
pensated by being made from Adam's rib, whereas Adam himself
was made merely from a lump of clay . . . Eve acted as the judicial
authority empowered to declare that the minor Adam had reached
the age of majority, after he seems to have been under the
guardianship of the worthy Eve . . . She shattered the fetters of
instinct which held reason in thrall and rejoiced at her work. In
her memory Eve and Reason should be called one and the same.[8]

Unfortunately, as a reward for her heroism Eve only found herself and
the whole of her sex in subjection to men. This alternative Fall takes
issue humorously with Kant, almost to the extent of parodying him.[9]
In 1786 Kant wrote a treatise entitled *Mutmasslicher Anfang der
Menschengeschichte* (Conjectural Beginning of Human History), in which
he reinterprets the biblical story of the Garden of Eden as a fortunate
fall. Man was then in the happy state of obeying instinct. However,
reason drove him out of the Garden, a development bringing about
much hardship to the individual but setting mankind as a whole on
the path to progress. We can detect one or two jibes at the author of
Was ist Aufklärung? in this section of Hippel's treatise:

The first major revolution, like every revolution, could not avoid
suffering and upheaval. These are so necessary as a result of human
nature that I know of nothing, whether practical or theoretical,
which, even if it has different distinguishing marks, was not
conceived and born in disorder and suffering . . . This eulogy to
Eve, which in view of the revolution of reason is so fitting to her,
would perhaps give the mind and the pen ample opportunity for
a theological, legal, medical or philosophical disputation or for an
article in some entertaining journal or other. (p.19–20)

Kant's argument about mankind's progression is in part an answer to
the lack of clarity in Rousseau's treatment of the state of nature and
whether the passage from instinct to reason brought gain or loss. Kant
argues that it did both. By setting up his rival conjectural history Hippel
is exposing the fact that women are not normally explicitly integrated
into this vision of secular salvation, that in fact their position is
extremely problematic. The Rousseauian rehabilitation of woman as
guardian of nature and helper towards the reintegration of instinct and

reason liberates woman from the stereotype of the weak and lustful Eve, while excluding her from the arduous pilgrimage that leads mankind to reintegration and true moral autonomy.[10] Kant constantly assumes that women will always be in need of the tutelage that is associated with a pre-enlightened state.

Hippel's approach to the question of male superiority, whether physical, intellectual or psychological, is to show that there is no 'scientific' evidence nor anything in normal experience which cannot as easily support the theory of equality as of male superiority. In doing so he shows clearly that he realizes that most of the arguments commonly put forward are feeble and self-serving, betraying the prejudices of those who employ them. He shows himself to be sceptical about the growing trend in thinking on sexual difference by asserting that compared with what men and women have in common physically, the difference in sexual function is really a very limited difference. This attitude was in conflict with the growing tendency to regard women, much more than men, as being dominated both physically, intellectually and psychologically by their sexual organs. While medical thinking at the time generally postulated a close causal connection between malfunctions of the mind and body, in the case of women a very direct connection between their reproductive organs and their moral and physical well-being was assumed.[11] Hippel shows that he recognizes how that could be, and was, used as a means of regulating and restricting women's lives. He rejects both the proposition that women are weak physically and that body and mind do exist in such a direct relationship, pointing out that many men of intellectual strength have had ailing bodies. It may be that Hippel's hidden opponent here is the Göttingen law professor Ernst Brandes.[12] In 1787 Brandes published a book entitled *Über die Weiber* (On Women) which began a lively controversy about gender roles and characters. Brandes was closely associated with medical men and natural scientists in Göttingen. The work is a diatribe against the false path taken by modern culture in giving too much authority and prominence to women and their opinions, whereas, like Rousseau's Sophie, they should be kept in a state of subordination and comparative ignorance. Brandes claimed that in view of the way women's heads were being turned by the influence given them it was no wonder they were becoming prone to nervous illness, infertility and consequent neglect of their vocation as mothers. Brandes's book is symptomatic of the harnessing of natural science to support a Rousseauian view of women and cultural development.

Hippel is equally sceptical about the use of anthropological evidence, showing how it can as easily support his case as well as the opposite by noting that explorers have discovered women in numerous parts of the world who are not physically smaller than men, the natives of Tierra del Fuego, for instance, amongst whom men and women are very similar in stature.[13] As far as weakness is concerned, he points out that women in primitive societies often have a very hard life, acting as beasts of burden and being expected to work alongside men in the field. What is more, the men come home and rest while the women are still having to work there. Childbirth in primitive societies is an altogether quicker and easier matter and ironically it is the men who seem worn out by it:

> As soon as she is relieved of her burden, she bathes it in the nearest stream, puts the new arrival to her breast, spares herself the bother of milk féver and of finding a good wetnurse and takes care of the household as before, while the man, prone on his bed, has to be looked after and receives the customary visits and congratulations of his neighbours for having—just think of the effort—born a child via his wife. (p.29)[14]

As far as intellectual inferiority is concerned, Hippel pillories the abuse of anthropology, that is, when it is used to put whole races of people on to a lower rung of the human ladder. He mentions the example of the American Indians who, because they had no beards, had been branded by some anthropologists as an inferior race. The implication is that similar methods are employed to brand women an inferior sex with as little justification. Like Wollstonecraft he recognizes the lack of distinction in most women but like her sees it as lack of opportunity and the result of having to conform to male requirements.

Hippel's own account of the prehistoric origins of the inequality between the sexes attributes women's inferior position not to the order of nature but specifically to the usurpation of power by men, who unfairly took advantage of women's temporary immobilization during childbirth. Childbirth gave women the impetus to lay up stores, leaving the hunting and thus the use of weapons to men. Thus women created the domestic sphere to which they could then be conveniently confined, while men held the weapons, which they could then put to use in warfare and finally exclude women from power. Having domesticated animals, Hippel wrily says, women found they had been turned into domesticated animals themselves. Hence women's apparent unfittedness now for anything outside the domestic sphere, a situation Hippel feels cannot be remedied by degrees:

> Why should I be reserved? As long as women merely have
> privileges and not rights; as long as the state treats them like
> parasitic plants who owe their civil existence and their value only
> to the man with whom fate has coupled them, will woman not
> always fulfil very imperfectly and the more imperfectly as time
> passes the great calling of nature to be the wife of her husband,
> the mother of her children and by virtue of these noble occupations
> a member, a citizen of the state and not simply a poor relation.
> (p.42)

The prevalent argument that women need no advancement because they
already exercise an influence on the state by virtue of being wives and
mothers is stood on its head when Hippel suggests that they cannot be
the kind of influence they should be if they are not citizens. This passage
is in fact almost the only time he alludes to the calling of being a wife
and mother. He rejects the tactic of dignifying women's role in the
domestic sphere for he wants them to enter the professions. Like
Wollstonecraft and Condorcet he believes that being treated as rational
beings would enhance rather than threaten women's fittedness to raise
the next generation. He wants to see women in the professions for two
reasons, first to transform the public sphere itself and secondly to give
women the opportunity to fulfil themselves, to become what men aspire
to be, namely autonomous individuals. Hippel is clearly unable to
conceive of fulfilment which excludes the chance of making an impact
in a sphere outside the home and he is concerned that women are denied
that vital component in individual autonomy:

> Activity has for its daughters Three Graces: Virtue, Knowledge
> and Riches. But what kind of activity? That to which men, in the
> plenitude of their power, have condemned the women, or that
> which one applies to occupations of one's own choosing? . . . When
> will activity of one's own choosing ever cease to be the royal
> prerogative of the men! When will women attain that human right
> to work not for bread, not for gain only, but wholeheartedly and
> for the love of it! (pp.103–04)

He neglects the practical implications of such suggestions and this
silence on such practicalities may be construed as part of his argumentative strategy. The treatise presents marriage in a very unfavourable
light. Discussing the nuts and bolts of how women could adapt their
domestic commitments to new possibilities would divert the treatise
from one its main objectives—to expose the need for men to think
differently. By allowing his revolutionary suggestions for women's

activities outside the home simply to stand, he implies, without the need to state, that the consequences for domestic life of the broadening of women's horizons simply have to be accepted.

This negative view of marriage, on the evidence of the present treatise, derives not from the deficiencies of women but from the tyranny of men. The home is presented not as a retreat from the oppressions of the world at large but as the scene of another despotism. In a key section of the treatise Hippel twice comes out with what he considers the root cause of the continued subjection of women:

> If I am not completely deceived, it was men's *fear of being subjugated* by the women which moved the former to overwhelm them with benefits and privileges. Just like courtiers, who tolerate no moral equinox where good and evil hold each other in check, so the men, who already count among their number so many enemies and adversaries, seem to want to cover their backs against attack by the women as well. Would it be the first time that people have tried to protect their dominion with the home remedy of depriving with care and deliberation those whom they have ruled and wish to rule forever of true knowledge and improvement? Has no voice cried in the wilderness to expose this male arrogance and call the attention of all to this state within a state? (p.101)[15]

These are arguments familiar from the censorship debates of the day and redeployed in the cause of women. Metaphors of warfare and despotism suggest the underlying psychology of men. If in fact Hippel was influenced by Brandes he would not have needed to look far for examples of the fear of domination, when the latter claimed, for example, that young women were in danger of becoming 'foolhardy rulers of the world'.[16]

In this key section Hippel's use of metaphor suggests that he sees the identification of the public and private spheres with the developing male/female polarity as being a mechanism by which to deny women their natural rights. He goes on the analyse the model husband:

> Look around! Even now you will find that men who *adore* their wives are the principal ones to avoid doing anything to improve the opposite sex. And why this disconcerting resistance? The sense of the merit of his excellent wife intensifies the husband's *fear*. The devotion which he accords her suppresses the idea of showing justice to her sex in her. Even the worthiest man is envious of the admirable qualities of his wife that may threaten him; he wants to stop her mouth with favours, restrict and mislead her reason

and will, so that she does not desire justice. It is a special kind of tactic—to subvert rights with gifts, to refuse to pay a debt but rather to make the creditor a gift that outweighs the debt. Such men make extraordinary efforts to show their best side to their wives, and since they well realise how far their wives outdistance them in all respects they place extraordinary weight on their civic duties and give themselves immense credit for performing the business of state, in order to keep their wives' respect . . . A Turkish ambassador who, when asked if he was pleased by the ladies from — is supposed to have replied: I do not know anything about painting. Is not every state official covered in make-up? (p.103)

In the first half of the quotation we find the language of the public sphere used to expose the true conditions of the private. Then, in the story of the Turkish Ambassador, we find a metaphor drawn from the frivolous world of female beauty being used to cut those in the public sphere down to size. Hippel regards this fear and the need to perpetuate this domestic despotism so fundamental that he recognizes that no mere reform of political systems will bring any significant change to the position of women, as the example of France had already shown.

Hippel saw that justice for women could come through increasing their economic independence. Women had not only to be educated but educated *for* something. He sees no reason for separating children before the age of twelve. Up to then boys and girls should be taught together. After the age of twelve they should be taught separately but not taught different things. Women, like men, have to receive education for citizenship. He does discriminate between the sexes when he suggests that boys should remain at school to eighteen and girls to sixteen, but his further suggestions for female 'career opportunities' imply that he believed women should be able to study at university where appropriate. Clearly these educational prescriptions have the professional middle classes in mind, since they would seem out of the question financially for lowlier families, and yet the education of the daughters of the prosperous in Germany at that time was frequently not more extensive than that of the daughters of fairly humble artisans.

Hippel advocates that women should become, amongst other things, teachers, administrators, judges and doctors. Of the law he says:

Should the civil improvement of women ever stretch to the administration of justice and law cease to be the monopoly of a particular salaried class of men, only then will people begin to realize that administering justice does not mean pronouncing in the tone of an oracle incomprehensible formulae which are effective only because the sword lies next to the scales but will see that an effort has to be made to instruct the parties concerned about law and wrongdoing and convince them. Only then can justice earn a *part* of the honour that it claims for itself so unreservedly and imperiously. (p.198)

The suggestion is that women would demand clarity and exercise humanity as judges. He knows he is being outrageous and provocative in making these suggestions but rather than plead for grudging acceptance that the odd woman might be up to these professions his tactic is to claim that women already have the appropriate qualities and that any right-thinking person with eyes in his head can see it. In this section of his argument he moves away from his own earlier position that physical and mental attributes are not sex-specific, claiming that women are already fitted physically and temperamentally by nature for the very fields of activity from which men exclude them. In the case of medicine, for example, he points out that women are constantly practising medicine in the home. They combine sharpness of observation with practical sense and hands suited to delicate work. Women already make a significant contribution to health through their interest in diet and preventive medicine. He also enters into the battle between *accoucheurs* and midwives by quoting a statistic which indicates that of those women in London and Dublin who have their babies delivered by a midwife, one in 70 dies, while of those delivered by an *accoucheur* the figure is one in 140. Rather than arguing for more accoucheurs or suggesting their inherent superiority, Hippel uses this as evidence that the men are better trained and so calls for the improved training of women in medicine.

Hippel's argumentative strategies may be thought to have misfired. The work was felt by some to be too ironical to be meant seriously. One contemporary critic even suggested it was a satire on emancipatory ideas. After Hippel's death in 1796 his authorship was finally established and the work shared something of the same fate as Mary Wollstonecraft's *Vindication*, that of being judged in the light of its author. Wollstonecraft's life lent some notoriety to her work. Hippel's secretive life and rumours of secret vices further undermined the chances of its being read seriously. Beyond that, it is a work that calls for a revolution in attitude on the part of men as well as women, one which was well-nigh impossible at the time. In particular, Hippel fails to glorify marriage in any way, or to take women's role as wives and mothers for granted, and perhaps this was another reason why the rising German women's movement in the nineteenth century entirely overlooked him and it has only been in the last fifteen years that this treatise has begun to receive full critical attention.

Notes

1. *Beantwortung der Frage: Was ist Aufkärung?*, *Immanuel Kant's Sämmtliche Werke in chronologischer Reihenfolge*, ed. by G. Hartenstein (Leipzig, 1867) IV p. 163 (my own translation).
2. For a detailed recent account of Hippel's life and works, see Joseph Kohnen, *Theodor Gottlieb von Hippel 1741–1796. L'Homme et l'oeuvre*, 2 vols (Bern and Frankfurt am M., 1983). For a concise survey of the argument of the treatise see 'The Feminist Manifesto of Theodor Gottlieb von Hippel (1741–96) by Ruth P. Dawson. In *Gestaltet und gestaltend. Frauen in der deutschen Literatur* ed. by Marianne Burkhardt, Amsterdamer Beiträge zur neueren Germanistik 10 (Amsterdam, 1980) pp. 13–32.
3. Some useful comment on points of comparison between Hippel and Wollstonecraft is to be found in Timothy F. Sellner's introduction to his translation of *Über die bürgerliche Verbesserung der Weiber*, *On Improving the Status of Women* (Detroit, 1979; see especially pp. 35–38). I should like to acknowledge the stimulus I gained from this translation for my own translation of various extracts. Emilie von Berlepsch's essay was published in the *Neue Teutsche Merkur* (1791) no. 5 pp. 63-102 and no.6 pp. 113–34. On Berlepsch see Claudia Honegger, *Die Ordnung der Geschlechter. Die Wissenschaften vom Menschen und das Weib 1750–1850* (Frankfurt am M. and New York, 1991) pp. 15–18; Ruth P. Dawson, ' "Der Weihrauch, den uns die Männer streuen": Wieland and the Women Writers in the *Teutscher Merkur*' in *Christoph Martin Wieland. Nordamerikanische Forschungsbeiträge zur 250. Wiederkehr seines Geburtstages 1983*, ed. by Hansjörg Schelle (Tübingen, 1984) pp. 225–50 (pp. 242–46 on Berlepsch); John McCarthy, *Crossing Boundaries. A Theory and History of Essay Writing in German, 1680–1815* (Philadelphia, 1992) pp. 287–92.
4. 'Einige Gedanken über den Einfluss des schönen Geschlechts auf Staatsgeschäfte und Staatsbegebenheiten' in *Amaliens Erholungsstunden. Teutschlands Töchtern geweiht* (1791) no.2 (June) pp. 270–76 (p.275). See also 'Über weibliche Erziehung überhaupt, und über Töchterschulen insbesondere' in *Amaliens Erholungsstunden* (1792) no.2, where Ehrmann again stresses the importance of women to the state (p.37). On Ehrmann see Helga Madland, 'Three Late Eighteenth-Century Women's Journals: Their Role in Shaping Women's Lives', *Women in German Yearbook* 4 (1988) ed. by Marianne Burkhard and Jeanette Clausen, pp. 167–86; Ruth P. Dawson, ' "And this shield is called —self-reliance". Emerging Feminist Consciousness in the Late Eighteenth Century' in *German Women in the Eighteenth and Nineteenth Centuries. A Social and Literary History* (Bloomington, 1986) pp. 157–74 (also mentions Berlepsch). On the use

of this argument by Republican women, particularly in France and in America, see Jane Rendall, *The Origins of Modern Feminism. Women in Britain, France and the United States, 1780–1860* (Basingstoke and London, 1985) pp. 33–65.

5. For a short appraisal of *Über die Ehe* see Marion W. Gray Jr., 'Radical Feminism and a Changing Concept of Marriage: Prussia's Theodor Gottlieb von Hippel' in *The Consortium on Revolutionary Europe 1750–1850. Proceedings to Commemorate the Bicentennial of the French Revolution*, ed. by D.D. Horward and J.C. Morgan (Tallahassee, Florida, 1990) pp. 807–14.

6. *Sur l'admission des femmes au droit de cité*. For a comparative discussion of Condorcet, Wollstonecraft and Hippel in relation to German Romantic attitudes to femininity, see Ursula Vogel, 'Rationalism and Romanticism: Two Strategies for Women's Liberation' in J. Evans et al. (eds) *Feminism and Political Theory* (London, Beverly Hills and New Delhi, 1986) pp. 17–46.

7. *Vindication of the Rights of Woman*, ed. by Miriam Brody (Harmondsworth, 1985) p. 122.

8. All quotations from *On the Civil Improvement of Women* are my own translations based on the text in volume 6 of Hippel's complete works, *Sämmtliche Werke* (Berlin, 1828). Following each translation is the page reference of the original quotation in that edition.

9. No-one, as far as I can discover, has drawn attention to the allusions to Kant or to Hippel's argument as connected with *Muthmasslicher Anfang der Menschengeschichte*. Two critics who mention Kant's influence on the treatise are Ursula Pia Jauch (*Immanuel Kant zur Geschlechterdifferenz. Aufklärerische Vorurteilskritik und bürgerliche Geschlechtsvormundschaft* (Vienna, 1988)) and Claudia Honegger, *Die Ordnung der Geschlechter*.

10. On this problem in relation to Rousseau see, for example, Silvia Bovenschen, *Die imaginierte Weiblichkeit. Exemplarische Untersuchungen zu kulturgeschichtlichen Präsentationsformen des Weiblichen* (Frankfurt am M., 1979) esp. pp. 164–81.

11. On this question in general see Londa Schiebinger, *The Mind Has No Sex? Women in the Origins of Modern Science* (Cambridge, MA, 1989) in particular pp.189–244; Ornella Moscucci, *The Science of Woman. Gynaecology and Gender in England 1800–1929* (Cambridge, 1990). See also my own article 'Über den Zusammenhang der tierischen Natur der Frau mit ihrer geistigen. Zur Anthropologie der Frau um 1800' in *Anthropologie und Literatur um 1800*, ed. by Jürgen Barkhoff and Eda Sagarra (Munich, 1992) pp.213–25.

12. This was first suggested by Emma Rauschenbusch Clough, *Mary Wollstonecraft and the Rights of Woman* (London, New York and Bombay, 1898) p. 212. See also Honegger, *Die Ordnung der Geschlechter* pp.75–77.

13. One of the most widely read treatises on the condition and duties of women was Joachim Heinrich Campe's *Väterlicher Rath für meine Tochter* (Brunswick, 1789). Campe specifically used anthropological 'evidence' to convince his female readers that they must accept their subordinate role.

14. A reference to 'couvade' or 'men's childbed'.
15. The *locus classicus* on the link between despotism and fear is Montesquieu's *De l'Esprit des Lois*. Hippel may be playfully reversing the normal assumption that fear is felt by the victims of despotism, whereas here it is felt by its perpetrators.
16. Quoted by Honegger, *Die Ordnung der Geschlechter* p. 47 (my translation).

Acknowledgement: I gratefully acknowledge the help I received from the British Academy under its Small Grants scheme towards my work on this article.

Seven

Literatures of Publicity and the Right to Freedom of the Press in Late Eighteenth-Century Germany: The Case of Karl Friedrich Bahrdt

John Christian Laursen

In 1787 a well-known German publicist brought out a small book that argued at length that the right to freedom of the press belonged to every man. This was a radical claim at the time and one that has been neglected subsequently by most of the secondary literature on this period or on the rise of the free press. The author of the book was Karl Friedrich Bahrdt, and the title was *Über Pressfreyheit und deren Gränzen. Zur Beherzigung für Regenten Censoren und Schriftsteller* (On Freedom of the Press and its Limits: For Consideration by Rulers, Censors, and Writers).[1] Bahrdt's book was 172 pages in octavo, divided into eighteen chapters. As we shall see below, previous writers in English, French, Dutch, and German had made a variety of claims for freedom of the press during the preceding century, but none of them had claimed repeatedly and in no uncertain terms, and over and over, as Bahrdt did, that freedom of the press was a right of man or human right (in his terms, *Menschenrecht* and *Recht der Menschheit*).

Bahrdt's book raises important questions. If this was the first extended defence of freedom of the press as a right of man, why was it the work of a German publicist in 1787? Another way of putting this question is, what were the elements that had to come together to make this possible? And then, why has it subsequently been forgotten? Let us start with the point that the idea that freedom of the press should be considered as a right of mankind does not have a single or definitive source. Many strands of political practice and political thought came together to produce it. The story of the practices has been better told than the history of the idea. After a brief survey of the practices, I shall concentrate on the idea.

An influential account of the practices that led to an increasingly open public sphere is that of Jürgen Habermas's *Strukturwandel der Öffentlichkeit*, first published in 1962.[2] By now all historians are familiar with the increasing literacy, the coffee shops in London, the salons in France, the reading societies in Germany, the importance of the stage, and so forth. Our information on these matters has grown steadily since Habermas's book appeared. In addition to studies of these practices, there is a wealth of material on the growth in the sheer numbers of books and journals published in the second half of the eighteenth century in Germany.[3] Taken all together, the foregoing public practices and means of communication contributed to *Publicität*, 'publicness' or 'publicity' in its German sense. This was the process of dissemination of ideas to the public, of open debate and discussion, of communication and the sharing of information. Freedom of the press was only one part of this process, but for obvious reasons it was a key one. Habermas's account must be supplemented in at least two areas. One is the importance of the publishing industry as an economic interest, and the other is the role of the Netherlands in the growth of publicity.

It is rather remarkable that a would-be Marxist author such as Habermas says very little about the economic interests behind eighteenth-century publicity. It is true that he talks in terms of the rise of capitalism and the bourgeoisie in general, but much more can be said about the particular economic interests of writers, printers, publishers, and booksellers of the period.[4] These people certainly did all they could to make markets for their work.[5] One does not have to be a Marxist to recognize the importance of material interests in the rise of publicity. Back in the nineteenth century, Macaulay alerted us to the role of very mundane motives in the rise of the freedom of the press. Habermas is probably right to attribute much of the rise of the public sphere in England to the lapsing of the Licensing Act in 1695, but he gives us no indication as to why it lapsed.[6] Macaulay explains:

> On the great question of principle, on the question whether the liberty of unlicensed printing be, on the whole, a blessing or curse to society, not a word is said [in debates in Parliament]. The

Licensing Act is condemned, not as a thing essentially evil, but on account of the petty grievances, the exactions, the jobs, the commercial restrictions, the domiciliary visits, which were incidental to it. It is pronounced mischievous because it enables the Company of Stationers to extort money from publishers, because it . . . detains valuable packages of books at the Custom House till the pages are mildewed. The Commons complain that it is made penal in an officer of the Customs to open a box of books from abroad, except in the presence of one of the censors of the press. How, it is very sensibly asked, is the officer to know that there are books in the box till he has opened it?[7]

These were clearly arguments of commercial interests, not ringing declarations of freedom or rights. Macaulay knows that Milton had written the *Areopagitica* (1644) decades before the Act, but finds no reference to it in the parliamentary debates. This account raises an important question concerning the rise of the free press. If Macaulay's account of a single instance is symptomatic of the structure of other breakthroughs in the liberty of the press, then we may be forced to conclude that the idea of the free press and all of the rights language associated with it are epiphenomena, or 'superstructure' as Marx would have it. Rather than being idea-driven, freedom of the press may have been on the whole practice-driven, and the ideas followed only at a safe distance. This would raise a general question concerning the public sphere as a whole: how much of it is idea-driven, and how much interest- and practice-driven?

Macaulay's account may apply as well to the origins of the free press in the Netherlands, beginning more than a century earlier. Historians have pointed to several factors that had nothing to do with ideology to explain the rise of the free press. One was the division of authorities and the reluctance of local magistrates to enforce orders from the centre; another was government exhaustion during and after the wars with Spain; a third was the presence and different language of the Huguenots in exile in the late seventeenth century, useful to the Dutch in their conflicts with France; and all of these given further support by the economic interests of writers and printers.[8] As in the English case, there were no influential declarations of principle.

The Dutch experience is of no small importance for explaining German developments because the latter may have at least as much in common with the former as with Habermas's English model. To take only one example, Germany actually boasted of substantial freedom of the press in the second half of the century, not because of any such government policy to that effect, but rather, as in the Dutch case, because of the division of jurisdictions. As one writer put it in 1814: 'Germany has always had a perfect freedom of the press . . . because what could not be printed in Prussia could be printed in Württemberg, what could not in Hamburg could in Altona . . . No book remained unprinted, none undistributed.'[9]

The implication here for Germany in the late eighteenth century is that there were numerous practices militating in favor of publicity and a vigorous press. But until Bahrdt, there were no substantial declarations of the right to freedom of the press. The following discussion will explore how he might have come to make that declaration.

I shall start with a point about the semantics of rights. Actual freedom of the press could exist without recognition of a right to it, and the notion of a right to freedom of the press could exist without actual freedom of the press. It is also technically possible to claim that a right exists although it has never been expressed or claimed, but for most purposes rights cannot exist without verbal expression. This is another way of saying that for most purposes rights *must be* declared; they are verbal constructs that will not be recognized if no one claims them. Therefore, the first declaration of a right is a particularly interesting intellectual phenomenon.

Since Bahrdt was apparently the first German to write a substantial work claiming that freedom of the press was a right, we must look for the sources of his claim. Even if we concede that single individuals can make major intellectual and linguistic changes, few who have read his work will believe that Bahrdt was such a genius that he invented the idea by himself. This essay can be conceived of as a reconstruction of the elements that made it possible for Bahrdt to put together his argument from existing ideas. What, then, were the intellectual circumstances that led up to and culminated in his book?

Like many of the more important developments in the history of ideas, more possible sources can be traced than one might expect. In order to keep control over the sheer number of possible influences, it is helpful to distinguish them into various 'literatures'. Each 'literature' has its own sociological characteristics and internal dynamic; each uses a different vocabulary and rhetoric to deal with different problematics via different media, and with different relationships to government. It should be emphasized, however, that these 'literatures' are more heuristic devices than natural kinds. They should not be conceived of as exclusive boxes for over-neat classification. Rather than trying to develop artificial categories, the attempt here is to identify literatures that contemporaries would have been able to distinguish. Naturally, these literatures sometimes overlapped with respect to important vocabularies, media, or strategies of argumentation. Sometimes, even often, an author could manipulate several of these literatures, empathizing and identifying with a literature even if the author had no other personal or professional connection with it.

In late eighteenth-century Germany, there were several literatures of publicity. That is to say, there were several literatures in which the concerns of the public sphere were discussed and debated. In the following discussion, the literatures relevant to freedom of the press will be distinguished as the literatures of (1) religion, (2) enlightened absolutism, (3) travel journals/comparative government, (4) political journalism and pamphleteering, and (5) the scholarly writings of professional philosophy, natural law, and *Staatswissenschaft* or political science. Each literature will be explained at greater length below, but for the sake of introducing the idea, let us simply sketch some key features of the literature of publicity with respect to religion. This was the literature of those who preached and wrote sermons and books on the importance of toleration and open discussion of religious matters, appealing largely to audiences of ministers of the church and other faithful, as well as to government officials who supervised religious matters. It could appeal to age-old metaphors in church dogma concerning light and truth to underpin its demands for enlightenment.

The foregoing list cannot pretend to be analytically or even historically exhaustive and exclusive, but in my judgment it covers most of what went into the history of the idea of a right to freedom of the press. Naturally, in this essay we can only identify a few representative texts and arguments for each literature.

Religion

We will start with the observation that notions of freedom of the press would have no sense if there were no such thing as differences of opinion. There would be little need to publish—or to prevent anyone else from publishing—if everyone thought the same about important issues. Therefore, we would expect these notions to arise concerning issues that are contested, and in the places where they are contested. A second point about the semantics of freedom and rights is that they are closely related to notions of toleration. Corresponding to a freedom or a right there must be some sort of obligation to tolerate the exercise of that freedom or right.

The issues that caused the most divisiveness and war in Europe during the sixteenth and seventeenth centuries were religious issues, so it is not surprising that the first major expressions of notions of toleration were concerned with religion. On most accounts, toleration of different opinions expressed in speech or in print grew out of the campaign for toleration of religious freedom.

Students of the history of the idea of the free press in England seem to agree that the first work devoted primarily to freedom of the press was John Milton's *Areopagitica* of 1644. This was a speech to Parliament intended to persuade it to repeal the Licensing Order of 1643. That order was a product of conflicts within Parliament concerning reformation of the church and toleration of dissidents.[10]

Milton's argument began with a history of censorship, showing that it began in earnest with the Council of Trent and the Inquisition. Providing a Catholic genealogy was, of course, designed to discredit censorship in Protestant England. Significantly, Milton excepted Catholics from the freedom of the press for which he was arguing. Milton's second argument concerned the nature of virtue. One cannot have virtue without a choice between good and evil, and one cannot truly know evil until one has had the chance to read about it. Thus, if we are to be virtuous, we must be tried by the knowledge of evil. Related to this is a third argument, the practical *reductio ad absurdum* that if we are going to license books to prevent temptation, we must also license diet, dress, conversation, company, and 'all recreations and pastimes'.

Milton's final point concerns the nature of truth. We cannot fully understand a truth unless it has been tested by questions, and thus censorship limits our access to truth. But at least one truth has been fully tested and confirmed, and that is the unique authority of the Scripture as God's word. Catholicism denies that uniqueness, and would prevent us from testing the lesser truths of religion, so it can be safely censored. So Milton's position in the tolerationist controversies was that any Protestant sect may have the truth, and if all can express their views, the truth will win out. Thus the Catholics were excluded from the free press partly because they had engaged in so much censorship themselves, but also partly because they were wrong on the crucial issue. Milton's argument for freedom of the press was an argument for freedom of the Protestant press only.[11]

The great texts on religious toleration of the later seventeenth century include Spinoza's *Tractatus Theologico-Politicus* (1670), Bayle's *La France toute catholique* (1686) and *Commentaire philosophique* (1686), and Locke's *Epistola de Tolerantia* (1689), all written in the Netherlands. Each of these works justifies freedom of thought and speech on the basis of religious freedom, but makes no specific reference to freedom of the press.[12] All of these writers seem poised on the brink of a declaration of a right to freedom of the press, but none of them makes it.

It is apparent that freedom of the press was not perceived as an issue of much importance by these writers. Why not? From one perspective, they may have considered it an obvious implication of the argument for thought and speech; if thought and speech of certain sorts were tolerated, it would follow that there was no reason to censor or suppress their expression in print. It may be the case that they thought freedom of the press was a trivial practical corollary of their principles. If so, we have a sort of paradox. Writers concerned with principle would not stoop to discuss the mechanics of the expression of ideas while the printers and writers who were engaged in the business of the press would not rise to define what they were doing as a right. Freedom of the press would not be declared a right until someone was ready to bridge this gap between abstract right and practical reality.

From another perspective, these writers also took it for granted that certain kinds of government control of expression were justified. They were arguing for freedom of thought and speech of certain types only, and not for *carte-blanche* freedom of thought and speech. Spinoza, for example, writes that criticism of the laws is acceptable, 'provided one does no more than express or communicate one's opinion, defending it through rational conviction alone, not through deceit, anger, hatred, or the will to effect such changes in the state as he himself decides'; 'if on the contrary the purpose of his action [i.e. speech] is to accuse the magistrate of injustice and to stir up popular hatred against him . . . he is nothing more than an agitator and a rebel'.[13] If freedom of expression applies only to 'rational' expression, freedom of the press would presumably apply only to that sort of expression. Similarly, Bayle distinguished thought and speech from public display of religious differences, and rejected a right to the latter. If publication in print is considered public display, then Bayle's arguments would not justify freedom of the press. Finally, Locke is notorious for his toleration of Protestant sects alongside intolerance of Catholics and atheists. Like Milton, his freedom of the press would only be freedom for his kind of people. None of these writers could justify anything approaching a thorough-going freedom of the press on religious grounds.

A century after these great texts, the tolerationist controversies that faced a German writing in the 1780s would have included the question of tolerance and civil rights for Jews (Lessing's *Nathan der Weise* (Nathan the Wise) of 1779 preparing the way for Dohm's *Bürgerliche Verbesserung der Juden* (Civil Improvement of the Jews) of 1781 and Mendelssohn's

Jerusalem of 1783)[14] and the questions of Spinozism and atheism raised in the Mendelssohn-Jacobi correspondence of 1785–86. None of these issues was posed as a question of the right to freedom of the press by the chief figures involved. Lessing might well have approved of such a right, but he spent his career playing the game of cryptic writing and pseudonymous publishing under absolute regimes. He was understandably sceptical of the claims of others to enjoy freedom of the press under those conditions: 'Your famous freedom to think and to write in Berlin . . . can be reduced to nothing more than the freedom to criticize religion', he wrote in 1769.[15] Mendelssohn probably knew, as a Jew, that he was going very far in defending civil equality for Jews, and that to demand freedom of the press on top of that would only have increased the opposition to his work and the risk to his own position. On the one hand, for many progressive Germans recognition of a right to freedom of the press probably seemed like icing on the cake which could be obtained after the principle of freedom of religion had been established. On the other hand, they may not have thought that an explicit declaration of freedom of the press was necessary, if they could have the virtual freedom of the press made possible by cryptic writing and other methods of getting around censorship.

Religion was clearly the most important influence on Bahrdt's intellectual development. The son of a professor of theology at Leipzig, Bahrdt was trained as a theologian. Under the influence of Semler and Heyme and other Biblical philologists he moved step by step toward the radical theology of natural religion. He gained notoriety for a modernized and naturalized translation of the Bible in 1773 that was banned by Imperial Decree in 1779, and for a ten-volume life of Jesus (*Ausführungen des Plans und Zwecks Jesu*) of 1783–5, which portrayed Jesus as simply a good man. So it is not surprising that *Über Pressfreyheit und deren Gränzen* insisted that the right to freedom of the press was a God-given right. And it is not surprising that Bahrdt's main opponent focused on the religious issue: J. C. Kinderling's *Auch etwas über Pressfreiheit und ihre Grenzen; oder: ist das Gesetz des Kaiser Joseph II., dass die christliche Religion nicht systematisch bestritten werden soll, ein weises Gesetz?* (More on Freedom of the Press and its Limits: or, is the Law of the Emperor Joseph against Systematic Refutations of the Christian Religion a Wise Law?).[16]

It is not unlikely that Bahrdt drew on the work of some or all of Milton, Bayle, and Locke. Like Milton and Locke, he argued that the absence of freedom of speech 'makes the perfection of their immortal souls impossible' (p. 39); freedom of thought, speech and the press and the testing of religious truths for oneself are necessary for true religion and salvation of the soul (pp. 54–59). But Bahrdt went further. For one thing, where Milton and Locke had explicitly limited toleration to Protestant sects and excluded Catholics, Bahrdt argued in favour of toleration of expression in print by Catholics, Muslims, and even Tahitians (see for example, pp. 87, 91–92).

Like Locke, Bahrdt shifts the issue from the epistemological matter of the truth of religion to the psychological matter of the sincerity of one's opinions and one's inability to change them. Like Locke, he insists that the only authority of the state is political, and that religion should not be a political matter.[17]

A number of considerations suggest a rather close connection to Spinoza. One is that in many of his books Bahrdt was at the forefront of rationalistic religion in its battles against what it took to be mystical *Schwärmerei* and priestcraft. In his book on freedom of the press he asserts that freedom to think saves us from superstition (p. 26), which is the source of barbarism, suffering, and the downfall of nations (pp. 30–31). He explicitly defends toleration of naturalists, free-thinkers, and atheists (esp. pp. 98–102, 143f.), where Locke had excluded atheists from toleration. In this period Spinoza was commonly labelled an atheist.[18]

Bahrdt's understanding of God, nature, and reason is Spinozan, in that he defines them as virtually equivalent (see for example, pp. 8, 24, 29). In addition, his definition of rights has Hobbesian and Spinozan roots. What is the sign of all God-given rights? he asks. It is in the powers, drives, and needs bestowed by God, which create rights (p. 40). This follows rather closely Spinoza's definition in chapter sixteen of the *Tractatus*. Also following Spinoza, Bahrdt claims that God gives rulers the power to rule, and that we know this because they have that power (p. 79).

Bahrdt's theory of hermeneutics may also have Lockean or Spinozan roots. Everybody interprets the Bible differently, Bahrdt asserts, and everybody believes that his or her own interpretation is the true one (see for example, p. 143). If we are justified in coercing others because we believe we are right and they are wrong, then the Romans, Jews, and anyone else would be justified in persecuting Christians.

The rhetoric of religion serves Bahrdt in a number of ways. On the one hand, it gives him an authority for overriding the authority of princes. Since freedom of the press is a God-given right, he writes, it has priority to the prince-given rights of residency and ownership of private property (pp. 39–40). On the other hand, his polemics against priestcraft were probably calculated to win over secular rulers: priests are would-be 'monopolists of the truth' who have often brought down thrones (see for example, pp. 35, 88).

Of particular importance to an account of Bahrdt's use of 'rights' language, one observes that throughout the book religion serves to endorse the concept of rights. The right to think and judge independently from priests is declared the 'holiest, most important, most inviolable right of mankind' (p. 39) and we read that Jesus himself made the right to think and speak 'a universal human' one (p. 139). We shall return to the language of rights below.

Enlightened Absolutism and Reform

A second 'literature' of publicity in Germany in the late eighteenth century can be described as the literature of enlightened absolutism and reform. This can be found in the writings of the often highly educated and sophisticated bureaucratic public service elite. Their world has been well described in recent scholarly work.[19] Bahrdt was surely familiar with the writings of the officials. Observe from the title that his book was addressed to the censors along with rulers and writers; the Preface addresses Frederick William and Joseph. Some of the arguments in the book are designed to appeal especially to the problems and way of thinking of enlightened reformers.

In order to capture some of the elements of the literature of the bureaucratic reformers, we shall focus here on only two examples: one short piece that deals specifically with freedom of the press, and then a scholarly work on the career of an influential pedagogue. The article we shall start with appeared in 1784, a few months before Kant wrote 'What is Enlightenment?' and three years before Bahrdt published his book. It contains much that is symptomatic of many other expressions of the mentality of the enlightened absolutists.

The article in question is Ernst Ferdinand Klein's 'Über Denk- und Druckfreiheit. An Fürsten, Minister und Schriftsteller' (On Freedom of Thought and of the Press: For Princes, Ministers, and Writers), which appeared in the *Berlinische Monatsschrift*.[20] Klein was an adviser to the Prussian High Chancellor von Carmer and eventually co-author with Carl Gottlieb Svarez of the Prussian Civil Code, a major project of enlightened legal reform which went into force in 1794. He was a member of the Wednesday Society in Berlin, along with other prominent officials.[21] We shall focus on three characteristics of his essay. The first is its subversive rhetoric, the second is its relation to the rhetoric of rights, and the third is its final ambivalence about the free press.

Klein's article purports to draw a defence of freedom of speech and of the press from the writings of Frederick II himself. Much of it paraphrases ideas in Frederick's French writings, and it is supported by quotations from them. It is probably true that Frederick had been generally sympathetic to Enlightenment ideals, at least where they did not threaten his power. But Klein must have known that he had not hesitated to crack down on his critics in the past.[22] And a close reading of Klein reveals that he is playing very fast and loose with his sources.

For example, Klein paraphrases some lines from Frederick's 'Eloge du Prince Henri' of 1767 to the effect that the true power of a country consists in its great men. Klein mentions Shaftesbury, Locke, Montesquieu, and Voltaire in this connection, and thus construes Frederick's poem as a call for freedom of the press in order to encourage the genius and talent of the people. But Frederick's original poem in honour of a Prussian prince[23] was an elegy in the aristocratic 'great man' tradition, taking for granted that great men were born princes. Klein has taken it out of context to support freedom of the press and men of talent from among the people.

A second example is Klein's use of Frederick's ode on the occasion of the re-establishment of the Prussian Academy in 1749. Klein twists the meaning by applying Frederick's stanzas in praise of reason into praise for English liberty. He was aided here by history. Frederick wrote of reason's achievements in describing the courses of the stars and weighing the air: by the time Klein was writing this would have reminded readers of scientists working in England such as Joseph Priestley (author of *Experiments and Observations on Different Kinds of Air* (1774–7)) and the German expatriate Herschel's discovery of the planet Uranus in 1781. Frederick surely would not have approved of Klein's fulsome praises for English liberty, and Klein must have known that. His work is typical of the cryptical writing of the sophisticated but dependent intellectuals who made up much of the reforming class.

The argument that Klein extracted from Frederick's writings was almost entirely in terms of prudence, not of rights. It was clearly intended to appeal to Frederick himself, as well as other officials, by describing the pride and power that freedom of the press could bring to a country. In a nutshell, the argument was that liberty of the press is part of the package of liberties that leads to courage, initiative, wealth, and rising power such as that of England, as opposed to the poverty, sloth, tyranny, and decline of countries that throttle the press, such as Spain and Portugal. Klein even had a reasoned argument for focusing on results rather than principles: freedom of the press indeed 'flows from the first principles of natural law', but it 'nevertheless will be secured more through the lively presentation of its results than through the development of its first principles'. Like Macaulay, he evidently believed that a free press would gain more support from the interests it fed than from ringing declarations of rights.

Klein's article made a strong case for freedom of the press, but he could not avoid the internal contradiction of enlightened absolutism. The enlightened part wanted to see freedom of the press, but the absolutist part wanted to maintain some sort of paternalistic control. In the last paragraphs, he enters caveats that could have the effect of swallowing the rule of freedom of the press. Prussia's ruler can and does suppress writings 'which impugn the state itself, which betray it to its enemies, which loosen the subjects from their duty of obedience, and stimulate civil disorder'. It is easy to see how interpretations of these exceptions could justify a rather wide censorship. Klein goes on to call for self-censorship on the part of writers: 'Not every truth is equally useful for all times and circumstances.' Accordingly, writers should take care not to endanger freedom of the press by imprudent or ignoble use.[24]

Closely related to the bureaucrat's paternalism is the educator's paternalism. Recent studies of the mentality of the eighteenth-century German pedagogue have focused on men like Friedrich Gedike, one of the co-editors of the *Berlinische Monatsschrift* and a member, with Klein, of the Berlin Wednesday Society (*Mittwochsgesellschaft*).[25] Like Klein, when pressed, Gedike pinned his hopes for enlightenment on reform from the top down. Like Klein, his claims to freedom and rights were subordinated to the imperatives of administration and paternalistic rule. In this, they were only following the inspiration of their employer. In 1779, Frederick II had written that it was fine to teach the farmers how to read, but 'if they know too much, then they run to the cities and want to become secretaries and so on; so the instruction of the people in the countryside must be arranged so that they learn that which it is most important for them to know, but in such a way that they do not leave the villages, but happily stay.'[26] His bureaucrats were quite comfortable with this kind of thinking, and thus the freedom of the press could never be more than a pragmatic matter, subject to control when other exigencies came up. Kant must have had this sort of paternalism in mind when in *What is Enlightenment?* he attributed the lack of enlightenment to thinking of people as legal minors. His answer to paternalism was that people will never grow up if they are never set loose on their own responsibility. This was, in fact, one of the arguments in Milton's *Areopagitica* and in Milton's pedagogical writings of the same period, so it is at least possible that Kant borrowed it from him.

Bahrdt had a similar answer to paternalism, and he also may have derived it from pedagogical theory. He had written several books purporting to interpret and expand on Basedow's popular Philanthropinum, and had served as a headmaster of a school. Examples from the education of children are sprinkled throughout his book on freedom of the press (see for example, pp. 11–12, 22, 51). His advice to educators was to cultivate the independent reason of their pupils (p. 30). Bahrdt's book includes the usual advice to rulers to the effect that freedom of the press will be useful to them in bringing important information to their attention (pp. 150ff). Another current topos that he follows is to cite Frederick and Joseph as the best and most progressive of the enlightened rulers, and hold up the freedom of the press that they allegedly support as models for other rulers (p. 149). Frederick's decree of 1781, allowing for partial freedom of the press, is quoted at length by Bahrdt (pp. 75–77), although he argues that it does not go far enough. Many pages of the book are dedicated to parsing out exactly what the limits of the free press should be, addressed to the bureaucrats who would be expected to enforce the laws.

But Bahrdt's book is much more radical than the bureaucrats would have been able to condone. There is plenty of anti-princely material, as in describing King Frederick William as a hateful name (p. 2), calling him a tyrant (p. 43), asserting that the idea behind his edict on religion (which appeared the following year) was a shameful trick (pp. 44–45). Raising his rhetoric to a level of high confrontation, Bahrdt writes that 'your minds are armoured with bronze and your backs covered with Russia leather, but I will smash the bronze and tear the skin, so that you will feel my blows' (p. 44). As we have already seen, the right to freedom of the press was a human right, above the prince's rights, and Bahrdt did not hesitate to assert that denial of this right by a prince amounted to rebellion against God (p. 68).

Bahrdt's book on press freedom was the opening salvo in the increasingly uninhibited *oeuvre* of his last years. Two years later he published an all-out satirical attack on Frederick William entitled *Das Religions-Edikt* (The Religion Edict), which earned him fifteen months in prison.[27] One of its characters asserts that 'as long as there are presses in Germany the skunks [*Scheiskerls*] will not keep us down' (p. 87). In *Briefe eines Staatsministers über Aufklärung* (Letters of a Minister of State on Enlightenment) of 1789, the sarcasm drips from the page as he signs his letters to the king with 'Dyingly, your most humble slave'. His *Handbuch der Moral für den Bürgerstand* (Handbook of Morals for the Middle Class) of 1789 has earned him the epithet 'the German Sieyès' in the scholarly literature.[28] It was followed up with a *Geschichte und*

Tagebuch meines Gefängnisses (History and Diary of my Imprisonment) of 1790 and then *Rechte und Obliegenheiten der Regenten und Untertanen* (Rights and Duties of Rulers and Subjects), which appeared in 1791 after some typical manoeuvering to get around the censors, who had rejected the book twice.[29]

Bahrdt was writing in part for enlightened reformers, but he himself had moved beyond them. We have observed at least two contributions of the literature of the enlightened reformers to Bahrdt's declaration of the right to a free press. One is the efforts by reformers like Klein to establish a moderately free press, which Bahrdt simply pushed further. The other is the theory of emancipation of the pedagogical literature of the day, applied by Bahrdt to the press.

Travel Literature/Comparative Government

The next 'literature' to be explored is the travel literature of the day, broadly construed. This consisted of a wide range of materials, from multi-volume reports of travellers in many parts of the world to occasional poetry in praise of particular foreign places or events. Some of what was available to Germans in the late eighteenth century was written in German, some of it was translated from other languages, and some was available only in other languages.

Such literature of this genre as was likely to discuss the press and its rights provided the forum for what we now term comparative government. There was a lively interest in the different ways in which political life was organized around the world, and references to travel literature were ubiquitous in political writings in Germany in this period. There is no justification for the shibboleth that German intellectuals were isolated and unaware of the political situation and political ideas elsewhere in the world. Although news of some foreign developments may have taken some months to spread across the German-speaking lands, anything important eventually got to almost anyone who was interested. The Republic of Letters in Germany was as cosmopolitan as it was elsewhere.[30]

Another shibboleth that must be rejected at the outset is the widespread notion that the Germans got the idea of a right to freedom of the press from the French Declaration of the Rights of Man of 1789.[31] This essay, of course, is exploring the possible sources of a German book on the right to freedom of the press dating to 1787. The grain of truth in the attribution of the idea to France is that the influence of France was probably the single greatest cultural influence in late eighteenth-century Germany. Francophilia could almost be labelled its own *Weltanschauung*, with Frederick II himself figuring prominently as a francophone writer.

Great figures of the French Enlightenment such as Voltaire and Rousseau were well known in Germany, so Voltaire's defence of liberty of the press in the *Dictionnaire philosophique* (1764) was probably familiar to Bahrdt. It is less clear how available early francophone works on the press such as that by Luzac (1749)[32] may have been. Other early statements from writers such as Malesherbes (1759, 1789), Diderot (1763) and Condorcet (1776) remained in manuscript until the 19th century. The crucial point here is that none of these precursors gave anywhere near the sustained attention to the press that Bahrdt was to do. The year after Bahrdt's book appeared, Mirabeau published the first French translation of the *Areopagitica*, and of course the press played an epoch-making role in Condorcet's later writings such as 'Des conventions nationales' (1791) and *Esquisse d'un tableau historique des progrès de l'esprit humain* (1793/5), but this was all too late to have influenced Bahrdt's book.

Meanwhile, in addition to the rather few French sources of the right to freedom of the press prior to 1787 mentioned above, there were also other possible sources. Admiration for England was another widespread topos, as we have already seen in Klein. Voltaire and Montesquieu had inspired a large literature on English liberty, with at least some reference to the liberty of the press,[33] whilst David Hume's short essay on the liberty of the press was available in German translation.[34]

England had produced the 'great text' declaration against censorship in Milton's *Areopagitica*, which was reprinted numerous times in English volumes of his collected works and elsewhere, and excerpted in Nicolai's *Allgemeine deutsche Bibliothek* in 1773. Other English discussions of freedom of the press ranged from Charles Blount (1679, 1695), Daniel Defoe (1704, 1715), Matthew Tindal (1704), John Asgill (1712), Samuel Buckley (1733), John Trenchard and Thomas Gordon (1720s), and James Ralph (1758) to debates from the 1760s down to the 1790s.[35] Much of this, of course, was pamphlet literature that might not have crossed the Channel. If it had, Germans might have realized that much of it was tailored specifically for English controversies and circumstances.

It would not be surprising if the most important influence on German thinkers of English freedom of the press was knowledge of the practices. This would have been similar to the demonstration effect of the Netherlands, which had apparently produced no ringing declarations of freedom of the press (besides Luzac's of 1749), but nevertheless had

had one of the freest presses in Europe during much of the preceding century. In his history of the free press published only a few years later, August Ludwig Schlözer also mentioned Sweden and Denmark as examples of countries enjoying a free press.[36]

And then there was America. America should certainly qualify as a literature of its own in late eighteenth-century Germany. There was already a widespread literature on America before hostilities began, and of course after the Revolutionary War broke out the Hessian troops sent back substantial reports on what they saw.[37] Two examples that were probably available to Bahrdt, Kant, and their contemporaries were 'Die Freiheit Amerika's', published in the *Berlinische Monatsschrift* in 1783, and J. C. Schmohl's *Über Nordamerika und Demokratie*, published in Kant's Königsberg in 1782. M.C. Sprengel's *Geschichte der Revolution von Nord-America*, first printed in Berlin in 1783, described the colonists as leaving their ploughs to fight for 'the most sacred rights of mankind: for liberty and the protection of property'[38]. Some of these materials referred, at least in passing, to American ideas or practices concerning the freedom of the press.

American newspapers such as John Peter Zenger's *New-York Weekly Journal* and Benjamin Franklin's *Pennsylvania Gazette* were writing about the liberty of the press (often reprinting Cato's letters) at least as early as the 1730s.[39] Several famous trials affirmed the importance of that liberty.[40] But by 1787 Germans did not have to rely on writers' interpretations or jury verdicts to understand American freedom of the press. They had access to it in official declarations. The Virginia Declaration of Rights of 1776 asserted 'That the freedom of the Press is one of the greatest bulwarks of liberty, and can never be restrained but by despotick Governments'.[41] This was followed by similar declarations in Pennsylvania (1776), Delaware (1776), North Carolina (1776), Georgia (1777), Vermont (1777), South Carolina (1778), Massachusetts (1780), and New Hampshire (1783).[42] As news of these declarations filtered into Germany,[43] they would have provided a stimulus to thinking about freedom of the press in terms of rights.

It is remarkable, however, that Bahrdt does not mention America in his book. Nor does he say anything about the British and Dutch experiences, or for that matter even about the French. The only persons mentioned are Frederick II and Frederick William of Prussia, and the Emperor Joseph. General references to the lessons of history are common in Bahrdt's book, and he asserted that we learn the most from history. But he did not take explicit advantage of the materials surveyed above. One possible explanation is that he assumed that these examples would be so obvious to his readers that there was no reason to spell them out.

The danger of provoking the censors may have prevented him from naming the American Revolution explicitly. Another possibility is that he thought of his project as an explication of the truths of reason, valid no matter what the historical experience had been. Although it seems likely that the language of travel literature and comparative government would have influenced Bahrdt by providing a context and support for his theories, he did not draw on it explicitly in this book.

Journalism and the Pamphlet Wars

A fourth 'literature' of publicity in late eighteenth-century Germany may be broadly classified as journalism, consisting largely of pamphlets and periodicals. Pamphlet discussions of freedom of the press ranged from anonymous pamphlets such as *Der Censor* (Frankfurt, 1775), *Über den Gebrauch der Freiheit der Presse* (On the Use of Freedom of the Press) (Vienna, 1780), and *Die heutige Pressfreyheit in Wien* (Freedom of the Press in Vienna Today) (Vienna, 1781) to Johann Baptist Strobl's *Über Publizität und Pasquill* (On Publicity and Pasquinade) (Munich, 1785) and Johannes Kern's *Briefe über die Denk- Glaubens- Red- und Pressfreiheit* (Letters on Freedom of Thought, Religion, Speech and of the Press) (Ulm, 1786). Bahrdt's book probably belongs to this genre.

Periodical discussions included Lamberg's 'Gedanken über Pressfreyheit' (Thoughts on the Freedom of the Press) in Schlözer's *Briefwechsel* of 1781, Kant's 'What is Enlightenment?' in the *Berlinische Monatsschrift* and Feder's 'Über die Censur' (On Censorship) in the *Neueste Staatsanzeigen* of 1784, and Wieland's 'Über die Rechte und Pflichten der Schriftsteller' (On the Rights and Duties of Writers) in his *Teutscher Merkur* of 1785. This literature expressed the goals and needs of the editors and writers of the burgeoning number of periodicals.[44] Some of these were modelled on the English 'moral weeklies' of the first part of the century;[45] some were modelled on the French scholarly journals of the preceding century, many of them published in the Netherlands;[46] and some of them were newspapers, the first real political journals.

Out of the large number of such periodicals and pamphlets, I will focus here on ideas expressed by the editors of just two. They are particularly relevant because they were likely to have been read by Bahrdt and Kant and other writers on the freedom of the press, and because they are symptomatic of many others of their ilk.

August Ludwig Schlözer was a professor of history, politics, and law at the University of Göttingen and the editor of two very important journals. From 1775 to 1782 he published *Briefwechsel, meist statistischen Inhalts* (Correspondence, mostly of Statistical Content), soon retitled *meist historischen und politischen Inhalts* (mostly of Historical and Political Content), and followed that with *Staatsanzeigen* (Government News) from 1782 to 1793. These periodicals consisted of reports from correspondents all over Europe plus Schlözer's own editorial comments. Circulation grew to 4,000 copies in the 1780's. His work was credited with such influence that when new policies were proposed, Maria Theresa of Austria was supposed to have inquired, 'What would Herr Schlözer say about that?'[47].

In 1785 Schlözer wrote a pamphlet entitled *Briefe nach Eichstädt. Zur Verteidigung der Publizität überhaupt und der Schlözerischen Staatsanzeigen insonderheit* (Letters to Eichstädt in Defence of Publicity in General and of Schlözer's *Staatsanzeigen* Especially).[48] He did not speak of rights, but of practical and political reasons for freedom of the news journal press. 'Now learn the ABC's of general constitutional law, which hold that every power must have a counter-power to keep it in its limits.' The church and morality no longer weigh against the state; the only remedy now is the power of writers (p. 57). Writers have been the impetus for eliminating torture and will eliminate serfdom (p. 59). The writer is an 'unpaid servant of civil society' (p. 58). Bahrdt evidently picked up on this kind of argument when he argued that princes should appreciate the criticisms of writers (pp. 149ff.).

Schlözer was, like Kant, a professor with a good income and job security as long as he did not get too far out of line. Toward the end of his life, when he wrote his book on freedom of the press, Bahrdt may have had more in common with 'freie Schriftsteller' or free writers; free, that is, of any job and any secure income.[49] He began his career with professorial appointments and his scholarship was widely admired in the more progressive circles, but he managed to get himself run out of jobs in Leipzig, Erfurt, Giessen, Marschlins, and Heidesheim for a combination of personal debts, sexual peccadillos, and doctrinal heresies. He ended his life as an innkeeper near Halle, reportedly much visited by admiring students.[50]

Wilhelm Wekhrlin published a journal titled *Das graue Ungeheuer* (The Grey Monster) in the years 1784 to 1787, and he expressed the views of the 'free writers'. He was able to make a living from his pen for a dozen years,[51] as Bahrdt was forced to do in his later years, and wrote that unlike the employed bureaucrats and professors, 'for whom injustices are profitable', uncompromised writers are the 'natural organ of public righteousness'.[52] He provided a metaphor that Bahrdt used over and over—'reason was monopolized'—and then used the rhetorical licence of the journalist to wax eloquent: 'then Providence spoke: let the human race become free! And 'publicity' appeared.' (*Das graue Ungeheuer* II p. 124.) In a widely used metaphor, he claimed that publicity would 'bring the abuse of power before the judgment seat of the public.' (*Das graue Ungeheuer* II p. 195.)

This very brief exploration of the journalists' and pamphleteers' rhetoric should serve to establish that some of these authors were self-consciously demanding freedom for their craft. These particular contemporary expressions, however, were not couched in 'rights' language, as Bahrdt couched his. We shall now turn to the sources of his move beyond them.

Philosophy/Natural Law/Staatswissenschaft

Bahrdt's polymathy, his ability to draw on and to synthesize widely divergent specialized literatures, is probably the basis for his achievement in crowning the demand for freedom of the press with rights language. The last 'literature' we will survey briefly here is the academic literature of moral philosophy, natural law, and political science. This was the original home of rights language. The late eighteenth century German academy was steeped in the modern natural law tradition going back to Grotius and Pufendorf, with Thomasius and Wolff as early and influential German representatives. In the second half of the century, *Staatswissenschaft* was coming into its own as an academic discipline.

Bahrdt's *Über Pressfreyheit und deren Gränzen* was his first venture into 'purely political' writing.[53] It is not surprising that when he turned to political matters he began to integrate the language of natural law and political science into his vocabulary. It may be surprising that he was apparently the first to combine the demands of the publicists with the language of the natural lawyers and political scientists, when professor/publicists such as Schlözer and Kant might have been expected to do it sooner. But perhaps his life-long practice of rummaging through all sorts of literatures prepared and predisposed him to it while others still maintained separate categories.

Diethelm Klippel's reasonably exhaustive survey of the use of 'rights' language in late eighteenth-century Germany attributes the first usage of the idea of 'freedom of speech, writing, and the press' as rights to Bahrdt, but to another book: Bahrdt's *System der moralischen Religion* (in two volumes, also published in 1787). He goes on to list a half a dozen works on natural law which *later* made the same claim, in the years 1790–98.[54] Klippel calls Bahrdt's later work *Rechte und Pflichten von*

Herrschern und Untertanen (1791; published as vol. 3 of *System der moralischen Religion* to avoid drawing the attention of censors, see above p. 118) 'a fundamental change of the whole of natural law' (p.115) because it rejects any state of nature and individualness whatsoever, insisting on social imbeddedness. But Bahrdt had already done that in our *Über Pressfreyheit*; however, the 1791 book also included a right to publicity, with fewer limitations than the ones he had previously allowed.[55]

Bahrdt had no great respect for the jurists. They could just as easily prove either side of any proposition, he wrote: 'the jurist's right is a waxen nose' (p. 41). When he established the right to a free press he insisted that 'no philosophizing applies here'; God's will is seen *a posteriori*, not *a priori* (p. 42). But Bahrdt's protestations of philosophical innocence are somewhat disingenuous. He reveals a fairly sophisticated epistemology when he writes of 'socially founded truth' (p. 59). He makes a point rather similar to Kant's point in 'What is Orientation in Thinking?' of the same year: that taking away the right to speak effectively takes away the right to think (pp. 47–48). He distinguishes universal human rights from the particular rights of princes, and gives the former priority (p. 43, 69).

Perhaps the most telling point about Bahrdt's reliance on philosophy and natural law is that he uses rights language at all. As we have seen above, many of the early defences of freedom of the press did not use the word or the concept of rights at all. Bahrdt must have thought that he was adding a powerful argument to the case for freedom of the press. It is noteworthy that he preceded the French at this, anticipating the rhetoric of the 'Declaration of the Rights of Man'. It is probably safe to say that he did so as a result of the same general conditions, intellectual and practical, that lead to the French declaration. His example demonstrates that it may well be counter-productive to think of Germany as somehow intellectually backward at the time: here we have a case of the 'periphery' anticipating the 'centre'.

In the foregoing survey, we have seen that although Bahrdt made no significant mention of the travel literature and foreign-language works concerning freedom of the press, he appropriated the literature and rhetoric of religion for his own purposes, went far beyond the mindset of the enlightened absolutists, and contributed to the fight for liberty of the press being carried on in the pamphlet literature and journalism of his day. He brought together many of the growing voices for freedom of the press, contributing to the increasingly rich movement of opposition to princely absolutism in late eighteenth-century Germany. All of this culminated in his appropriation of the 'rights' language of the scholarly literature of his day for what is apparently the most uncompromising defence of freedom of the press as a human right to appear on the Continent before the French Revolution.

Notes

1. *Über Pressfreyheit und deren Gränzen. Zur Beherzigung für Regenten Censoren und Schriftsteller* (Züllichau, 1787). Reprinted under the title *Über Pressfreyheit und deren Grenzen. Ein Wort für Regenten und Schriftsteller* in 1794 (see Karl Goedeke, *Grundriss zur Geschichte der deutschen Dichtung*, 3rd ed., Berlin, 1955, p. 827); Danish translation, *Om Trykkefrihed* (Copenhagen, 1797). I have translated about a third of the book for publication in James Schmidt (ed.) *What is Enlightenment? Eighteenth Century Answers and Twentieth Century Questions* (Berkeley, forthcoming). On Bahrdt, see Dieter Schwab, 'Pressefreiheit als Menschenrecht—Zur Theorie der Gedanken- und Pressefreiheit bei Carl Friedrich Bahrdt' in Otto Triffterer and Friedrich von Zezschwitz (eds) *Festschrift für Walter Mallmann* (Baden-Baden, 1978) pp. 245-58; Ludger Lütkehaus, 'Karl Friedrich Bahrdt, Immanuel Kant und die Gegenaufklärung in Preussen (1788–1798)' *Jahrbuch des Instituts für Deutsche Geschichte* 9 (1980) pp. 83–106; Günter Mühlpfordt, 'Bahrdts Weg zum revolutionären Demokratismus' *Zeitschrift für Geschichtswissenschaft* 29 (1981) pp. 9962D1017; G. Mühlpfordt, 'Radikale Aufklärung und nationale Leserorganisation. Die Deutsche Union von Karl Friedrich Bahrdt' in Otto Dann (ed.) *Lesegesellschaften und bürgerliche Emanzipation* (Munich, 1981) pp. 103–22; Gerhard Sauder and Christoph Weiss (eds) *Carl Friedrich Bahrdt (1740-1792)* (St. Ingbert, 1992); John Christian Laursen, 'Publicity and Cosmopolitanism in Late Eighteenth Century Germany' *History of European Ideas* 16 (1993) pp. 117–22; and the very amusing book by Sten Gunnar Flygt, *The Notorious Dr Bahrdt* (Nashville, 1963).
2. *Strukturwandel der Öffentlichkeit* (Darmstadt and Neuwied, 1962), cited below in the English translation by Thomas Burger in *The Structural Transformation of the Public Sphere* (Cambridge MA, 1989).
3. See, for example, Dann (ed.) *Lesegesellschaften*; Ulrich Im Hof, *Das gesellige Jahrhundert: Gesellschaft und Gesellschaften im Zeitalter der Aufklärung* (Munich, 1982); Horst Möller, *Vernunft und Kritik* (Frankfurt, 1986); Hans-Erich Bödeker, 'Aufklärung als Kommunikationsprozess' *Aufklärung* 2/2 (1987) pp. 89–111.
4. I find one place where he specifically refers to such interests, and that is to downplay them: he writes that 'it is questionable whether the interests of those who made a living by writing news pamphlets would have provided a sufficiently strong impetus' for the growth in the news journal industry (p. 21).
5. Schlözer, discussed below, is an instructive example; and see my article,

'The Beneficial Lies Controversy in the Huguenot Netherlands, 1705–1731' in *Studies on Voltaire and the Eighteenth Century* 319 (1994) pp. 67–103.

6. Habermas, *Structural Transformation* p. 59

7. Thomas B. Macaulay, *The History of England* (New York, 1866) VII pp. 189f. A more recent scholarly account is Raymond Astbury, 'The renewal of the Licensing Act in 1693 and its lapse in 1695' *The Library*, Fifth Series, XXXIII (1978) pp. 296–322.

8. See the articles in A. C. Duke and C. A. Tamse (eds) *Too Mighty to be Free: Censorship and the Press in Britain and the Netherlands* (Zutphen, 1987) and John Christian Laursen, 'The Politics of a Publishing Event: The Marchand Milieu and *The Life and Spirit of Spinoza* of 1719' in *Heterodoxy, Spinozism and Freethought: The Traité des Trois Imposteurs* ed. by S. Berti, F. Charles-Daubert and R. H. Popkin (Dordrecht, 1995).

9. Helmut Kiesel and Paul Münch, *Gesellschaft und Literatur im 18. Jahrhundert* (Munich, 1977), p. 118. Habermas does not recognize the practice of getting around French censors through the Netherlands (p. 67); and says that only the British had a free press (p. 59).

10. See Ernest Sirluck's Introduction to *Complete Prose Works of John Milton* (New Haven, 1959) II, esp. pp. 53–136.

11. The *Areopagitica*'s claim to freedom of the press was preceded in the same year by similar claims in William Walwyn's *The Compassionate Samaritane* and Henry Robinson's *Liberty of Conscience*, and followed by arguments for freedom of the press by Richard Overton, John Lilburne, and Leveller petitions to the Parliament. Some of the arguments these men made drifted rather far from the religious issues, including appeals to economic laissez-faire and Englishmen's rights (compare the discussion in Frederick Siebert, *Freedom of the Press in England, 1476–1776* (Urbana, 1952) pp. 192–201 and Sirluck pp. 83–92). But none of these texts dedicated more than a few sentences to freedom of the press, usually mentioning it without special attention in conjunction with freedom of speech and of conscience. And it is not particularly likely that these English pamphlets had the kind of circulation that would have crossed the Channel and reached Germany.

   A further peculiarity of Milton's position was that in 1651 he served as the official censor of newsbooks. As one commentator suggests, 'Either Milton had by 1651 changed his mind on the subject of licensing the press or he had never intended . . . that this freedom, enjoyed by serious and scholarly books, should be extended to newsbooks of ephemeral as well as explosive contents' (Siebert 196–97.) We shall return to the question of Bahrdt's debt to Milton.

12. Later, Locke prepared a memorandum opposed to the renewal of the Licensing Act in 1695, arguing that 'I know not why a man should not have liberty to print what ever he would speake and to be answerable for the one just as he is for the other if he transgresses the law in either' (*The Correspondence of John Locke* ed. by E. S. De Beer (Oxford, 1979) pp.

785ff.) Locke's arguments are largely those described by Macaulay, concerned with the practical effects of the law.

13. Spinoza, *Tractatus Theologico-Politicus* trans. Samuel Shirley (Leiden, 1991), p. 293.

14. Although I have not found any explicit reference to freedom of the press in Mendelssohn, Mendelssohn's twentieth-century editor suggests that Mendelssohn may have considered the right to freedom of the press a civil right (as distinguished from a human right). See Alexander Altmann's 'Commentary' to Moses Mendelssohn, *Jerusalem* (Hanover, 1983) p. 154. Bahrdt's move was to make freedom of the press a human right rather than a civil one, as we shall see below.

15. Letter of 25 August 1769 in G.E. Lessing, *Werke* ed. by Paul Stapf, I p. 1134.

16. *Auch etwas über Pressfreiheit und ihre Grenzen; oder: ist das Gesetz des Kaiser Joseph II., dass die christliche Religion nicht systematisch bestritten werden soll, ein weises Gesetz? Wider Herrn D. Bahrdt erwisen von einem Freunde der Wahrheit* (Quedlinburg and Leipzig, 1788).

17. See James Tully, 'Toleration, Skepticism and Rights: John Locke and Religious Toleration' in E. J. Furcha (ed.) *Truth and Tolerance* (Montreal, 1990).

18. See David Bell, *Spinoza in Germany from 1670 to the Age of Goethe* (London, 1984).

19. See, for example, H. M. Scott (ed.) *Enlightened Absolutism: Reform and Reformers in Later Eighteenth Century Europe* (Ann Arbor, 1990); Eckhart Hellmuth, *Naturrechtsphilosophie und Bürokratischer Werthorizont* (Göttingen, 1985); Claudia Langer, *Reform nach Prinzipien: Untersuchungen zur politischen Theorie Immanuel Kants* (Stuttgart, 1986); Günter Birtsch (ed.) *Der Idealtyp des aufgeklärten Herrschers*, special issue of *Aufklärung* 1 (1987); Anthony J. La Vopa, 'The Politics of Enlightenment: Friedrich Gedike and German Professional Ideology' *Journal of Modern History* 62 (1990) pp. 34–56; Franco Venturi, *Settecento Riformatore* (Torino, 1969–90).

20. The article appeared anonymously in vol. III, pp. 312–30. Klein acknowledged it in his *Kurze Aufsätze über verschiedene Gegenstände* (Halle, 1797) p. 91. See Norbert Hinske (ed.) *Was ist Aufklärung?: Beiträge aus der Berlinischen Monatsschrift* (Darmstadt, 1981) p. 517. I have also translated Klein's article for Schmidt (ed.) *What is Enlightenment?* (see note 1).

21. For further information about Klein see Eckhart Hellmuth, 'Ernst Ferdinand Klein: Politische Reflexionen im Preussen der Spätaufklärung' in Hans Erich Bödeker and Ulrich Hermann (eds) *Aufklärung als Politisierung—Politisierung der Aufklärung* (Hamburg, 1987) pp. 222–36; Gerd Kleinheyer, 'Klein, Ernst Ferdinand', *Neue Deutsche Biographie* (Berlin, 1977) XI pp. 734–35.

22. See Franz Etzin, 'Die Freiheit der öffentlichen Meinung unter der Regierung Friedrichs des Grossen' *Forschungen zur brandenburgischen und preussischen Geschichte* 33 (1926) pp. 89–129, 293–326; Edoardo Tortarolo,

'Zensur, öffentliche Meinung und Politik in der Berliner Spätaufklärung',
*Leipziger Beiträge zur Universalgeschichte und vergleichenden Gesellschafts-
forschung* 3 (1991) pp. 80–90, and Tortarolo's chapter in this volume.

23. Note that this was *not* an elegy for that well known 'Prince Henri', Henry
    IV of France.

24. Here, Klein is repeating the classist substance of a lecture he gave in
    1780 and published as 'Vom Edeln und Niedrigen im Ausdrucke',
    Litterarische Chronik II (1786) pp. 374–93.

25. Anthony La Vopa, *Grace, Talent, and Merit* (Cambridge, 1988); and 'The
    Politics of Enlightenment'.

26. Quoted in Kiesel and Münch, *Gesellschaft und Literatur* p. 163. On Klein's
    later growing conservatism see also Günter Birtsch, 'Freiheit und
    Eigentum, Zur Erörterung von Verfassungsfragen in der deutschen
    Publizistik im Zeichen der Französischen Revolution' in Rudolf Vierhaus
    (ed.) *Eigentum und Verfassung. Zur Eigentumsdiskussion im ausgehenden 18.
    Jahrhundert* (Göttingen, 1972), pp. 179–92.

    On Frederick's paternalism, Habermas cites a famous rescript from
    1784: 'A private person has no right to pass public judgment [on the
    government] . . . For a private person is not at all capable of making such
    a judgment, because he lacks complete knowledge of circumstances and
    motives' (p. 25). This may have been suggested to Frederick by a
    bureaucrat such as Klein.

27. There is a modern edition of *Das Religions-Edikt*, edited with an afterword
    by Ludger Lütkehaus (Heidelberg, 1985).

28. Günter Mühlpfordt, 'Ein Rigaer Revolutionsbuch. Das Werden der
    Staatslehre Karl Friedrich Bahrdts 1786–1791' in E. Donnert (ed.)
    Gesellschaft und Kultur Russlands in der 2. Hälfte des 18. Jahrhunderts I
    (Halle, 1982) p. 217.

29. Mühlpfordt, 'Ein Rigaer Revolutionsbuch', pp. 225ff. There is a modern
    reprint, *Rechte und Obliegenheiten der Regenten und Untertanen* (Scriptor,
    1975).

30. See Venturi, *Settecento Riformatore*, as a corrective to the recent vogue of
    national histories of the Enlightenment.

31. For example, Ernst Cassirer, *The Philosophy of the Enlightenment* (Princeton,
    1951), gives only French examples in his chapter on the rights of man;
    and see Diethelm Klippel, *Politische Freiheit und Freiheitsrechte im deutschen
    Naturrecht des 18. Jahrhunderts* (Paderborn, 1976), p. 123; Horst Dippel,
    Germany and the American Revolution, 1770–1800 (Chapel Hill, 1977) pp.
    165–66. Habermas's suggestion (p. 70) that 'the German term for the
    public sphere, 'Öffentlichkeit', was formed after the French . . . in the
    days of the revolution' is effectively refuted by Lucian Hölscher's attention
    to earlier sources in Latin, English, German, and French in *Öffentlichkeit
    und Geheimnis* (Stuttgart, 1979).

32. Elie Luzac, *Essai sur la liberté de produire ses sentimens* (Amsterdam, 1749).

33. Elie Luzac dedicated his booklet on freedom of the press to the English:

Essai sur la liberté de produire ses sentimens pp. 1–4. See also Dippel, *Germany and the American Revolution* p. 143.

34. David Hume, *Vermischte Schriften*, tr. H. A. Pistorius, 1754-6.
35. See Eckhart Hellmuth, ' "The palladium of all other English liberties": Reflections on the Liberty of the Press in England during the 1760's and 1770s' in Hellmuth (ed.) *The Transformation of Political Culture: England and Germany in the Late Eighteenth Century* (Oxford, 1990) pp. 467–501.
36. A. L. Schlözer, *Allgemeine StatsRecht und StatsVerfassungsLere* (Göttingen, 1793) p. 92.
37. Dippel, *Germany and the American Revolution* pp. 73ff.
38. Dippel, *Germany and the American Revolution* p. 140.
39. See Leonard W. Levy, *Freedom of the Press from Zenger to Jefferson* (New York, 1966), esp. pp. 3–43.
40. See Levy, *Freedom of the Press from Zenger to Jefferson*, esp. pp. 43–61 (the Zenger case) and pp. 105–27 (the McDougall case).
41. Bernard Schwartz (ed.) *The Roots of the Bill of Rights* (New York, 1980) II p. 235.
42. Schwartz (ed.) *Roots of the Bill of Rights*: PA: 'the people have a right to freedom of speech, and of writing, and publishing their sentiments; therefore the freedom of the press ought not to be restrained' (p. 266); DE: 'the liberty of the press ought to be inviolably preserved' (p. 278); MD (p. 284); NC (p. 287), GA (p. 300), VT (p. 324), SC (p. 335), MA (p. 342), and NH (p. 378).
43. For example, Johann Jacob Moser reprinted article 16 of the Massachusetts Bill of Rights of 1780 in *Nordamerika nach dem Friedensschlüssen vom Jahr 1783* (Leipzig, 1784–85) III p. 505.
44. At least 754 new periodicals were founded between 1741 and 1765 alone, and in the 1780s one count found 217 periodicals at one time (see Gisbert Lepper, Jörg Steitz et al., *Einführung in die deutsche Literatur des 18. Jahrhunderts, Band 1: Unter dem Absolutismus* (Opladen, 1983) pp. 210, 336). For more of this literature see Jost Hermand (ed.) *Von deutscher Republik, 1775–1795, Texte radikaler Demokraten* (Frankfurt, 1975); Zwi Batscha (ed.) *Aufklärung und Gedankenfreiheit* (Frankfurt, 1977); and Eckhart Hellmuth, 'Zur Diskussion um Presse- und Meinungsfreiheit in England, Frankreich und Preussen im Zeitalter der Französischen Revolution', in Günter Birtsch (ed.) *Grund- und Freiheitsrechte im Wandel von Gesellschaft und Geschichte* (Göttingen, 1981) pp. 205–26.
45. The classic survey is Wolfgang Martens, *Die Botschaft der Tugend. Die Aufklärung im Spiegel der deutschen Moralischen Wochenschriften* (Stuttgart, 1968).
46. This would include Wieland's *Teutscher Merkur*, the *Göttingische Anzeigen von gelehrten Sachen*, Nicolai's *Allgemeine deutsche Bibliothek*, and so on. For a good survey of many of these journals, see Hans Erich Bödeker, 'Journals and Public Opinion' in Hellmuth (ed.) *Transformation of Political Culture* pp. 423–45.
47. For more on Schlözer, see the text and notes in John Christian Laursen,

'Kant and Schlözer on the French Revolution and the Rights of Man in the Context of Publicity' in Timothy O'Hagan (ed.) *Revolution and Enlightenment in Europe* (Aberdeen, 1991) pp. 30–40.

48. Published Frankfurt am Main and Eichstädt.

49. See Hans-Jürgen Haferkorn, 'Der freie Schriftsteller' *Archiv für Geschichte des Buchwesens* 5 (1962–64) pp. 523–712; and Henri Brunschwig, *Enlightenment and Romanticism in Eighteenth Century Prussia* (Chicago, 1974), pp. 138ff.

50. These are the stories that make Flygt's book so entertaining (see note 1).

51. Jean Mondot, 'W.L. Wekhrlin et le Jacobinisme allemand' *Annales historiques de la Révolution française* 255/6 (1984) p. 26. See also Mondot, *Wilhelm Wekhrlin: un publiciste des lumières* (Bordeaux, 1986).

52. *Das graue Ungeheur* II p. 192.

53. Mühlpfordt, 'Ein Rigaer Revolutionsbuch' p. 206.

54. Klippel, *Politische Freiheit* p. 123. The sources are: Eggers, *Staatsrecht* (1790), Becker, *Vorlesungen über die Pflichen und Rechte des Menschen* (1791–92), Schaumann, *Kritische Abhandlungen* (1795), *Neues System* (1796), and Buhle, *Lehrbuch des Naturrechts* (1798).

55. Klippel, *Politische Freiheit* p. 143; Mühlpfordt, 'Ein Rigaer Revolutionsbuch' p. 206.

Eight

Censorship and the Conception of the Public in Late Eighteenth-Century Germany: Or, are Censorship and Public Opinion Mutually Exclusive?

Edoardo Tortarolo

Very recently the idea of public opinion has become a crucial element in the discussion about the end of the *ancien régime* in Europe.[1] In fact, Jürgen Habermas and Reinhart Koselleck had already investigated the importance of public opinion in the eighteenth century in the 1950s and early 1960s. The former underlined the exemplary value of the Enlightenment idea of public opinion as a socio-historical category in contrast to its subsequent evolution in the late nineteenth century and in the twentieth century; the latter considered public opinion a major factor in the pathogeny of bourgeois civilization.[2] Their works had no impact on international discussion until disenchantment with the traditional patterns of explanation called the attention of historians to such entities as public opinion, whose importance grew as the relevance of economic and social structures decreased. The translation of Koselleck's and Habermas's works into English in the late 1980s has contributed to the emergence of public opinion as a central category in dealing with the late eighteenth century.[3] This reorientation of interest has been most apparent in the discussion about pre-Revolutionary France. According to influential historians such as Keith Baker and Mona Ozouf, public opinion became central in France in the last decades of the eighteenth century: an invisible, all-powerful, self-appointed tribunal, making decisions nobody actually signed. Public opinion in France was the alternative to the corrupt absolutist state, whose crimes and decay it mercilessly exposed. In France public opinion was therefore above all a form of language that society created: it turned out to be an impersonal force whose outcome was the sapping of the state institutions. In recent historiography on the French Revolution public opinion is a decisive factor in the fall of the *ancien régime*.

A similar pattern prevails when historians deal with Germany at the end of the eighteenth century. To quote a recent and authoritative book about eighteenth-century Germany, 'the emergence of a literate public sphere led to a polarization between public opinion and the absolutist state . . . The private sphere outside the state developed into a public sphere against the state.'[4] In this statement the influence of Habermas's and Koselleck's point of view is evident; the general validity of its long-term implications is beyond doubt. The reference to the rapidly growing number of journals and newspapers, to the changes in the patterns of reading behaviour (the so-called revolution in reading) and to the increasing interest in public affairs substantiate the claim that public opinion in Germany was emerging as a political factor opposed to the absolutist state.[5]

Still, as Habermas has recently remarked in the new and strikingly innovative *Introduction* to his ground-breaking *Strukturwandel der Öffentlichkeit*, historical research is concerned with empirical realities as they are expressed in documents, while sociological categories have to emphasize outstanding features of an epoch and therefore tend to create an oversimplified image.[6] In this essay I will focus on Berlin in order to grasp some social and political features of public opinion at the end of the eighteenth century, taking it as a multifarious historical phenomenon rather than as a sociological category (in the style of Habermas) or as a 'political invention' (in the style of Baker). While both scholars have contributed seminal insights into this topic, a rather different constellation will emerge from my essentially historical investigation. I argue that public opinion in late eighteenth-century Berlin was neither a sociological category expressed ultimately by the ascending bourgeoisie (Habermas) nor a political invention appearing in the context of a crisis of absolute monarchy (Baker). An analysis of the Prussian censors and their political culture and attitudes, of the debate on the liberty of the press and, finally, of the eighteenth-century meaning of public opinion will show the outstanding characteristics of *öffentliche Meinung* in its eighteenth-century German context.

I

Censorship and public opinion can be considered correlative entities. Their relationship is usually explained as follows: while the latter stands for unfettered creative activity of a literate community expressing the needs of civil society, the former represents the repressive activity of state institutions concerned about the subversive dangers public opinion can embody. On closer inspection, this view is inappropriate for most of eighteenth-century Germany.[7] On the whole, censorship in early modern Germany was rather inefficient, in the sense that only rarely could governments ban a book if considered dangerous. Most German states (including Prussia under Frederick II) and the Holy Roman Empire as a whole had various offices entrusted with censorship.[8] The most comprehensive level should have been the Imperial level, which was also the most ancient. But the sheer multiplicity of censoring officials belonging to different institutions and divided by conflicting loyalties prevented censorship from becoming a powerful force, as in France and in the Austrian *Erblande*. Territorial state governments often resisted Imperial, that is Habsburg, censorship. An anonymous critic writing in 1757 attacked the confiscation and suppression of anti-Habsburg books by the *Reichsfiscal* and praised Prussian policy with this argument: 'The Emperor, being a party to the suit, declares himself to be the judge. He fears that the impartial public, this fair judge, might not be easily cheated. Therefore an attempt is made to prevent the public from judging the truth by banning all writings that show the justice of the Prussian cause.'[9] Conflicts between different territorial states concerning the way censorship functions should be exercised and divergences between Protestant and Catholic states were frequent; ecclesiastical princedoms, particularly in the 1770s and 1780s, often accused the Prussian monarchy of being too lax and of allowing Prussian printers and booktraders to flood Catholic Germany with dangerous books and journals.[10] It should also be remarked that in the different states censorship was not managed by one institution alone. Many officials were charged with the censorship of specific sorts of books and journals: standards of judgement were different and conflicts between officials broke out frequently. One should also remember that institutions such as the universities, the Academies of Sciences as well as some individual writers enjoyed liberty from censorship. Scepticism about the positive consequences of censorship was widespread. According to the *Deutsche Encyklopädie* in 1780, censorship was one of the institutions of the *Polizey*: it must prevent 'dangerous and shameful books' from entering the country and also protect the local booktrade by enacting wise, that is to say moderate and fairly liberal, measures. Even the *Deutsche Encyklopädie* underlined the fact that excessive strictness on the part of the censors was a self-defeating strategy.[11] As a matter of fact, censorship was especially sensitive to external priorities; as a rule censorship was managed with a high degree of flexibility, according to the political, diplomatic and economic context of each territory.

The example of the Prussian monarchy is for many reasons an interesting case study. Berlin was considered by contemporaries as the seat of a very liberal government with regard to the freedom of the press, though in fact there were forms of censorship. Many writers lived in Berlin (172 in 1783, according to Zöllner, 145 in 1795 according to Schmidt and Mehring);[12] social life was lively and attracted many foreigners; activities connected with book printing and book trading were widespread. None the less, the myth that Frederick II was an enemy of censorship can be easily dispelled. In the two first decades of his reign he reorganized Prussian censorship many times.[13] The original arrangement was fragmentary, having arisen without a systematic plan. The Lutheran Consitorium was to control religious books. The Department for Foreign Affairs was responsible for books dealing with foreign politics and *jus publicum*. Moreover there was a commission consisting of individual censors: each of them had to examine specific topics like history, philosophy and jurisprudence, or specific authors. Usually these censors were members of the Academy of Sciences or occupied official positions in the civil service. None was in the first instance and above all a censor. In 1747 Frederick II tried to restructure the censorship system and appointed the Academy of Sciences as the only censoring institution: all books and all journals had to be deposited there for examination before being printed. This would have led to a regular procedure, a form of modern censorship, but was resented by book printers for financial reasons (censorship fees were increased to meet the needs of the Academy) and commercial reasons (censorship was expected to become stricter and that would curtail production) and by the academicians as well, who resisted the prospect of additional work for no additional revenue. This scheme failed, showing the limits of the absolute rule, and in 1749 the king re-established the previous system. The edict of 1749 became a milestone in discussions about censorship and freedom of the press in the second half of the century: it stated that censors had to pass books that were not against religion, state and morality.[14] It was up to the censors to decide what these three concepts actually meant. A similar, but slightly more rigid system was adopted for newspapers: the censors had to take care that nothing offensive to foreign powers was published and that censors' decisions were carefully followed by the printers. Frederick's subsequent instructions to the censors show that reality almost never lived up to absolutist theory and royal intentions, despite the efforts of such officials as the Berlin *Generalfiscale*, who sometimes, usually very haphazardly, confiscated those books at the booksellers' premises that they thought were breaching the edict's provisions. In this case it was apparent that the laxity of the censoring system gave free rein to two competing ideas of what a dangerous book was. The legal structure of censorship in the Prussian monarchy did not change until 1788, when the new king, Frederick William II, enacted a censorship edict that aimed at tightening practice above all in the religious field, while leaving the whole system as it was.

The basic features of the censorship system under Friedrich II were that it was preventive, that it was based on the decisions of the individual censors and that it was a highly informal, case-to-case system, in which person-to-person relationships played an important role. Three elements had to work together in order to allow the printing industry to flourish: censors, publishers and authors. Roles were not as clear-cut as one might expect: many publishers were no mere businessmen, were proud of their prestige in the Republic of Letters and sometimes wrote books and edited journals themselves. Authors only rarely made a living by their pen: they were often state officials or members of the clergy. Last, but not least, censors were in most cases *hommes de lettres*, convinced that on the one hand freedom of the press was necessary to the improvement of mankind, but on the other hand, that censorship was necessary to safeguard the state's morality and order to prevent what they thought were plain and objective mistakes from becoming widespread. This led to a peculiar interpretation of the idea of freedom of the press, which I will touch on later.

In this censorship system the individual personalities of the censors were a decisive factor, as their political culture, their intellectual commitment and their social relations deeply influenced the practice of censorship and therefore determined what issues were liable to be discussed in public. Many censors were members of the Academy of Sciences and distinguished scholars in their field, such as Pellouttier, Kahle, and Sulzer. We owe to Sulzer, a famous Swiss *Popularphilosoph* who had lived in Berlin since 1747, a telling remark on censorship in a letter to his friend Gleim in 1748. According to Sulzer, German writers had nothing to fear from Prussian censorship, as its principles were tolerant.[15] Other Prussian censors included the theologian Teller, Dohm, the well-known author of the book advocating the emancipation of the Jews, and Steck, the expert in public law. For all of these men their dual role as censors and as writers was natural; subordination to the king's approval and to the public's judgment were not contradictory.

Two lesser known censors are particularly worth investigating; Marconnay and Beausobre were examples of censors who, while serving in the state bureaucracy, were actively engaged in the second-rank literary life of Berlin. Marconnay was appointed censor in 1767 after serving as a Prussian diplomat during the Seven Years' War; as a young student of law, he also studied Wolff's philosophy, became acquainted with Formey and other academicians, wrote literary pamphlets and commented extensively and with passionate interest on *La Nouvelle Heloïse* and on Coyer's *Vie de Sobieski* in his correspondence with Formey.[16] In his *Schreiben eines Reisenden aus Danzig* (Writings of a Traveller from Danzig), a pamphlet he wrote in 1756 to defend the good cause of Frederick II against the Saxon king at the beginning of the Seven Years' War, he appealed many times to the German *Publikum* as a superior judge, showing that diplomacy could not overlook the importance of the prevailing mood in Germany. Marconnay was indeed a state official with a literary and philosophical background, a censor with a clear intellectual stance and far-reaching connections with the literary elite: in 1782, for instance, he forbade the publication of an announcement of a *Prière pour obtenir de Dieu un ministre selon son esprit dans l'Eglise française du Werder, à Berlin. Par une âme dévote.*[17] It is clear from this and other examples that Marconnay took advantage of his position as a censor to influence public debate in favour of the Enlightened theology of Erman and Reclam against backward superstitions and religious enthusiasm. Louis de Beausobre, the son of the famous Huguenot theologian and learned historian, was one of Marconnay's colleagues from 1755 until his death in 1783; like Marconnay, Beausobre was linked to Formey and was conversant with the German and French philosophy of his time. As a young man, he spent more than one year in Paris in 1752 and 1753; during his stay in France he wrote a polemical essay against Raynal in the *Mercure de France* and was acquainted with Condillac. In *Le Pyrrhonisme du sage*, written in 1754, Beausobre claimed that certainty and *esprit de système* must be replaced by likelihood, that time and experience have increased man's knowledge of the world and that man must always be humble and reasonable. In a later essay on the principles of politics and economic thought Beausobre combined his sceptical attitude with a firm commitment to the well-being of the state as a supreme value.[18] This position suited a Prussian civil servant better than extreme scepticism: still, Beausobre kept a lively interest in the literary world.

A look at the censorship documents in the Prussian archives in

Merseburg shows that the working of censorship in its repressive function was relatively smooth and discreet. Lessing's complaints about Prussian censorship were the exception and his indictment of Prussian censorship as a despotic and enslaving institution, in a private letter to Nicolai, should not be interpreted as an outlook shared by his contemporaries.[19] The contrary was usually considered to be true. Most of the books and journals that were actually confiscated were attacks from outside the kingdom against Prussian foreign politics, as during the War of the Austrian Succession and at the time of the first partition of Poland in 1772, or dealt with minor quarrels between private individuals who felt themselves insulted in journals. The famous literary journal *Briefe, die neueste Literatur betreffend* (Letters on Most Recent Literature), for instance, was banned in 1762 upon the denunciation of Justi, who was insulted by a book review. Some confiscated books were considered to be libellous against foreign powers, above all Russia. The point is that until the early 1780s, that is until the last years of Frederick II's rule, cooperation between Enlightened writers, state officials entrusted with censorship and publishers worked to almost everybody's satisfaction. This cooperation sometimes resulted in a complete lack of censorship. In 1759 Kahle accepted the appointment as a censor only when he was told that 'in a whole year not a single book was brought to the censor'.[20]

The cohesive force was a common understanding of some basic principles of the Enlightenment, including commitment to toleration of criticism in public discussion. This does not mean that censors, writers and book-traders (who in most cases were also publishers) agreed on the desirability or even feasibility of an absolute freedom of the press. Not at all. What they agreed on, was that free communication and exchange of ideas and innovations was in itself a positive contribution to the well-being of the state. Enlightenment was interpreted as a major factor in the modernization of Prussia and as a basis of the monarchy's strength. Bringing the Prussian monarchy to the status of a great power meant also stimulating public debate which could develop only under favorable conditions. What ran counter to the state, religion and morals (*die guten Sitten*) was considered not to belong to the Enlightenment, as the intellectual and political elite understood it under Frederick II. As a consequence the Prussian censors, together with the writers and the publishers, contributed to the emergence of a public sphere in Berlin and were instrumental in shaping it. To put it in clear terms: a public sphere in Berlin owed its existence to the state, had a political origin, and began to make itself independent only in the 1780s. The features of this public sphere, controlled and supported by members of the state structure, were indeed very complex. Some peculiarities are remarkable. Looking at the list of books confiscated before 1788 we find, alongside German publications, books that were the stock-in-trade of the clandestine book trade in France. For instance, in 1743 the *Generalfiscal* Uhden deplored the fact that at a public auction such books as *La putain errante* by Aretino, *L'école des filles, ou les mémoires des fantaisies de Constance* by Milot, and *Les Fantaisies de Bruscambille* by Deslauriers were being sold.[21] A trade in pornographic books was apparently going on in the capital. As to the *livres philosophiques*, the reaction of the Prussian authorities was ambiguous; they were against the *Mémoires d'une reine infortunée* and against some of Rousseau's writings, as the French government was. Voltaire's *Pucelle d'Orléans* was confiscated in Berlin as was Lamettrie's *Homme-machine* by very zealous *Generalfiscale* for the same reason as their French counterparts.[22] Some works, such as C. F. Moser's *Was ist gut kaiserlich* (What is truly Imperial) or Locatelli's *Lettres moscovites* were prohibited for purely internal reasons, as they jeopardized the Prussian position in the Empire (nevertheless Moser's book was widely reviewed in learned journals!).

On the other hand, and in contrast to France, if we compare Robert Darnton's list of forbidden books, smuggled over the border into the French Kingdom, we find quite a few examples of books that were prohibited in France and legally published and openly sold in Prussia.[23] A striking, if secondary case, is Mouffle d'Angerville's *La vie privèe de Louis XV*, ordered 198 times from the *Société typographique de Neuchatel*, apparently a best-seller in the underground market. The translation into German was submitted to the censor Schlüter in 1780 by the publisher, Friedrich Nicolai: Schlüter suggested a few minor changes dealing with the Prussian role in the *Kartoffelkrieg* (Potato War) against Joseph II, overlooked some satirical paragraphs against Frederick II and finally permitted the work to be printed.[24] A detailed analysis of Schlüter's reading would indeed confirm that desacralization of the king's role and personality was well under way. *La vie privée de Louis XV* shocked nobody in Berlin. If one reads Darnton's list of forbidden books, many substantial divergences will be found from the Prussian situation. D'Holbach's works were translated and published in Berlin without difficulty; the *Système social* was reviewed in the *Journal littéraire* edited by members of the Academy of the Sciences and was cited in 1788 as an authoritative source along with Raynal's *Tableau de l'Europe* in Brunn's apology of the Prussian monarchy.[25] Voltaire was widely read and translated into German, despite occasional interference from the *Generalfiscale* in the 1750s and Frederick II's occasional fits of rage against him. Masonic literature was available at any bookshop.

As the printer suffered the most severe consequences of a confiscation, he often changed the censor by one means or the other. Friedrich Nicolai, the most significant Berlin publisher, is again evidence of this. In 1775 Nicolai was asked for the first time, by the *Generalfiscal* d'Anières, to produce the written approbation of the censor for his *Allgemeine Deutsche Bibliothek* (General German Library), the major forum of learned public opinion in Germany since 1765. Nicolai replied first that his journal had never been submitted to censorship in the last ten years; second, that what he called a *decent* freedom of the press in Prussia ('eine anständige Freyheit zu drucken') had promoted learning in the kingdom; third, that the royal censor Teller had been a prominent contributor to the *Allgemeine Deutsche Bibliothek* from the beginning and had read many manuscripts before their publication: Nicolai therefore felt, as he said, legitimated enough ('genugsam legitimiert') by Teller's participation.[26] On the other hand, Nicolai was careful in suggesting changes to the authors, when their texts seemed not to fulfil the requirements of an Enlightened book. In the case of Dohm's famous work *Über die bürgerliche Verbesserung der Juden* (On the Civil Improvement of the Jews) (1781), there is a revealing exchange of letters between Nicolai and Dohm (himself a royal censor) about the most appropriate way to have the book positively censored; in the end, they agreed that Teller was the most liberal censor available and that he should censor it, which indeed he did.[27] It is noteworthy that most of the repressive interventions were initiated by the *Generalfiscale*, that is by the administrative and executive institution at the local level, whose responsibility it was to look after order and tranquillity in the town; as a rule, the *Generalfiscale* opposed the decisions of the censors *ex post* and lamented their laxity, as d'Anières did in 1769.[28]

II

In the 1760s and 1770s the agreement between censors, writers and publishers worked basically without strain. A public sphere emerged out of this consensus; the limits of this public sphere defined a free area in which discussion in journals and pamphlets could take place; these limits were basically set by the political and intellectual elite in Berlin. The discussion about the nature of this public sphere and about the opinions put forward in it was carried on in journals. The diffusion of journals in Berlin and throughout German-speaking countries has been correctly considered a fundamental feature of the emergence of public opinion in the late eighteenth-century.

I would like to point out two aspects of this phenomenon that seem to me worth considering. The first element is that all journalists were aware of the reading public they addressed and editors shaped the content of their journals accordingly. This is especially evident in those ephemeral journals edited for the lower classes; they were predecessors in the 1760s of the boulevard press and, in sharp contrast to the *Aufklärer*'s press, appealed to the virtues of sentimentality, religious orthodoxy and subordination to the great men in society and government. Systematic research into this sort of press would be a rewarding undertaking. Also, the learned journals addressed a socially defined public, while asserting they were the voice of reason. Hartmann, the anti-Jewish editor of the *Hieroglyphen*, claimed that the 'political society' of his readers 'consisted not of people of low standing, but of merchants, private citizens, army officials and even a learned lady'.[29] In 1781 the notorious journalist Cranz wrote in his *Charlatanerien*: 'The voice of the public is my judge . . . As long as I enjoy the support of thousands of readers, not from the common people, but only from that class which because of its origins and education is likely to be absolutely reasonable, I will continue to satisfy the taste of this public. The others may leave me alone.'[30] In 1782 the editors of the *Historisches Portefeuille* addressed 'officials, traders and in general civilized citizens' ('gesittete Bürger').[31] In the public sphere, different discussion areas were formed, appealing to different social groups with different outlooks and interests; sometimes these areas intertwined, but more often they were opposed to each other in polemical terms. Contemporaries realized that a single public opinion in Berlin did not yet exist, although some wished for it. In his *Ideal einer vollkommnen Zeitung* (Ideal of a perfect journal) Karl Philipp Moritz pointed out in 1784 the distance between the people and the cultivated elite and argued in favour of a 'public journal' ('eine öffentliche Zeitung') that becomes 'the voice of truth . . . [and] penetrates into the huts of the humble'.[32]

The second element is that in the 1760s, in the 1770s and, more markedly, in the 1780s discussion about freedom of the press intensified. This discussion had obvious philosophical presuppositions. However, I will examine only a few representative positions concerned with its political implications. The first point to make is that this discussion was public: in essays for popular and learned journals, in pamphlets, even in gazette reports, intellectuals confronted each other on the question of press freedom and its consequences; the implicit idea was that the practice of each of them embodied the right sort of liberty. The highly interesting (and indeed secret) debate held at the *Mittwochs-gesellschaft* (Wednesday Society) during 1783 and 1784 represented different interpretations which the members of this society also expressed in public debate.[33] Discussion was secret, ideas that issued from that discussion were public.

The second point is that by far the majority of the participants in this debate claimed to be in favour of press freedom, thus showing that the real issue at stake was the interpretation of its meaning and of the relationship between the press and the public. There was no doubt about the desirability of press freedom. When it came to some sort of definition of freedom of the press, limits were put forward to preserve the core of freedom, while excluding abuses. Communication between members of the society was to be preserved; the well-being of the country, in the interior and in foreign relations, was a prevailing goal. For example, the influential theologian Erman wrote in 1756 that 'la liberté de la presse ... n'est point faite pour des querelles personelles et pour les petits différens de quelques particuliers ... Prétendre que de telles misères soyent dignes de l'attention du public c'est ne le point respecter' ('freedom of the press ... is not intended for personal quarrels and for petty differences of detail ... To claim that such trifles are worthy of public attention is not to respect the public').[34] State control over writings on religion, in order to prevent enthusiasm from spreading, was usually accepted. In the *Allgemeine Deutsche Bibliothek* Nicolai and his collaborators came out in favour of freedom of the press, as in 1773, when a long passage from Milton's *Areopagitica* was reprinted. In 1775 a review of the *Encyclopädisches Journal* gave occasion to criticize censorship in the *Allgemeine Deutsche Bibliothek*.[35] At the same time (1775), the famous jurist Johann Jakob Moser gave ample evidence of the contradictions of the German system of censorship; he ended his detailed examination of censorship in the Empire calling for the restoration of 'die alt-Teutsche, herkömmliche, und unschädliche, Freyheit der Presse' ('the restoration of the old-German, customary, and harmless freedom of the press').[36] Freedom of the press was still a perspicuous idea.

In the 1780s things changed. An increasing number of journalists and writers appealed to the idea of freedom of the press in a way that provoked conflicts between them and the government, and sometimes between the censors and the government. Two simultaneous essays show this growing divergence. In 1784 Johann Georg Heinrich Feder wrote an essay in favour of press liberty in the *Neueste Staatsanzeigen* and claimed that every man should be allowed to publish a self-defence if he felt persecuted by the authorities of his country and be able to turn 'an den auswärtigen höchsten Richter, das Oberhaupt der Nation, oder das ganze Publicum' ('to the highest judge abroad, the head of the nation or the whole public') for an impartial judgment so that his grievances would be redressed. Thus, freedom of the press and appeal to the public were considered a means of opposition to established power in case of abuse.[37] In the same year the prominent Berlin journal *Berlinische Monatsschrift* published an anonymous essay under the title 'Über Denk- und Druckfreiheit' (On Freedom of Thought and of the Press), whose author was Ernst Ferdinand Klein. According to this essay freedom of the press in Prussia was complete and was a substitute for political freedom. Freedom of the press was linked to the progress achieved by the intellectual elite in Prussia, as the latter, according to the author, actually lived up to the expectations of an enlightened age. 'The freedom to think out loud is the most efficient weapon of the Prussian state . . . If the Prussian king wants writings against the State to be suppressed, he means just those writings that attack the State, betray it to its enemies, set the subjects free of their duty to and provoke civil disorder; he does not mean modest opinions about orders given by the sovereign or by his stewards . . . This freedom of the press is the clearest sign of a wise government.'[38] In other words, freedom of the press was based on a preliminary consensus among the participants in the discussion; access to the public was subordinated to the acceptance of the Prussian, state-oriented version of the Enlightenment. A central element in this interpretation was the idea of 'collision' between human rights (freedom of the press belonged to them) and the well-being of the state: as Karl Friedrich Bahrdt put it, in case of collision the state prevailed over the rights of the subjects.[39] As Frederick II was usually considered to be the embodiment of the Enlightenment, identity between freedom of the press and commitment to an Enlightenment in the public discussion was taken for granted. This idea of the interaction between discussion and public sphere inspired the decision in favour of a public debate about the revision of the Prussian laws in 1781. The chancellor, Carmer, thought that a free discussion and a free press were useful. 'Really able and competent men should open and communicate to the King their thoughts and proposals concerning these matters, also through print; nonetheless I cannot be indifferent if this way the public is given writings that can only lead it astray and worry it with prejudices and false ideas.' Prime Minister Hertzberg subscribed to the same concept when suggesting the prohibition of an essay by Hess against the town government of Hamburg: 'il ne convient pas de permettre dans les Etats de Votre Majesté l'impression publique d'un ouvrage rempli d'assertions fausses, d'invectives et de critiques la plupart mal fondées contre des gouvernmens respectables, et meme contre celui de Votre Majesté, et qui n'a au fond aucun but réel que celui d'une animosité et vengeance personelle' ('it is not right to permit in Your Majesty's territories the public printing of a work full of false assertions, invective and criticism, mostly ill-founded, against respectable governments and even against that of Your Majesty and which at bottom has no real purpose other than that of personal animosity and revenge').[40]

The divergence between the latter conception of freedom of the press and of access to the public debate, and the former, more liberal idea increased in Berlin in the 1780s. More and more writers were attracted by the relatively free conditions in Berlin and by its enlarging market; outsiders joined in shaping the public sphere. More and more journalists took the idea of public discussion seriously and some of them breached the practice based on this 'consensus theory'. In 1785 the editors of the *Ephemeriden der Litteratur und des Theaters*, published in Berlin, assessed as an obvious fact that 'Nowhere else do people talk about the state, the king, this or that new institution with more freedom'.[41] Others tried to address this potentially unstable part of the reading public in Berlin. In 1782 the unknown journalist Uhden, for example, started printing a *Freimaurer-Zeitung* (Freemasons' Newspaper), in which he appealed to a larger readership than that usually interested in Masonic affairs. The *Freimaurer-Zeitung* dealt especially with Rosicrucian theories; despite Uhden's protests and appeals to the edict of 1749, the journal was mercilessly suppressed by Hertzberg.[42] The same thing happened to the *Predigt-Kritiken* (Sermon Reviews), a periodical publication dealing with the sermons held at the Protestant churches in Berlin: even if the editors claimed to be in the spirit of the Enlightenment, their journal was suppressed on suspicion of spreading dissension among the public.[43] A French teacher at the *Académie des nobles*, a zealous admirer of Frederick II's government, later a Jacobin leader in Strasbourg, Jean Charles Thibault de Laveaux, wrote a satirical novel under the title of *Eusèbe* and various essays, in which Prime Minister Hertzberg was ridiculed. As a consequence Laveaux' writings were confiscated and in 1786 he had to leave Berlin.[44] Cranz' attempt at combining popular Enlightenment, political gossip and plain entertainment was also suppressed in the late 1780s, after much trouble to his personal censor Dohm. In 1788 a writer dared to criticize the Prussian military organization, the so-called *Cantonverfassung*, and its negative impact on the country; he appealed explicitly to the *Publikum* and his pamphlet was confiscated.[45] It is also worth mentioning that at the same time the *Militärische Monatsschrift* (Military Monthly) discussed those problems in a similar vein, addressing apparently a much more restricted public of officials.[46]

The crucial point seems to be that in the 1780s there were different public spheres: the church, Masonic lodges, learned discussion, the tavern, popular science, the theatre-going public, and handprinted newspapers, which experienced a new boost in the late 1780s. All these were tentatively put in contact with each other by some journalists and writers taking advantage of the peculiar conditions of the Prussian capital. Public discussion acquired a life of its own and developed well beyond the intentions of the leading figures in the Berlin government, who nonetheless in most cases still stuck to the Frederician idea of freedom of the press in the 1790s (for example in the *Prinzenvorträge*[47]), as the reactionaries around King Frederick Wilhelm II and Wöllner pushed for a draconian limitation of press freedom. To put it in simple terms: in Berlin the 1780s saw the transition from a multiplicity of public spheres, rather easily controlled by the intellectual elite in its various functions, to a potentially single, mobile public sphere, interested in an increasing range of topics. In this new situation the foundation was laid for a fresh approach to the meaning and functions of censorship. The edict of 1788 assessing the limits of the freedom of the press was just a first and very rudimentary step in this direction. The policy of censorship changed: the number of forbidden and confiscated books increased dramatically, at first in the field of religion, then in politics too, following the expanding interest in the French Revolution. By 1791–1792 a repressive strategy was organized in Berlin against subversive literature; the traditional elite noted in those years that political discussion was now going on in all social strata and reacted in a defensive way. As an active policy of persuasion and because it was thought that public education was bound to fail, journals were suppressed and the book trade was severely hampered. The consensus between the government and the intellectual elite began to crumble, as the 1792 correspondence between Biester, the outstanding Enlightenment figure and editor of the *Berlinische Monatsschrift*, and the new censor Hermes concerning the writings of Kant shows very clearly.[48] The impact of the French Revolution boosted the evolution of phenomena that were already taking place in the 1780s.

III

Ideas of public debate and public opinion changed accordingly. It has been remarked that the term *öffentliche Meinung* (public opinion) was imported into the German-speaking area from France. The German

Jacobin Georg Forster is traditionally considered the first one who used this term in German; that he did when commenting on the Revolution has also been underlined. I will discuss neither the implications of this assessment nor the more general and controversial issue of the relationships between words and historical realities. Suffice it to say that *öffentliche Meinung* has in German an earlier origin than is usually thought and was used in 1785 to describe public opinion in Vienna at the time of the reforms of Joseph II,[49] in 1789 by the Swabian Karl Friedrich Reinhard in a report from Bordeaux referring to the German situation[50] and in 1791 by the Prussian jurist and political writer Klein, who described in detail what he meant by the term.[51] On the other hand, Mirabeau, during his stay in Berlin in 1786, referred to the *opinion publique* in the capital many times in his letters to Mauvillon, taking for granted that such a thing existed in the Prussian capital.[52] *Öffentliche Meinung* was not a mere import from Revolutionary France.

It goes without saying that *Öffentlichkeit* (as an abstract term) and *Publikum* (as a concrete one) were more common words that indicated by and large the same entity. Kant and Fichte used both in 1784 and 1793 respectively. Divergences in meaning are noteworthy. When Kant spoke of an *Öffentlichkeit* as a universal tribunal of morality, judging matters solely from the point of view of reason, he clearly referred to the actual public sphere existing in Prussia, assuming that the public of learned men, writers, officials and so on was *the* public sphere *par excellence*. As this public was in agreement with the government on basic issues in the actual development of the public discussion, an idealization of its features was obvious. Rather than being a check on state action, Kant's *Öffentlichkeit* belonged in part to the sphere of the state and represented its Enlightened prop, and that was what had actually happened until then in Prussia under Frederick II. Kant had not yet noticed that *Öffentlichkeit* could also convey opposition to the state, that private and public use of reason could merge into one single practice.[53] Fichte's *Publikum* was indeed this sort of oppositional force against absolute rulers; *Publikum* comprised all social strata as it dealt with universal rights. That public opinion is separate from and potentially opposed to the state and to its rulers, as Fichte implied, was in fact an outstanding feature of the modern meaning of public opinion.[54] This meaning of public opinion certainly emerged as a consequence of the social and above all intellectual unrest of the late 1780s and early 1790s and signalled the surfacing of the longing for a new set of political arrangements based on the separation between civil society and the state and in particular between a self-sustaining, although easily manipulated and fickle, public opinion and a merely repressive censorship. A hard time was coming for smugglers of ideas (*Ideenschmuggler*).[55]

Notes

1. See K. M. Baker, 'Politics and Public Opinion under the Old Regime. Some Reflections', in J.R. Censer and J.D. Popkin (eds) *Press and Politics in Pre- Revolutionary France* (Berkeley and Los Angeles, 1987) pp. 204–46 (revised version reprinted in Baker, *Inventing the French Revolution* (Cambridge, 1990) pp. 167–99); M. Ozouf, 'L'opinion publique' in *The Political Culture of the Old Regime* vol. I: *The French Revolution and the Creation of a Modern Political Culture* ed. by K.M. Baker (Oxford, 1987) pp. 419–34; S. Maza, 'Le tribunal de la nation: les mémoires judiciaires et l'opinion publique à la fin de l'Ancien Régime' *Annales ESC* 42 (1987) pp. 73–90; D. Gordon, '"Public Opinion" and the Civilizing Process in France: The Example of Morellet' *Eighteenth-Century Studies* 22 (1989) pp. 302–38; E. Tortarolo, ' "Opinion publique" tra ancien régime e rivoluzione. Contributo a un vocabolario storico della politica settecentesca' in *Rivista Storica Italiana* 102 (1990) pp. 5–23; R. Chartier, *Cultural Origins of the French Revolution* (Durham NC, 1991); A. Farge, *Dire et mal dire. L'opinion publique au XVIIIe siècle* (Paris, 1992); Gordon, 'Philosophy, Sociology, and Gender in the Enlightenment Conception of Public Opinion' *French Historical Studies* 17 (1992) pp. 882–911; *Pouvoir et légitimité. Figures de l'espace public.* Textes réunis par A. Cottereau et P. Ladrière (Paris, 1992); J.C. Laursen, 'Publicity and Cosmopolitanism in Late Eighteenth-Century Germany' *History of European Ideas* 16 (1993) pp. 117–122; J.A.W. Gunn, 'Opinion in Eighteenth-Century Thought: What did the Concept Purport to Explain?' *Utilitas* 5 (1993) pp. 17–33.
2. J. Habermas, *Strukturwandel der Öffentlichkeit. Untersuchungen zu einer Kategorie der bürgerlichen Gesellschaft* (Frankfurt a/M, 1990, 1st edn. 1962); R. Koselleck, *Kritik und Krise. Eine Studie zur Pathogenese der bürgerlichen Welt* (Frankfurt a/M., 1989, 1st edn. 1959)
3. Koselleck, *Critique and Crisis: Enlightenment and the Pathogenesis of Modern Society* (Cambridge MA, 1988); Habermas, *The Structural Transformation of the Public Sphere: An Inquiry into a Category of Bourgeois Society* (Cambridge, MA, 1989). See A.J. La Vopa, 'Conceiving a Public: Ideas and Society in Eighteenth-Century Europe' *Journal of Modern History* 64 (1992) pp. 79–116; J.D. Popkin, 'The Concept of Public Opinion in the Historiography of the French Revolution: a Critique' *Storia della Storiografia* 20 (1991) pp. 77–92; D. Goodman, 'Public Sphere and Private Life: Toward a Synthesis of Current Historiographical Approaches to the Old Regime' *History and Theory* 31 (1992) pp. 1–20; C. Calhoun (ed.), *Habermas and The Public Sphere* (Cambridge, MA, and London, 1992).

4. H. Möller, *Vernunft und Kritik. Deutsche Aufklärung im 17. und 18. Jahrhundert* (Frankfurt a/M, 1986) pp. 285–86.

5. See H.E. Bödeker, 'Journals and Public Opinion. The Politicization of the German Enlightenment in the Second Half of the Eighteenth Century' in E. Hellmuth (ed.), *The Transformation of Political Culture. England and Germany in the Late Eighteenth Century* (Oxford, 1990) pp. 423–45.

6. Habermas, *Strukturwandel*, 'Vorwort zur Neuauflage 1990'.

7. See D. Breuer, 'Stand und Aufgaben der Zensurforschung' in H. G. Göpfert and E. Weyrauch (eds), *Unmoralisch an sich . . .': Zensur im 18. und 19. Jahrhundert* (Wiesbaden, 1988) pp. 34–60; E. Weyrauch, 'Zensur-Forschung' in W. Arnold, D. Werner and B. Zeller (eds), *Die Erforschung der Buch- und Bibliotheksgeschichte in Deutschland* (Wiesbaden, 1987) pp. 475–88.

8. U. Eisenhardt, *Die kaiserliche Aufsicht über Buchdruck, Buchhandel und Presse im Heiligen Römischen Reich Deutscher Nation (1498-1806). Ein Beitrag zur Geschichte der Bücher- und Pressezensur* (Karlsruhe, 1970); F. Schneider, *Pressefreiheit und politische Öffentlichkeit. Studien zur politischen Geschichte Deutschlands bis 1848* (Neuwied, 1966); B. Plachta, *Damnatur-Toleratur-Admittitur: Studien und Dokumente zur literarischen Zensur im 18. Jahrhundert* (Tübingen, 1993).

9. *Wie weit geht das Recht eines Reichs-Fiscals in Ansehung der Bücher-Censur?* Solches beantwortet Anton Well Esq. und übersetzt aus dem Englischen T. (no place, 1757) p. 13.

10. See A.L. Veit, *Das Aufklärungsschriftum des 18. Jahrhunderts und die deutsche Kirche. Ein Zeitbild aus der deutschen Geistesgeschichte* (Cologne, 1937) and H. Molitor, 'Zensur, Propaganda und Überwachung zwischen 1780 und 1815 im mittleren Rheinland' in A. Gerlich (ed.), *Vom Alten Reich zu neuer Staatlichkeit. Alzeyer Kolloquium 1979. Kontinuität und Wandel im Gefolge der französischen Revolution am Mittelrhein* (Wiesbaden, 1982) pp. 28–44.

11. 'Bücherzensur' in H.M.G. Köster and J.F. Roos, *Deutsche Enzyklopädie: oder allgemeines Real-Wörterbuch aller Künste und Wissenschaften von einer Gesellschaft Gelehrten* vol. IV, Blat-Cam (Frankfurt a/M, 1780) p. 562.

12. V.H. Schmidt and D.G.G. Mehring, *Neuestes gelehrtes Berlin oder literarische Nachrichten von jetztlebenden Berlinischen Schriftstellern und Schriftstellerinnen* (Berlin, 1795).

13. *Acta Borussica. Denkmäler der preussischen Staatsverwaltung im 18. Jahrhundert* (Berlin, 1892-1936) vol. VII pp. 408–9; VIII pp. 403–4; X p. 315; XI p. 518; XI p. 522 footnote 1.

14. *Edict wegen der wieder hergestellten Censur, derer in Königl. Landen herauskommenden Bücher und Schriften, wie auch wegen des Debits ärgerlicher Bücher, so ausserhalb Landes verlegt werden.* De dato, Berlin den 11ten May 1749.

15. W. Körte (ed.), *Briefe der Schweizer Bodmer, Sulzer, Gessner aus Gleims litterarischem Nachlasse* (Zurich, 1804) p. 79.

16. Nachlass Formey, Staatsbibliothek Preussischer Kulturbesitz Berlin.

17. Geheimes Staatsarchiv Preussischer Kulturbesitz (Hereafter cited as GSAPrK), Merseburg, Rep. 9, F2a, Fasz. 10.

19. Lessing to Nicolai August 25 1769 in G.E. Lessing, *Briefe in einem Band* (Berlin and Weimar, 1983) pp. 186–87.

20. GSAPrK, Merseburg, Rep. 9, F2a, Fasz. 12. See C. Porset, 'Louis Martin Kahle et Voltaire sur les causes finales', in P. Brockmeier, R. Desné, J. Voss (eds), *Voltaire und Deutschland. Internationales Kolloquium der Universität Mannheim zum 200. Todestag* (Stuttgart, 1979) pp. 357–58.

21. GSAPrK, Merseburg, Rep. 9, F2a, Fasz. 1.

22. GSAPrK, Merseburg, Rep. 9, F2a, Fasz. 12.

23. See the list of the forbidden books in R. Darnton, *Édition et sédition. L'univers de la littérature clandestine au XVIIIe siècle* (Paris, 1991).

24. Mouffle d'Argenville, *Geschichte des Privatlebens Ludwigs XV* (Berlin und Stettin, 1781). See Schlüter to Nicolai, 13 November 1780, Nachlass Nicolai, vol. LXXXVII, Staatsbibliothek Preussischer Kulturbesitz Berlin.

25. See *Journal littéraire* 7 (1773) pp. 216–17 and *Berlinisches Journal für Aufklärung* 5 (1789): 'Der Preussische Staat, der glücklichste unter allen in Europa. Eine Rede, am Geburtstage des Königs Friedrich Wilhelms II den 25. September 1789 in Königl. Joachimsthalischen Gymnasium zu Berlin gehalten von dem Professor Brunn' p. 127.

26. GSAPrK, Merseburg, Rep. 9, F2a, Fasz. 14.

27. Dohm to Nicolai, 11 May 1780, Staatsbibliothek Preussischer Kulturbesitz Berlin, Nachlass Nicolai, vol. XV.

28. GSAPrK, Merseburg, Rep. 9, F2a, Fasz. 14. The role of the *Generalfiscale* in the Prussian bureaucracy is stressed in the seminal work by H. Rosenberg, *Bureaucracy, Aristocracy and Autocracy. The Prussian Experience 1660–1815* (Cambridge MA, 1958) chapter V, and H.C. Johnson, *Frederick the Great and His Officials* (New Haven and London, 1975) p. 121.

29. *Hieroglyphen*, 1781 p. 236.

30. A.F. Cranz, *Charlatanerien in alphabetischer Ordnung als Beyträge zur Abbildung und zu den Meinungen des Jahrhunderts* (Berlin, 1781) vol. IV pp. 12–13.

31. *Historisches Portefeuille*, 1782, I, n. p.

32. K.P. Moritz, *Ideal einer vollkommnen Zeitung* (Berlin, 1784) pp. 4–5.

33. See E. Hellmuth, 'Aufklärung und Pressefreiheit. Zur Debatte der Berliner Mittwochsgesellschaft während der Jahre 1783 und 1784' *Zeitschrift für historische Forschung* 9 (1982) pp. 315–6.

34. J.-P. Erman, *Lettres sur le Diogene décent et la cause bizarre de M. de Prémontval* (Amsterdam: n.p., 1756).

35. *Allgemeine Deutsche Bibliothek* 24 (1775) pp. 296–301.

36. J.J. Moser, *Von der Reichsverfassungsmässigen Freyheit, von Teutschen Staats-Sachen zu schreiben* (Göttingen und Gotha, 1772) p. 110.

37. J.G.H. Feder, 'Ueber die Censur der zum Druck bestimmten Schriften und deren gerechte Grenzen', *Neueste Staatsanzeigen; ges. und hersg. von*

Freunden der Publicität und Staatskunde, als eine Fortsetzung der Schlözer'schen Staatsanzeigen 4 (1784) pp. 250–58.

38. *Berlinische Monatsschrift* April 1784, pp. 312–30.
39. K.F. Bahrdt, *Ueber Pressfreyheit und deren Gränzen. Zur Beherzigung für Regenten, Censoren und Schriftsteller* (Züllichau, 1787).
40. GSAPrK, Merseburg, Rep. 9, F2a, Fasz. 15.
41. 3 December 1785, issue 49, pp. 353–54: 'Nirgends wird wohl freier, über den Staat, über den Monarchen, über diese oder jene neue Einrichtung gesprochen als in Berlin (. . .) Eben die Freiheit, die der Monarch uns in Meinungen, im Denken und Handeln gestattet, gestattet er uns auch im Sprechen (. . .) Die weisesten Anordnungen für's Ganze können einzelnen Theilen nachtheilig sein, worauf der Monarch weder Rücksicht nemen kan noch darf: der unzufriedene Berliner nutzt die allgemeine Freiheit, und sucht seinen Missmut einigermassen dadurch zu kühlen, dass er öffentlich murrt. In anderen monarchischen Staaten herrscht diese Freiheit nicht'.
42. See *Bibliothek für Denker und Männer von Geschmack* 7 (1783) p. 568.
43. GSAPrK, Merseburg, Rep. 9, F2a, Fasz. 18. See B. M. Hoppe, *Predigt-kritik im Josephinismus. Die Wöchentlichen Wahrheiten für und über die Prediger in Wien (1782–1784)* (St. Ottilien, 1989).
44. See J.-C.-T. de Laveaux, *Eusèbe ou les beaux profits de la vertu dans le siècle où nous vivons. Virtus post nummos* (Amsterdam, 1785).
45. Arnim, *Ueber die Canton-Verfassung in den Preussischen Staaten und die von den Obristen von Brösecke verweigerte Verabschiedung des Enrollierten Elsbusch* (Frankfurt und Leipzig, 1788); see Johnson, *Frederick II and His Officials* pp. 263–64.
46. See *Militärische Monatsschrift*, 1785.
47. C.G. von Svarez, *Vorträge über Recht und Staat*. Ed. by H. Conrad und G. Kleinheyer (Cologne, 1960).
48. See F. Kapp, 'Aktenstücke zur Geschichte der preussischen Zensur- und Pressverhältnisse unter dem Minister Wöllner 1788–1793' *Archiv für Geschichte des deutschen Buchhandels* 4 (1879) p. 200.
49. See P. Mitrofanov, *Joseph II. Seine politische und kulturelle Tätigkeit* (Vienna und Leipzig, 1910).
50. 'Briefe über die Revolution in Frankreich' *Schwäbisches Archiv* 1790, p. 517.
51. E.F. Klein, 'Anmerkungen eines Bürgerlichen über die Abhandlung des Herrn Oberappellationsrats von Ramdohr, die Ansprüche der Adligen an die ersten Staatsbedienungen befreffend' *Berlinische Monatsschrift* 17 (1791) p. 460.
52. H.G.R. de Mirabeau, *Lettres du Comte de Mirabeau à un des ses amis en Allemagne* (Brunswick, 1792).
53. See I. Kant, *Was ist Aufklärung? Aufsätze zur Geschichte und Philosophie* (Göttingen, 1975). See S. Lestition, 'Kant and the End of the Enlightenment' *Journal of Modern History* 65 (1993) pp. 57–113.

54. See A.J. La Vopa, 'The Revelatory Moment: Fichte and the French Revolution' *Central European History* 22 (1989) pp. 130–59.

55. W. Siemann, 'Ideenschmuggel. Probleme der Meinungskontrolle und das Los deutscher Zensoren im 19. Jahrhundert' *Historische Zeitschrift* 245 (1987) pp. 71f. See also on Hessen-Kassel F. Ohles, *Germany's Rude Awakening. Censorship in the Land of the Brothers Grimm* (Kent, Ohio, 1992).

Nine

Opinion's Metamorphosis: Hume and the Perception of Public Authority

Dario Castiglione

Was ist Modernität?

Since 1784, when the question 'Was ist Aufklärung?' was asked by the *Berlinische Monatsschrift*, philosophers, and philosophically minded historians, have sought to represent the Enlightenment as part of the project of modernity. Kant's own answer,[1] that the Enlightenment was humanity's coming of age, has been the model for all modernist interpretations, even for those, like Adorno's and more recently Foucault's,[2] based on more sceptical views of humanity's own ability to sustain and bring to conclusion the on-going project of self-emancipation. Kant's representation of the spirit of the age as an 'exit' (*Ausgang*) from immaturity, a break of the stronghold that authority and myth had over the philosophical mind, was meant, as Foucault has noted, both as the illustration of a historical process in which men (in the restrictive, gendered sense of the word) were collectively participating, and as an individual moral act: *sapere aude*.[3] From this perspective, the philosophy of the Enlightenment—both in its epistemological illuminations (its rejection of myths) and in its normative stance (its pretention to recognize no authority beyond reason)—already contains the programme of modern philosophy as a philosophy of the 'present', where reason and will are happily reunited in a world brought under human control. Answering the Enlightenment question, therefore, does not seem very different from answering the question about modernity, and whether this is fully understood by paying sole attention to its projectual, Promethean, and present-focused characteristics.

The problem with such philosophical interpretations of the Enlightenment is one of circularity between evidence and definition. But the risk of false reification is intrinsic to all historical generalizations, and, as John Pocock has noted, in historical reconstruction 'large patterns and even Whig interpretations have their uses, and are worth putting together in order to see where they may be used to take us'.[4] Pocock himself has been arguing for some time that there is not one Enlightenment, 'denoting a radical liberation of the mind from traditions of oppression', but several. Within the common perception of 'new ways of thinking' opposed to those associated to 'ancient Hellenic and medieval Latin pasts' which was experienced by a diffuse philosophical elite in Europe and across the Atlantic, there lay conservative as well as radical attitudes. The former, prevalent in Protestant cultures, were both intellectually conservative, encouraging the self-limitation of reason, and also politically conservative, attempting to entrench traditional aristocracies and clergies within rapidly forming commercial societies. The bugbear of this conservative Enlightentment was enthusiasm in its religious, philosophical and eventually political forms, all representing threats against settled sovereignty and social stability, which were considered the preconditions of ordered life, civility, natural liberty and the diffusion of wealth. The project of the 'enlightened *ancien régime*' was to find a *via media* on both social engineering and moral control, and, according to Professor Pocock, if this is the main heritage of the Western vision of things, all considered 'it seems to work'.[5]

The Public Sphere: Ideas and Institutions

The projectual Enlightenments to which I have just referred need not be taken as teleological representations of some hidden pattern of history; nor should they be considered in a reified sense as the characteristics of a particular world epoch. Indeed, both Pocock and Foucault, for instance, emphasize that their Enlightenments are shorthand expressions for a series of attitudes, which, as such, both operate at the same time as opposite postures (counter-enlightenment) and may take more than one form (conservative, radical, and so on).

There are, however, other projectual visions of the Enlightenment, which tend to underplay the purely intellectual and ideological aspects of the phenomenon by focusing on a broader conception of *mentalités*, and in particular on the institutions, groups and social practices which fostered enlightened attitudes. One such interpretation was offered more than thirty years ago by Jürgen Habermas in a book which, as other contributors to this volume also remark, seems to have come to new life by its diffusion in the English-speaking academic world.[6] There are at least two reasons for this new lease of life, linked on the one hand to the sociological and philosophical import of the book and on the other to its historical dimension. The former has much to do with Habermas's more recent work on the inner morality of communicative action as a foundation for rational public discourse, a topic which has intrigued English-speaking political philosophers at least since the Rawlsian revolution; the latter is to be found in the influence that Habermas's conceptualization of the public sphere seems to have exercised on recent historical work on both practices of sociability in the eighteenth century and the growing phenomenon of public opinion within the machinery of government.

In this essay, I shall not deal with the philosophical dimension, besides remarking that Habermas has since shifted his position considerably.[7] Although the book was conceived as a correction of the Frankfurt School's vision of the dialectic of the Enlightenment, as one where the progress of 'positive' thought and science harboured within itself new mystifications and a technologically sophisticated barbarity, *Structural Transformation* was particularly insistent on the halting of the process of human emancipation that appeared to be inscribed in the rational and universalizing features of the *modern* public sphere. This was due to the erosion of the space of rational freedom, represented by the institutions of the public sphere itself, following on the emergence of the social state. The new Habermas is less pessimistic on the manipulative uses of culture, less inclined to take a totalizing view of the evolution of social relationships, and more positive on the self-rectifying features of the public sphere in pluralist and complex societies. In brief, his position is less inclined towards the critical theory of the Frankfurt School and more open to liberal persuasion.

This said, I am here more interested in exploring some of the historical issues arising from *Structural Transformation*. As already suggested, two main lines of historical research have been directly influenced by Habermas's early work. Margaret Jacob has recently synthetized one of them as the study of the socially structured kinds of interaction in which speech acts take place.[8] This mainly consists in taking the new enclaves of sociability typical of the eighteenth century as the focus for historical research, in an attempt to go beyond both the purely ideological and quantitative ways in which the investigation of these phenomena was conducted by previous scholarships. By paying attention to both the 'forms' of these enclaves and the 'content' of the available discourses in the same fora, Margaret Jacob believes that it is possible to overcome one fundamental impasse of traditional Enlightenment scholarship, incapable as this is, according to her, of reconciling the 'intellectual' with the 'popular' elements of the Enlightenment and so of explaining the particular historical process through which political modernity came about.

The other line of enquiry has focused on the emergence of both the idea and the institutions of public opinion. Keith Baker and others have studied its appearance in France after the middle of the century and investigated the particular role that the appeal to public opinion played in the pre-Revolutionary and Revolutionary periods.[9] Baker himself has suggested that early modern public opinion is mainly a 'political invention', which emerged as the result of a combination of strategic moves on the part of differently motivated political actors in the course of the Revolutionary crisis. The creative force attributed to political discourse partly undermines the more socially-oriented vision underlying Habermas's early position. But two things need stressing in order to clarify the crucial part that the discussion of public opinion played in *Structural Transformation*. First, public opinion is only one of the phenomena which, according to Habermas, comprise the early modern public sphere as a social space growing in between the realm of the public and that of the private. Nonetheless, public opinion has a particular importance as the institution that more than any other gives expression to the rationalizing and moralizing aspects of the public sphere. Secondly, the idea of public opinion is the intellectual and ideological construct through which contemporary authors understood and conceptualized the kind of phenomena which Habermas considers under the public sphere, thus representing the self-conscious manipulation to which social and intellectual groups subjected the public sphere itself.

For these reasons it appears that the reconstruction of the idea of public opinion and of how it became an important feature of modern democratic politics needs to figure highly in any re-assessment of the historical import of Habermas's theory of the public sphere. As said, a number of scholars have explored the French side of that history. Some contributors to this volume discuss some of its aspects in relation to the German experience. In this essay, I turn to the British case by examining Hume's intellectual contribution to the formation of modern ideas of the role of opinion in politics.[10] It is my contention that such a discussion indirectly shows a number of limitations in Habermas's own historical reconstruction of this intellectual chapter of the public sphere. Habermas's suggestion that early eighteenth-century appeals to 'public spirit' are the origins of the more general and critical use of the idea of public opinion—such as, in his view, later Burkean appeals to 'general opinion' in a 'free country'—is misconceived,[11] because it misses the particular civic humanist dimension of discourses on public spiritedness in eigtheenth-century Britain. Moreover, Habermas underplays the diffusion of sceptical attitudes in Enlightenment thought, and how these resulted in a more circumspect view of processes of democratization already evident at the time. Hume's own theory of opinion as the support of government clearly illustrates both failings in Habermas's theory, and to this I shall now turn.

The 'Phantasticke Voyce'

In one of his political essays, Hume famously contended that 'governors have nothing to support them but opinion. It is therefore on opinion only that government is founded.'[12] This statement can be, and indeed has been, variously interpreted, mainly because of the ambiguity of the word 'opinion' itself. As we know, the word has two main connotations corresponding to our own current usage. By 'opinion' we mean a belief entertained about something and the esteem in which someone is held: his or her reputation. Although the two meanings are distinct, they often reinforce each other, as happens in the famous statement that 'opinion is the queen of the world'.[13]

The two meanings share two characteristics which make their occasional identification the more telling. For they both refer to a world of appearances where imagination, more than real knowledge, seems to rule, with the effect that our beliefs and reputations are in a state of continuous fluctuation. Moreover, it is in their nature to be *subjective* constructions which, largely owing to the reinforcement they receive by being widely accepted, become *objective* facts. Obviously, when taken by themselves either meaning has only neutral value that must be qualified by an attribute: an opinion can be either true or false; we can have either a good or bad opinion of someone or something. Yet, it is this neutrality that devalues opinion in both philosophical discourse and the practical world.

Opinion, in the sense of 'belief', was usually set against scientific knowledge and reason, which were represented as the only certain guide to things practical and theoretical. This opposition arose early in Greek philosophy, where *doxa* (opinion, belief) was used in an antithesis to either *episteme* (science) or *phronesis* (prudence and practical knowledge).[14]

It is not necessary to cite much evidence of the negative value that uncertainty, oscillation and subjectivity have traditionally implied in philosophical discussion (unless the author wanted to make a case for sceptical belief). However, it should be noted that until the seventeenth and the eighteenth centuries, and probably afterwards, in strict philosophical discussions, opinion was rarely understood to mean 'knowledge in formation', but only what we are left with when we have no knowledge of something. This can be seen in Hobbes's discussion of the issue in Chapter 7 of *Leviathan*, where he denied that opinion can have any meaning in scientific discourse, which in itself is only a form of 'conditional knowledge'.[15]

This view of opinion may also have been the result of the 'social' connotations of the word. Until the eighteenth century, by opinion was meant only 'popular' or 'vulgar' belief, which were normally associated with superstitions and prejudices. Voltaire, for one, was explicit on the subject. In a short piece on 'opinion', he mainly discussed the social formation of opinions (in the plural), which were said to be absent amongst primitive populations or between those people in more advanced societies who are 'solely occupied with the painful and continual care of providing their subsistance'. Voltaire maintained that only when a nation rises from its backward conditions will it have opinions, but that these will at first be quite false, and that only after centuries will this *opinion populaire* be put right. Voltaire's epigrammatic conclusion to this short piece echoed old themes: 'Opinion is called the queen of the world; it is so: for when reason opposes it, it is condemned to death. Reason must rise twenty times from its ashes gradually to drive away the usurper.'[16]

It may seem that Voltaire's treatment of the notion was not very different from those traditional positions which pretended that opinion ought only to be reason's 'slave or shadow': in the words of an Elizabethan poet, opinion was 'but the hisse of Geese, the people noyse, the tongue of humours, and phantasticke voyce of haire-braind Apprehension'.[17] But this is not entirely true. For Voltaire's suggestion that opinion is the product of civilization introduced a rather disconcerting element into the traditional image of irrational beliefs. These are certainly stubborn prejudices against which reason had to struggle, yet, at the same time, they are the first manifestation of the rationality (*perfectibilité*, in Rousseauean terms) of man.

The social and civil dimension of opinion posed a problem for eighteenth-century philosophers, who, through their battle against superstition and authority, became progressively more interested in a sort of natural history of the rise and fall of various popular beliefs.[18] The change of attitude is graphically illustrated by D'Alembert's introductory discourse to the *Encyclopédie*, where he condemned the Scholastic pedants for having hardened their 'opinions particuliers' into dogmas, in order to oppose the progress of true philosophy; but where, a few pages later, he also maintained that Scholasticism could be subverted only by 'opinions hardies et nouvelles'.[19] Even before the middle of the century this tendency could be clearly seen at work, and Saint Aubin's *Traité de l'Opinion*, a book which may well have influenced some of the *philosophes*, was only its most remarkable manifestation.[20]

There is nothing surprising in this development, which aptly fits the spread of toleration and a taste for rational debate. Hume's use of the word 'opinion' did not refer to irrational and violent beliefs, which he usually designated as 'superstition' and 'enthusiasm'. In his usage, opinion did not contradict reason, nor was it outside the dominion of the latter, as many authors were instead keen to suggest. On the contrary, in Hume's work opinion is generally deployed in a positive context, where progress in manners and tempers is attributed to the general development of civilized and commercial society. The evidence for this reading, and the sense in which we must take Hume's position on the issue, will be discussed later. We should turn first to the more particular meaning that he gave to the word when he contended that government stands on opinion. For it may be suggested, as indeed it has been, that until the middle of the eighteenth century political references to the dominion of opinion over the world referred to the questions of reputation and interest rather than to the influence of rational beliefs on the administration of things public.[21]

The meaning of opinion as 'esteem' and 'reputation' did not in fact develop along similar lines to those I have indicated for 'belief'. As Lester Crocker has shown in his analysis of the function that the word has in Rousseau's writings,[22] when opinion is meant in the sense of reputation, its *objective* aspects are seen as a limitation to the natural development of the individual, who is caught, as Crocker holds that Rousseau was, in the dialectic between dependence and autonomy, from which there is no easy escape. In choosing one of these alternatives, one seems to renounce either the 'social' or the 'natural' aspects of one's identity.

If, by stating that government depends on opinion, Hume meant only to imply that the fortunes of governors are entirely based on the *reputation* they might have made for themselves among their own people, opinion would be little more than the 'phantasticke voyce' of Elizabethan times—the same voice that Shakespeare's Henry IV claims helped him to the throne:

> Had I so lavish of my presence been
> So common-hackney'd in the eyes of men,
> So stale and cheap to vulgar company,
> Opinion, that did help me to the crown,
> Had still kept loyal to possession,
> And left me in repouteless banishment,
> A fellow of no mark nor likelihood.
>
> (*Henry IV Part I*, III, ii, 39–45)

Natural Principles of Authority

There may indeed be a strong case for maintaining that Hume's maxim was rooted in a traditional conception of politics. Few scholars have remarked that Hume's general contention was taken almost verbatim from William Temple's 'An Essay upon the Original and Nature of Government'.

The gist of the argument, at least at first glance, appears to be the same. Hume began his essay by pointing out that it appeared surprising to a 'philosophical eye' with what facility the vast multitude of men were governed by the few: 'when we enquiry by what means this wonder is effected, we shall find, that as *Force* is always on the side of the governed, the governors have nothing to support them but opinion' (p. 32). In Temple's essay, written in 1672 and published eight years later together with other works, it is also emphasized (the passage was indeed in italics) that 'power arising from Strength, is always in those that are governed, who are many: but Authority arising from opinion, is in those that govern, who are few'.[23]

The problem posed by Hume, which in Temple's quotation seems to be resolved in a rather unphilosophical affirmation, was certainly not new. It had already been treated by Montaigne's friend and mentor Etienne de la Boetie in a short work, written by the author in his youth and published posthumously in a collection of Huguenot pamphlets.[24] The work enjoyed a certain revival during the eighteenth century, when it was published as an appendix to Montaigne's *Essais* and also translated into English (1735). The main argument advanced by La Boetie was that the reason for which people would endure tyranny was to be found in the maxim that people follow custom rather than nature. Thus, even though it could be argued that, apart from parental authority, men were free beings who followed their own reason, it was also true that, once they were subjugated by force or circumstances, they peacefully resigned themselves to their enslavement and accepted it through sheer habit.

If we turn back to William Temple, we will find that the specific sense that he gave to opinion was not very different from what La Boetie meant by *custom*. The passage from Temple's essay that I have quoted represents the culmination of the argument he develops throughout the first part of his pamphlet. His main interest was to show that government is, by itself, a restriction upon liberty, and therefore various forms of government do not differ in the freedom they allow to their subjects: 'all Government is a restraint upon liberty; and upon all, the Dominion is equally absolute, where it is in the last resort.'[25] Whenever people contend for liberty, their actual desire is merely to change either their rules or the form of their government. Men, or so Temple held, cannot live without government and authority—a fact which is emphasized by the many instances in which we see the mass willingly subjugating themselves, their lives and fortunes, to the commands of one ruler. This cannot be the result of 'want of heart', rather it is the result of 'the force of *custom*, or *opinion*', which is 'the true foundation of all Government, and that which subjects Power to Authority'.[26]

Within this context, opinion is not an active force which expresses the preferences of the governed, but only the passive registration of the *reputation* (the authority) of the governors. Temple illustrated his distinction between power (strength) and authority (opinion) by referring to the Roman state of classic times, where law was passed by *auctoritate senatus ac jussu populi*: the force of the people was thus guided by the reputation for wisdom, goodness and valour that the senators and their families had acquired. Besides these characteristics there are other aspects, such as the favour of the divinity, piety and fortune, which contribute to the candidate's authority, but with the possible exclusion of material wealth, they are also mediated by the opinion that the people have formed themselves of the presence of such qualities in a particular person. Finally, this reputation is said to be greatly enhanced by custom: 'for no man easily distrusts the persons, or disputes the things which he and all men that he knows of, have been always bred up to observe, and believe; or, if he does, he will hardly hope, or venture to introduce opinions wherein he knows none, or few of his own mind, and thinks all others will defend those already received.'[27]

However, in Temple's argument, the establishment of the principles of opinion and custom on which he believed authority to be generally founded served to introduce his main contention that one does not need to revert to the idea of a contract to explain political power. The principles of opinion and custom, together with 'natural authority', are sufficient to account for the origin of government. Nor is it necessary to dispute the true nature of man, whether he is a sociable being or a 'creature of prey', for these questions are clearly redundant. According to Temple, the only explanation of political power consists in the analysis of how it gradually developed from the authority of the father—authority which is ultimately based on the 'great opinion' that his children have of 'his Wisdom, his Goodness, his Valour, and his Piety'.[28]

This leads us back to the question of the exact meaning that Hume intended to give to his maxim. Firstly, we may note that he did not use opinion in the narrow sense of 'custom' and 'reputation'. Whereas Temple had only considered opinion in its passive dimension, Hume endowed it with a more active and dynamic function as the cement which bound governors and governed. It is true that he held *force* to be the most usual way in which government commenced; but force, like consent, can work only sporadically and for a limited period. It cannot guarantee the smooth running of government, which requires the continuous exercise of power and authority to maintain order in civil society. Therefore, in Hume's treatment, opinion assumed a more specific meaning, anticipating modern theories of legitimacy, which stress that power and authority do not work in a vacuum, but need a variously founded disposition to obedience that constitutes the source of their legitimacy.[29]

This has been described as a 'belief-theory' of legitimacy. By contrast with the 'power-theory' of legitimacy, it is a *de facto* construction, which has no normative validity. Nor does it explain the ground on which the rulers appeal to the people in their claim to power.[30] But the limits of this theory, which are evident even in the more sophisticated version of Max Weber, do not diminish its importance as one of the avenues through which Hume's political thought moved towards a pre-occupation whose 'sociological' character will perhaps appear more clearly from a brief examination of the different kinds of opinion which, according to Hume, contribute to the maintenance of government.

Hume distinguished three kinds of opinion: of 'interest', of 'right to power' and of 'right to property'. These principles do not work in isolation; they are modified by secondary principles such as self-interest, fear and affection. Governments are rarely founded on one principle alone. As a result, political power is a very complex social mechanism where no single principle prevails. Moreover, in politics there are no abstract interests or rights which are not mediated by the subjective perception that people have of them.

By 'opinion of interest' Hume understood men's faith either in the actual advantageousness of their present government, or in the knowledge that the advantages of that government are equal to those of any other that might take its place. By 'right of power', he inferred the concepts of personal authority and tradition; and he pointed to the 'attachment which all natives have to their ancient government, and even to those names, which have had the sanction of antiquity' (p. 33) as proof of the sway which this form of opinion has over mankind. That right that Hume called 'right of property' was instead a modification of Harrington's theory that power followed property.

The reference to Harrington is of some importance, for it introduces a consideration which goes beyond the question of political obligation and touches upon the more general issue with which eighteenth-century authors were confronted: the possibility of a modern science of politics. Significantly, the essay on the first principles of government followed one in which Hume summarily sketched the sense in which politics can be reduced to science.[31] This science was only possible because the actions of men depended more on laws and institutions than on their temper and humours. This vision of a *regular* world—a vision which Hume further clarified in other essays in which he explained the difference between causes and chances in human affairs[32]—was tempered by his conviction that in politics there is a concurrence of causes which makes it difficult to predict the general course of events, and that general maxims may sometimes have irregular results, depending on the particular social and cultural conditions to which they apply.[33]

Hume's criticism of Harrington, which he made more explicit in another essay,[34] was not directed simply at the Harrington's mistake in believing that the balance of power entirely depends upon that of property, but more generally to his narrow view of causation in politics—a view which implied that the reduction of politics to a demonstrable science was only possible through the mechanical application of a single principle. Harrington had maintained that the correspondence between the balance of power and that of property was such a principle.[35] Experience had shown, or so Hume held, that Harrington had been mistaken, and that power was not always distributed according to property; though Hume readily admitted that the stability of a commonwealth would certainly increase in those cases when there was a clear correspondence between the two kinds of balance.

As on the question of legitimacy, where Hume considered *opinion* to be a more adequate description than *consent* of the flexible basis on which allegiance was founded, so with the balance of power, where *opinion* more than simple *interest* or *property* seemed to possess all the required nuances with which to stress the objective and subjective aspects on which power was founded.

A Gentle Form of Government

The flexibility of the concept of opinion is perhaps the key to an understanding of Hume's preference for it, and of how, in the use that he made of it, his descriptive and normative intentions overlap. In this, Hume's analysis of opinion is closely related to another central concept of his political philosophy: stability, which, as well as functioning as a descriptive criterion for understanding the organization of social and political life, acts as an ideal by which particular political systems may be judged. The pervasive presence of this concept in Hume's political work, together with that of 'moderation', partly reflects that general social and ideological climate which J.H. Plumb has described as the growth of political stability in England from 1688 onwards. This stability seemed to have been sanctioned by Walpole's regime which some of the Scottish literati of the mid-century interpreted, and partly justified, in the light of their 'sceptical Whiggism'.[36]

In examining Hume's theory of opinion we find a subtle interplay between his realism and his more directly political inclinations. Hume profited greatly from the flexibility of the concept of opinion, which he partly used to overcome several of the traditional antitheses that characterized the political language of the time. The question of the validity of the various forms of government, usually schematized in the opposition between republics and monarchies, was certainly one of these. One of the fundamental charges that Hume made against consent theories of government was that they denied legitimacy to most governments. This was particularly true in the case of absolute monarchies. Hume, who occasionally expressed the opinion that, ideally, the republican form of government was preferable, was convinced that the civilized monarchies of modern Europe were better equipped than republics to guarantee peace, stability and respect for justice. Monarchies, even those of the absolute kind, seemed to have the necessary requirements for being considered legitimate governments. Besides, despotic governments themselves, though they might contradict the principle of legitimacy in several ways, also guaranteed order in society—something that was certainly to be preferred to chaos and civil strife. As Hume remarked, the principle of opinion was sufficiently flexible to accommodate all forms of government; such a 'maxim extends to the most despotic and most military governments', since the sovereign depends upon the support of the army or militias, which he must lead 'like men, by their opinion' (p. 33). This was not to say that there was no difference between the various forms of government. Hume admitted that those governments that had been founded on consent and in which civil liberty was preserved and esteemed were preferable. Yet the very existence of despotic governments and absolute monarchies could not be lightly dismissed; on the contrary, they needed to be adequately explained—something that opinion certainly did better than consent or force.

A second question on which opinion seemed to have a positive effect was that of the balance between authority and liberty. Hume clearly rejected the identification of liberty with a particular form of government, an opinion held by republicans and radical Whigs. It has rightly been noted that his conception of liberty—in the sense of the regular rule of law[37]—was not in conflict with the conviction that this could be better guaranteed under monarchy. However, Hume's opposition of liberty to authority was often intended to be part of a more general opposition between license and despotism. Hume preferred to refer to the 'rule of law' as the regular functioning of justice. He usually deployed the word *liberty* in more strictly political contexts, where questions such as the liberty of the press, the relation between the executive and parliament, or the role of factions and parties was being discussed. Although he was inclined to give weight to the necessary role that authority plays in civil society, he held that liberty was the 'perfection of civil society' (p. 41). Both authority and liberty were essential ingredients of political life; and Hume maintained that 'in all governments, there is a perpetual intestine struggle, open or secret, between AUTHORITY and LIBERTY; and neither of them can ever absolutely prevail in the contest.' (p. 40)

In this intestinal struggle, though perhaps only occasionally, opinion plays a positive role, as Hume's didactic and 'philosophical' use of political essays and historical writing seems to suggest. The intervention of enlightened opinion can be considered as a double process which is fostered by the general progress of manners and knowledge and also by a specific act of philosophical education. Hume illustrated the former process in his history of England, where he remarked that manners had had a direct influence on government, strengthening the case of liberty. He expressed the same conviction in the essay which he dedicated to the inner tendencies of English government. There he remarked that 'there has been a sudden and sensible change in the opinions of men within these last fifty years, by the progress of learning and liberty'.[38] This change is said to have undermined any superstitious reverence to name and authority, thereby reducing the general credit of the clergy, and balancing the great power that the king derived from his property and influence. In another place the same change is also said to have softened the temper of men and, consequently, to have exerted a positive influence on political life by making factions less inveterate, revolution less tragic, authority less harsh, and seditions less frequent.[39]

Nevertheless, this natural progress of knowledge is inadequate to solve the complex problems of politics, whose comprehension required particular attention to the multiplicity of causes. The enlightenment of politicians and of men of middling rank in general has a definite importance in Hume's system of practical politics. This process of education primarily consists in the diffusion of a spirit of 'moderation' and 'impartiality' which Hume claimed to inform his way of writing political pieces. He hoped that his design would 'be acceptable to the moderates of both Parties; at the same time, that, perhaps, it may displease the bigots of both'.[40] However, moderation and impartiality are mere attitudes of mind which only serve to prepare the terrain for the act of understanding and analytic discernment. Political actors must examine dispassionately, but be able to judge in a strict philosophical way. This is the lesson that Hume derived from his analysis of the myths current in British politics: the Whiggish theory of the original contract, the Tory belief in passive obedience, and the opinion that the English mixed form of government had its roots in the Ancient Constitution. None of these seemed to be solid enough ground for the order and stability that are necessary in society because they were historically and theoretically fallacious. As Hume said of the myth of the Ancient Constitution, 'there is not a more effectual method of betraying a cause, than to lay the stress of the argument on a wrong place, and by disputing an untenable post, ensure the adversaries to success and victory' (p. 501).

Hume's belief in natural enlightenment and in the positive effect of philosophical education is however to be taken with circumspection. Although, as has already been noted, he generally used the word 'opinion' in a positive context, it remains true that, as Donald Winch has argued for both Hume and Smith, their sceptical attitude towards progress and utopian constructions inclined them to take notice of those aspects of prejudice and ignorance which were part of general opinion. They seemed aware that opinion 'could also be swayed by more pathological conditions of "terror", "rage", and "enthusiasm" '.[41] This made the accommodation of legitimate interests and general opinion a particularly difficult task for the politician and the legislator. Furthermore, the results of this accommodation could not be taken for granted; they were often unintended, and sometimes frankly regressive. One could conclude that Hume's idea of opinion was mid-way between the Shakespearean 'souvereign mistress of effects' and the Kantian optimistic faith in the public's self-illumination: 'There is more chance that a public will become enlightened by itself; this is indeed almost inevitable, if only the public concerned is left free.'[42] In Scotland, we can indeed see that the generation that followed Hume and Smith showed a more confident attitude towards enlightened opinion and the power of education. Somewhat paradoxically from a Humean perspective, this new confidence seems to have been founded partly on an appeal to a providential deism which Hume had ridiculed and Smith kept in the background.

Although we can discover no sign of excessive optimism in Hume, he acknowledged that those features of modern society which pointed towards an increase in the role of the public at large in political life could not be brushed aside. This was the gist of his position on the question of factions and parties in British politics. In general, he regarded them as inventions to be detested and hated; he thought that the influence of factions was contrary to that of laws and institutions in so far as they 'subvert government, render laws impotent, and beget the fiercest animosity among men of the same nation, who ought to give mutual assistance and protection to each other' (p. 55). But he also agreed that to abolish all distinctions of party was not practicable, or even desirable, in a free government, where the very form of mixed government required an opposition of forces. As long as the parties did not disagree on the essentials of the constitution, on which compromise would have been difficult to achieve, Hume believed that there was no danger to political society. Reason was rarely on one side of a dispute; beliefs were a product of the imagination, which operates on the passions and characters of men. Beliefs and opinions, or so Hume held, are hardly at our disposal. On the contrary, he insisted that wars of philosophical and religious principle were as risible as the Moorish civil wars which blacks and whites were supposed to have fought on account of their complexions: one can do nothing more than tincture a complexion, or camouflage an opinion. In politics, Hume concluded, the most effective manner of contributing to the public good was 'to prevent all unreasonable insult and triumph of one part over the other, to encourage moderate opinions, to find the proper medium in all disputes, to persuade each that its antagonist may possibly be sometimes in the right, and to keep a balance in the praise and blame, which we bestow on either side' (p. 494)

Hume's argument, which overtly seems to devalue opinions to an almost irrational level, in fact legitimizes their presence in civil society and that of parties in politics. Hume also believed that certain sources of faction, such as interest, were not only ineradicable, but also 'the most reasonable and the most excusable'. Anywhere in society that we find two or more orders of men whose authority in a government is not perfectly balanced, we have naturally to expect distinct interests; 'nor can we reasonably expect a different conduct, considering the degree of selfishness implanted in human nature' (p. 59). To overcome the differences between such parties is akin to discovering the secret of the grand elixir, or perpetual motion—a thing, Hume stressed, that 'may amuse men in theory, but can never possibly be reduced to practice'. Even despotic governments, though their appearances often belie it, are riddled with dissenting minds because 'the distinct orders of men, nobles and people, soldiers and merchants, have all a distinct interest; but the more powerful oppresses the weaker with impunity, and without resistance; which begets a seeming tranquillity in such governments' (p. 60).

The question of differing interests had been debated in England since the beginning of the century with reference to the conflict of landed and trading interests. In Hume's opinion the conflict was not of such momentous import to the 'commonwealth' as it had been represented: the 'interests of these two bodies are not really distinct, and never will be so, till our public debts increase to such a degree, as to become altogether oppressive and intolerable' (p. 60). However, within the present context Hume's discussion of the conflict is relevant to an understanding of how the different principles which govern politics can be checked and adjusted.

On the question of the public debt, for instance, we find that Hume's interest in it was eminently political. There were, as he remarked, strictly economical consequences which were pernicious to the general good; yet they were partly tempered by some advantage, and, in any case, they were 'trivial, in comparison to the prejudice that results to the state considered as a body politic' (p. 59). In the first version of the essay that Hume dedicated to the subject, he insisted on the general effects that an increase in taxation resulting from the increase of the public debt would entail to the economical and political fortunes of the state. In 1760, however, he added six long paragraphs putting forward his central contention. In them he argued that the first and more immediate effect of the public debt was to weaken the power of those social and institutional bodies which mediated between the executive and the people, thereby drastically reducing their capacity to ensure political stability. Public debt would substitute for the natural aristocracy of land, commerce and industry one based on stock-holders, whose only claim to power and authority consisted of paper. Besides creating a situation in which the alternatives became 'insurrection' or 'tyranny', an increase in public debt multiplied the chances that continuous adjustment in the system of taxation would gravely damage trade and commerce, throwing the system of government into further confusion.

Since the question of public debt was the only one on which Hume was alarmist, it can be inferred that he considered the role of men of middle rank to be of great consequence for the balance of power and that he regarded commercial interests as having a prominent role to play in politics. As John Pocock has suggested, this approach can best be placed in the context of a general 'counter-ethics' or 'counter-politics' which largely drew upon a language based on the mitigation of the concepts of fantasy and imagination. Passions, interest and opinions became, therefore, the most appropriate linguistic vehicles for expressing this mitigation. In the process, they marked the decline of more objectivistic terms like *virtue* and *rights*.[43] The language of commerce, in particular, seemed to confirm this process by giving great relevance to a word such as credit, which Genovesi defined as the faculty of using someone else's power as if it were one's own, and which depended on the opinion that others had of the security of their credit.[44]

Yet there is no reason to conclude that Hume's arguments were primarily intended to establish a new moral identity for the citizens of modern polities. Forbes' contention that in Hume's politics the 'scientific' dimension was the predominant one is certainly more convincing.[45] This can be seen from the 'realistic' criteria Hume used in his arguments on matters of political economy, where Hume's main interest was clearly in the stability of civil society, the power of the state, the authority of government and the wealth and security of subjects.

This does not mean that Hume had no preference in terms of social morality or political organization. On the question of maintaining a 'middle force' which would guarantee the transmission of values and the preservation of authority, Hume clearly held that the gentry should be considered as its main component, and their position preserved with a certain tenacity, even beyond strict justice.[46] In the British system this could be exercised through the existing 'popular government', where Lords and Commons were the natural representative of the gentry.

But this structure also seemed to be able, in its flexibility, to guarantee the gradual political ascendancy of those social groups which, though they might have little power, had an increasing share in property. As he wrote in the essay on the principles of government:

> A government may endure for several ages, though the balance of power, and the balance of property do not coincide. This chiefly happens, where any rank or order of the state has acquired a large share in property; but from the original constitution of the government, has no share in the power. . . . But where the original constitution allows any share of power, though small, to an order of men, who possess a large share of the property, it is easy for them gradually to stretch their authority, and bring the balance of power to coincide with that of property. This has been the case with the house of commons in England. (p. 35)

The combination of this flexibility towards property and the balance between authority and liberty that was expressed in the English form of mixed government represented the characteristics which shaped what Hume called that form of 'gentle government' for which he had a preference. As he remarked, 'it is hoped that men, being every day more accustomed to the free discussion of public affairs, will improve in the judgement of them, and be with greater difficulty seduced by every idle rumour and popular clamour'.[47] Perhaps this form of government was not a perfect commonwealth, but this did not disturb Hume: 'it is sufficient incitement to human endeavours, that such a government would flourish for many ages; without pretending to bestow, on any work of man, that immortality, which the Almighty seems to have refused to his own productions' (p. 529).

This outcome could not be guaranteed, but enlightened opinion and moderation would certainly contribute towards its realization. The diffusion of what Hume once called the 'genius of philosophy' would not therefore herald a society founded on Reason, but rather more modestly and imperfectly —though perhaps still utopistically—one founded on 'good reasoners'.

Notes

1. I. Kant, 'An Answer to the Question: What is Enlightenment?' in *Political Writings* ed. by H. Reiss and trans. by H.B. Nisbet (Cambridge, [1970] 1991), pp. 54–60.
2. M. Horkheimer and T.W. Adorno, *The Dialectic of the Enlightenment* (New

York, 1972); M. Foucault, 'What is Enlightenment' in *The Foucault Reader* ed. by P. Rabinow (Harmondsworth, 1991) pp. 32–50.

3. Foucault, 'What is Enlightenment' pp. 34–35
4. J.G.A. Pocock, 'Conservative Enlightenment and the Democratic Revolutions: The American and French Cases in British Perspective' *Government and Opposition* 24 (1989) p. 81.
5. Pocock, 'Conservative Enlightenment' p. 105.
6. J. Habermas, *The Structural Transformation of the Public Sphere: An Inquiry into a Category of Bourgeois Society* (Cambridge, MA, 1989)
7. Cf. J. Habermas, 'Further Reflections on the Public Sphere' in C. Calhoun (ed.) *Habermas and the Public Sphere* (Cambridge, MA and London, 1992) pp. 421–60. On Habermas's more critical position towards Adorno's and Horkheimer's reading of the Enlightenment Project, cf. 'The Entwinement of Myth and Enlightenment: Max Horkheimer and Theodor Adorno' in *The Philosophical Discourse of Modernity. Twelve Lectures* (Cambridge, 1987) pp. 106–30.
8. M. Jacob, 'The Enlightenment Redefined: The Formation of Modern Civil Society' *Social Research* 58 (1991) pp. 475–95.
9. Cf. K. M. Baker, *Inventing the French Revolution* (Cambridge, 1990), in particular ch. 8: 'Public Opinion as Political Invention' pp. 167–99; M. Ozouf, 'L'opinion publique' in K.M. Baker (ed.) *The Political Culture of the Old Regime* vol. I: *The French Revolution and the Creation of a Modern Political Culture* (Oxford, 1987) pp. 419–34; D. Goodman, 'Public Sphere and Private Life: Towards a Synthesis of Current Historiographical Approaches to the Old Regime' *History and Theory* 31 (1992) pp. 1–20; D. Gordon, ' "Public Opinion" and the Civilizing Process in France: The Example of Morellet' *Eighteenth-Century Studies* 22 (1989) pp. 302-38; E. Tortarolo, ' "Opinion publique" tra ancien régime e rivoluzione. Contributo a un vocabolario storico della politica settecentesca' in *Rivista Storica Italiana* 102 (1990) pp. 5–23; R. Chartier, *Les Origines Culturelles de la Révolution Française* (Paris, 1991), in particular ch. 2: 'Espace Public and Opinion Publique' pp. 32–52.
10. For a discussion more concerned with the moral aspects of conceptions of public and private in British discourse, see Pesante's essay in this volume.
11. Cf. Habermas, *Structural Transformation* ch. 4
12. D. Hume, 'Of the First Principles of Government' in *Essays Moral, Political and Literary* ed. by E.F. Miller (Indianapolis, 1987), hereafter *Essays*. All pages given between brackets in the main text refer to this edition of the *Essays*.
13. Cf. Blaise Pascal: 'L'opinion est la reine du monde': in *Pensées* ed. by P. Sellier (Paris, 1976) no. 200 [311]; James Howell: 'Opinion is that high and mighty Dame which rules the world', *Vocal Forest*, Introduction; and Gervase Markham: 'Yet it is but opinion, and that must be the world's master always', *English House-Wife* l. 70.
14. Aristotle used 'opinion' to describe the particular virtue that the good

citizen ought to possess when he obeys the orders of the political leader. Even in this case, in which 'true opinion' is considered a virtue, it is only considered as an instrumental virtue which is inferior to the virtue of the leader (*phronesis*), because it is completely dependent on the latter: cf. *Politics* ed. by E. Barker (Oxford, 1948) p. 122 [1277b].

15. Cf. Hobbes, *Leviathan* ed. by R. Tuck (Cambridge, 1991) p. 48.
16. Voltaire, *Oeuvres Complètes* (Paris, 1885) XX pp. 135-36 (my translation).
17. Guilpin, *Skialetheia* (1598) in *Satyre* IV.
18. Cf. J. Shklar, *Men and Citizens. A Study of Rousseau's Social Theory* (Cambridge, 1969) *passim*.
19. D'Alembert, *Discours Preliminaire de L'Encyclopédie* (Paris 1965) pp. 88–91. Cf. also the article 'Opinion' in *Encyclopédie, Ou Dictionnaire Raisonné* (Lousanne and Berne, 1780) XXIII, pp. 754–56, where it is said that 'opinion' is a 'feeble light' in the world of scientific knowledge, though opinion is here also discussed in connection with the sceptical question of 'doubt'.
20. P. Tedeschi, *Saint-Aubin et son Oeuvre* (Paris, 1968).
21. Cf. J. Gunn, *Beyond Liberty and Property* (Montreal 1983) pp. 263–65.
22. See Crocker, 'Rousseau et l' "opinion" ' in *Studies on Voltaire and the Eighteenth Century* 55 (1967) pp. 395–416.
23. W. Temple, *An Essay upon the Original and Nature of Government* [1680] (repr. Los Angeles 1964) p. 54.
24. La Boetie, *Le Discours de la servitude volontaire* ed. P. Leonard (Paris, 1978). See also Montaigne's essay 'De l'Amitié' in *Essais* (Paris, 1935) I pp. 239–56.
25. Temple, *Essay* p. 53.
26. Temple, *Essay* p. 54 (my emphasis).
27. Temple, *Essay* p. 58–59.
28. Temple *Essay* p. 65.
29. See Max Weber, *Economy and Society* ed. by G. Roth and C. Wittich (Berkeley, 1978) I, ch. 3, i.
30. See J. Merquior, *Rousseau and Weber. Two Studies in the Theory of Legitimacy* (London, 1980).
31. Cf. 'That Politics may be Reduced to a Science' *Essays* pp. 14–31. In *Gulliver's Travels*, Swift ridiculed the fashionable idea of making politics into a demonstrable science.
32. Cf. 'Of the Rise and Progress of the Arts and Sciences' in *Essays* pp. 111–37.
33. Cf. 'Of some Remarkable Customs' in *Essays* pp. 266–76.
34. Cf. 'Whether the British Government Inclines more to Absolute Monarchy, or to a Republic' in *Essays* pp. 47–53.
35. Cf. J. Harrington, *The Prerogative of Popular Government* in *Political Works of James Harrington* ed. by J.G.A. Pocock (Cambridge, 1977) p. 404.
36. See J. Plumb, *The Growth of Political Stability in England* (London, 1967); H.T. Dickinson, *Liberty and Property. Political Ideology in Eighteenth-Century Britain* (London, 1977); D. Forbes, 'Sceptical Whiggism, Commerce and

Liberty' in A. Skinner and T. Wilson (eds) *Essays on Adam Smith* (Oxford, 1975) pp. 179–201; and also S. Collini, D. Winch, J. Burrow, *That Noble Science of Politics* (Cambridge, 1984) ch. 1.

37. See D. Forbes, 'Hume and the Scottish Enlightenment' in S.C. Brown (ed.) *Philosophers of the Enlightenment* (Brighton, 1979) pp. 94—09; D. Winch, *Adam Smith's Politics* (Cambridge, 1978); and Collini, et al., *That Noble Science*.

38. D. Hume, *The History of England from the Invasion of Julius Caesar to the Revolution of 1688* (London, 1770) V, App. III, pp. 520 and *passim*.

39. Cf. 'Of the Refinement in the Arts' in *Essays* p. 274; 'The Rise' *passim*; and 'Of Civil Liberty' in *Essays* pp. 87-96 *passim*.

40. D. Hume, 'Preface' to the first edition [1741] in *Essays Moral, Political Literary* ed. by T.H. Green and T.H. Grose (London, 1875) I pp. 41–42.

41. Winch, *Adam Smith's Politics* p. 170.

42. Respectively: *Othello*, I, 3, 225; and I. Kant, 'An Answer' p. 54.

43. See J.G.A. Pocock, *The Machiavellian Moment* (Princeton, 1975) chs. 13–14, *passim*.

44. Cf. Antonio Genovesi's discussion of credito in *Lezioni di Economia Civile* (Milano, 1803) II pp. 352–67; see also Pocock's analysis of the question of 'credit' in *Machiavellian Moment* pp. 452-57.

45. Cf. Forbes, 'Sceptical Whiggism' *passim*.

46. Cf. 'Of Public Credit' in *Essays* pp. 349-65, *passim*.

47. 'Of the Liberty of the Press' in editions A [1741] to P [1768] of *Essays*, cf. 'Variant Readings' p. 603. The elision of this passage from the last few editions shows that Hume was less sanguine on the positive effects of the liberty of the press.

Ten

An Impartial Actor: The Private and the Public Sphere in Adam Smith's Theory of Moral Sentiments

Maria Luisa Pesante

In this essay I wish to discuss whether in Adam Smith's *Theory of Moral Sentiments* there is a conceptualization of a public sphere as an arena of human action.[1] In addressing this historical question I am employing Habermas's vocabulary as it appears in recent English translations, which sound quite different from the original German as well as from the Italian translation published (and read) in 1971 in a rather orthodox Frankfurt School context. Habermas is now read and translated in the Anglophone world within the context of his later philosophical writings, which are seen as providing one of the possible versions of the liberal philosophy which is meant to have started with the Enlightenment. It is from this perspective that, as a historian, I find *Strukturwandel der Öffentlichkeit* less interesting as a piece of historical writing than as part of an ongoing historical process, generally referred to as the unfinished project of the Enlightenment, to which Adam Smith also belongs.

The Anglophone Habermas shows strong resonances of a line of liberal moral philosophy. Thus, if we look at *Strukturwandel* from the vantage point of the theory of communicative action, we can see that in the 1950s Habermas was asking a very similar question to the one addressed by Koselleck on the relationship between politics and morals as envisaged by the philosophers of the Enlightenment. However, he developed the political possibilities implied by the public dimension of private virtue in a direction opposite to Koselleck's *Staatsraison*. Koselleck, writing as a critic and an enemy of the Enlightenment, identified in the moral pretensions of the *Bürger* against the secret sphere of politics the roots of the permanent crisis which in his view was haunting modern man.[2] Habermas, writing as both a critic of and an heir to the Enlightenment, was careful not to place public and private in stark opposition to each other, while he made their shifting relationship the focus of his own reflections. Since Habermas's research was carried on against a background in which a classical civic perspective was proposed by Hannah Arendt, the structure of the debate can be seen as revealing strong eighteenth-century roots.[3]

From Adam Smith's natural law perspective, the distinction of private and public appeared as obviously constituting a great dichotomy. However, Smith eventually dismissed this way of treating the distinction for a number of complex reasons, which I shall here attempt to explain.[4] Civic humanist writers maintained that, in modern societies, citizens' private concerns (that is, their rights to and over both things and persons as mediated by things) might be effectively protected by and from governments. But they also contended that the public and political dimension of life was often put into jeopardy by the citizens' involvement in the very pursuit of private wealth for which they sought protection.[5] Natural law philosophers faced with such a challenge felt they could not avoid endorsing some absolutist theory of sovereignty, if they wanted to defend the freedom of private concerns and the pursuit of wealth, refinement and civilization.

However, the kind of argument advanced by the civic humanists was also threatening to destroy the proper object of moral inquiry, universal moral agency. To understand this point we can refer to a piece of reasoning implied, though not fully elaborated, by John Pocock in his account of the eighteenth-century debate on virtue and commerce. This debate emphasized the precariousness in the relationship between the material preconditions of human personality and political agency in a world of Protean variability of property. There comes a moment in the eighteenth-century debate at which neo-Harringtonian discourse against public credit, standing armies and patronage, as ways in which the citizen is dispossessed of his autonomous activity by his representatives, is set into the wider perspective of division of labour and specialization. Those processes were shown as dissolving human agents' ability to address with full and undivided responsibility the challenges of their social, political and moral world. At this point more than just political agency was at stake. Moral agency was also seen as severely impaired, and moral philosophers arguing from within a jurisprudential framework faced a particular challenge, for which their conceptual armoury provided no obvious help. As the long eighteenth-century debate on how to deal with the poor showed so clearly, if property is recognized as the ground of personality, as in civic discourses, then lack of property means not just political disenfranchisement as a citizen, but also moral inability to rule over one's own behaviour. At the same time, in a world of mobile property and fictitious values no proxy can be found to ground a personality which is prevented by specialization from maintaining itself by exercising virtue. Therefore the moral philosopher found himself under the necessity of discussing afresh the foundation of personality in order to defend the possibility, not of political, but of moral, agency. It was precisely the structure of political argument that made it imperative for him to answer a problem in moral philosophy. I would submit that in *The Theory of Moral Sentiments* Smith had to redefine moral agency in terms of motives, not of ends, because showing the hierarchy of ends, as between private and public, could not answer a crucial question about the ability people actually had to behave according to given ends. In so doing he had to transform the classical dichotomy of public and private as ways of categorizing kinds of concern which were commonly taken to be active among men's motives.

Representative Publicness and Private Men's Motives

It may be useful here briefly to recall Smith's general moral argument, which is mainly centred on a factual inquiry into the way in which moral judgments are formulated. These are shown to be grounded in the emotional response of the sympathy we feel when we consider other people's situations. We react sentimentally in different ways when we consider their different actions. It is all-important that this emotional source of our moral life should be preserved intact. This is why Smith is at pains both to identify the causes of corruption of our moral sentiments and to find ways in which these causes can be resisted. He identifies the main source of this corruption in our tendency to concur with the sentiments of the great and the rich. As this tendency is also the foundation of the order of society, the antinomy is central to Smith's vision. This very situation is at the centre of Smith's analysis of 'private men'.

Private men, categorically distinguished from those who are not private, but who are not necessarily considered public figures, come upon the stage in *The Theory of Moral Sentiments* for the first time at the end of Part I to epitomize talents and solid virtues, the absence of which is notable in 'the great'. Their traits are carefully delineated to fit a variety of social circumstances and jobs, and different organizations of society, provided they are open to upward mobility. Their aim is not private opulence, but public conspicuousness. The activities in which they may be engaged and try their chance are various. The occasion they look forward to is one of troubled times:

> The most perfect modesty and plainness, joined to as much negligence as is consistent with the respect due to the company, ought to be the chief characteristics of the behaviour of a private man. If ever he hopes to distinguish himself, . . . he must acquire dependants to balance the dependants of the great, and he has no other fund to pay them from, but the labour of his body, and the activity of his mind. He must cultivate these therefore: he must acquire superior knowledge in his profession, and superior industry in the exercise of it. He must be patient in labour, resolute in danger, and firm in distress. These talents he must bring into public view, by the difficulty, importance, and, at the same time, good judgement of his undertakings, and by the severe and unrelenting application with which he pursues them. Probity and prudence, generosity and frankness, must characterize his behaviour upon all ordinary occasions . . . With what impatience does the man of spirit and ambition, who is depressed by his situation, look around for some great opportunity to distinguish himself? No circumstances, which can afford this, appear to him undesirable. He even looks forward with satisfaction to the prospect of foreign war, or civil dissension; and, with secret transport and delight, sees through all the confusion and bloodshed which attend them, the probability of those wished-for occasions presenting themselves, in which he may draw upon himself the attention and admiration of mankind.[6]

Ambitious private man thus appears on the stage almost as a kind of Machiavellian hero, ready to exert his abilities in offering some sort of rescue. He is the non-identical twin brother of deferential private man, the man disposed 'to go along with all the passions of the rich and the powerful'. They are both actuated, although to different outcomes, by the universal desire to be at the center of the scene where 'the abstract idea of a perfect and happy state' is being staged.[7] The former endeavours to get among the actors, perhaps to substitute some of them; the latter is satisfied with identifying himself with the great by means of worshipping them. The public space introduced by Smith as the arena where the natural formation of our moral judgments meets the severe and tempting challenge of *fortuna* is fundamentally a space of visibility. It is neither public in the sense of being defined by common deeds, activities, and pursuits; nor is it a place for common action or for common discourse. Politeness is not here the common virtue by which men refine themselves in intercourse; politeness itself is the preserve of the great, contemptible in the others, and the fiction of a superiority which excludes any personal capacity. This space is public only because men expose themselves in it to 'the public admiration', either by playing their roles, or by competing for roles, or by so intense an admiration as to be almost subsumed among the admired. As a consequence, men are public if they can rely on visibility and admiration, but admiration is bestowed simply on the condition which allows for visibility: 'To be observed, to be attended to, to be taken notice of with sympathy, complacency, and approbation.'[8]

I have been talking of a public space in order to emphasize that it is not Habermas's modern public sphere, but old representative publicness, the space in which authority was represented in the sense of being made present.[9] The public space so defined is both fractured and dominated by the representation of sovereignty. In order to understand the role it plays within Smith's theory we have to identify both its source—which perhaps is not so obvious—and a number of other relevant facts. The kind of situation here represented is as much Mandevillean as it is Machiavellian; it is portrayed as both displaying basic human drives and presenting a crucial problem for the development of moral life. Finally, it does not allow for a dimension of publicness.

Machiavellian ambition presented Smith with a problem in his system of morality very much as Mandevillean vanity did. This was so, because Smith's system consisted in an analysis of motives rather than a prescription of ends. If the possibility of moral life depends upon the reasons actually listened to by people, then no approved-of end can transform the character of a motive, however useful it may be for the structuring of social life. The point about the impossibility of manipulating the actual character of our motives had been made by Hutcheson against Mandeville, as is well known. Smith's description, with its emphasis upon the virtuous deeds prompted by ambition, tells us that he was making the same point also, but now against a civic conception of the way private motives of an otherwise not commendable kind were connected to a public good by the good orders of the republic. 'Fame, ambition and avarice, the common inducements to all great undertakings of this kind', Moyle wrote with admiration, 'reign very strongly in popular assemblies, where the spoils or the honour are to be divided among a multitude; which is more hard to satisfy, than the private glory of a prince or a senate.'[10] But, if a preconceived good is not there to change the character of avarice, ambition, and aggressiveness, the civic prescription is morally unacceptable. Thus new problems appear in the understanding of our moral world once the moral philosopher shifts from an ethics of ends to one of motives. And a primary consequence of this move is a challenge to the accepted distinction and distribution of private and public.

The description of man's existential impulse to recognize authority in the powers that be might be termed a secularized version of what Schochet has called anthropological patriarchalism.[11] This was 'not so much a political theory as it was a presumed description of the pre-political world', an account of the ways natural subjection worked and developed. While responding to theories of contract with their connected vision of the natural independence of man, it could be tempting for different kinds of divine right theorists to describe an alternative psychology of man, one accounting for his easy bowing to monarchical sovereign authority. It might be further recalled that, as the description could be easily deprived of specific normative implication, even authors who were not inclined to patriarchalism at all might find the theory useful against contractualism. Smith's contemporary, the modern Whig Josiah Tucker, knew this very well. Recognizing Smith's crucial description as a piece of patriarchalist anthropology should warn us against too easily taking it as the whole of Smith's theory of authority.[12] Moreover, it might suggest that such a description has to be interpreted as the first condition in a developmental series which is both historical and notional.

Nevertheless, a less generic origin of Smith's moral problem with deference and ambition can be located in Pierre Nicole's *De la grandeur*. Smith took from the French moral essay almost everything in his description, including the formulation of the problem and the wording itself.[13] However, he emphatically rejected the Jansenist solution. The greatness admired because it displays the most natural objects of concupiscence was, in Nicole's account, 'a participation of the power of God to men, which he communicated to some for the good of others'. Therefore, 'in so much as this submission having for its object, that which is truly worthy of respect, it ought not only to be exteriour and a bare ceremony, but must be likewise interiour; that it must include the acknowledgement of a real superiority and greatness in those who are honoured after this manner'. At this point Nicole was accepting the risk of the corruption of our moral judgments, something that Smith could not do, since in his meta-ethics moral judgments are the motives that make moral choice possible. The corruption of those judgments would make moral life impossible. The consequence was the enjoined separation of the criterion of moral judgments from the orders of civil society.

Smith might not have found Nicole's formulation so crucial, if Hutcheson had not readily accepted, in a secularized form, 'this ordinary connection in our imagination between *external grandeur, regularity* in *dress, equipage, retinue, badges* of *honour*, and some *moral abilitys* greater than ordinary'.[14] Hutcheson's positive presentation of such a confusion between rank and virtue was an outcome of his shifting between an ethics of motives, one that requires rigorous scrutiny of the reasons why we act as we do, and an ethics of ends, where our moral world is given and the reasons out of which we pursue the common good are less important, provided we do so. We can see therefore that Smith was raising the same problem. His refusal of Jansenist stabilizing deference, along with beneficent vanity and stirring ambition, tells us that he was articulating a theory of how men can construct for themselves a moral world for which they bear ultimate responsibility. Smith employed what he considered important and problematic accounts of the relation between human personalities and the moral world to describe a basic human condition. But, as he was at the same time attempting to transform moral philosophy from being a discourse about ends given before human moral agency into a discourse about the way men and women—and children as well—learn moral agency by defining to themselves the laws of their behaviour, the prescriptions implied in those accounts were declared defective, and the behaviour they commended rather a problem for virtue than a model for it. Such is both the civic (or cynical) vindication of independence and ambition, and the absolutist anthropology of deference.[15] Smith's answer to those accounts of moral life was an exit from a natural jurisprudence framework, in which the moral world is given to us in the form of already existing laws in such a way that our compliance with them is more important than our motive for so doing. All that is left in his discourse is a human faculty for moral legislation, grounded on a feeble natural sentiment. Thus the risk to be absolutely avoided is the corruption of the moral judgments, which are the basis for moral legislation. We can see here that, while the language of the law is retained, Smith abandons the main version of the natural law conceptual paradigm on a crucial point.[16]

I have tried so far to analyse the sources and implications of the description Smith gives of a situation where power and the order of society are strictly personalized, and in which no man can be public in the normative positive sense we know Smith was employing elsewhere. All men here are private, that is, acting out of private concerns, although some of those concerns are invested with power and representative publicness. The space in which publicness is represented appears so fully saturated that any road to the public sphere looks absolutely closed. We have to ask now whether Smith discovered other modes of behaviour within a public scene besides the lack of sympathy for inferiors in the man of high rank (that is the lack of a ground for moral relationships), the temporary passage through virtue of the man of ambition, and the abject meanness of those who 'have forgot the desire, and almost the very wish, for superiority'.[17] But I have still to insist on the point that the description I have chosen as the starting point for reconstructing the relation of private and public in Smithian moral discourse occupies a crucial place at the end of Part I of the *Theory*. In a section that bears the revealing title, 'Of the effects of prosperity and adversity upon the judgment of mankind with regard to the propriety of action', Smith concludes the foundation of his theory by defining the challenge that the hierarchy of civil society brings to the morally harmonious social world analysed in the former two sections. We know that, although the public space was described as an area of moral fragility since the first edition of the *Theory*, it was only in 1790 that Smith designated the disposition to worship the hierarchy of one's own society as 'the great and most universal cause of the corruption of our moral sentiments'.[18] And so we might further inquire whether Smith took this last step because he had been able to find an adequate counterpoise; yet this point is not to be made without previously providing specific instances of the corruption of moral sentiments.

The fractured public space whose tensions I have been sketching does not allow for an impartial spectator, that is a spectator who is indifferent to, and detached from, the pursuits of the three kinds of actors Smith described. As the impartial spectator is the central device in Smith's moral theory, which accounts for men's ability to develop and further articulate a growingly complex and autonomous moral life, I may be allowed briefly to recall that the impartial spectator, whose judgment is the moral standard, is initially a real man, but finally becomes a metaphor of men's ability to split in two and to act as moral judges of themselves *qua* agents. This internalized impartial spectator, Smith's 'man within', is the device by which a moral judgment that is formed only within the framework of social intercourse can eventually be formulated in a context-free decision. Saying that the fractured public space does not allow for an impartial spectator is not meant to imply that there can be no impartial spectator to look on in this realm, but that no process can be thought of by which impartiality of conscience may be formed on this ground. The impartial spectator grows up in the domain of private lives, in which the domestic side is dominant. The archetypal moral situation, that which defines the moral possibilities entailed by sympathy, is a situation in a private life, but one lived in the open. Two persons are quarrelling, and a third one is looking at them. That may happen in a family or at the market; but it seems that in either case people are observed, whether they like it or not. In that they are observed, all people are brought into the light of publicity, and the only domain that cannot be moralized is that which is withdrawn from scrutiny. The moral articulation of the private domain, so identified because it is not a general arena of interaction, but a circumscribed field of activity and intercourse, acquires in this way its character of basic moral structure. And a particular part of it can work as a model for the whole.

This is the domain of domestic law, as differentiated from private law. It is as a member of a family that man first learns to 'bring down his passions and restrain his will and so accommodate it to that of others as that they can go along with him'[19] and to look for sympathetic spectators to whom to appeal. It should not be taken as obvious that the elaboration of feelings, the ground for morality in Smith's theory, happens within the field of family relationships. The history of the family Smith recounted in the *Lectures on Jurisprudence* was the history of the ways in which the domestic sphere set between public jurisprudence and private law, a domain of relationships natural and at the same time political, that is of biology and of power, was reshaped into one of law and affection. Smith had to explain both historically and notionally how a domain of power relationships could be moralized. We are touching here on the crucial problem of the ways in which the abstract process of the formation of moral judgments is connected in Smith's writings to specific historical processes in European society.

If the process described is one of moralization and juridification, that is, a process by which direct exercise of power is substituted in many ways by feelings and laws, once again public and private are not pitted against each other in any simple way. As private and public are fields of activity and not modes of moralized behaviour, they are institutionally distinguishable, but not morally separable. There are moral and political consequences to this. Smith exploited the well-known lack of private virtues in times of public virtue to re-define virtue with the aid of a minimal natural and indivisible endowment—sympathy—as a device for achieving universalization. The abstract impartial spectator enables empirical observers to recognize that ancient virtue is defective, and in the end self-defeating, because the civic capacity of the *oikosdespotes* is grounded in the morally un-reconstructed sphere of his household. At the same time the internalized impartial spectator, once born, may be not prepared to exempt public men from his judgment. While no morally charged assault by private men is to be expected upon the government, it is to be expected that historically articulated human morality should make strictures upon the ways in which political power can be exercised.

Autonomous Agents from the Private to the Public Sphere

It has been said in several different ways that in Smith's moral theory, as in Hume's, human practical reason is left eventually defenceless against the contingencies of society.[20] As societies exist in history, any reconstruction of Smith's discourses that directly connects his view of the formation of personality as moral agency with his historicizing strategy in the analysis of origins, grounds and forms of government, and of systems of social and cultural relations, is bound to imply the same charge. Although the reflective elaboration of the natural senti-ment of sympathy which in Smith's view produces our articulate moral judgments may only with difficulty be subsumed under the law of opinion, it is certainly tempting to read into the impartial spectator a kind of enlightened public opinion. The natural feeling, which is meant to provide a barrier against human practical reason being penetrated by non-human agents in a causal chain, is avowedly weak. This natural endowment can be shown to be manipulable, and corruptible, possibly even tainted at the source, in a way that authorizes saying that sociologically determined opinion rules the moral world. The historical problem we face here is to understand what happened when authors employing a jurisprudential language abandoned the tenet of a state of nature and the law of the divine corporation, and attempted to explain that it was part of the nature of mankind to give laws to itself in history. Smith's defence of the autonomy of the self as moral agent might have been ineffective if measured by either an historical or a conceptual standard. But it certainly was no part of his intention (which is what I wish to reconstruct) to dismiss the importance of such a defence.

Smith in fact followed two roads in order to counter this ever present danger. In the first place he built a model of the ways it is possible for the individual to elaborate his natural feelings. It has to be emphasized that sympathy is just the thin ground on which the articulated and connected moral activity that is the formation of moral judgments takes place. It was shown to be a crucial part of this elaboration that the real impartial spectator could be reshaped into an 'abstract man, the representative of mankind'. This process of abstraction was being forced in human history by the experience of the conflict of interests and of injustice:

> When we first come into the world, from the natural desire to please, we accustom ourselves to consider what behaviour is likely to be agreeable to every person we converse with, to our parents, to our masters, to our companions. We address ourselves to individuals, and for some time fondly pursue the impossible and absurd project of gaining the good-will and approbation of every body. We are soon taught by experience, however, that this universal approbation is altogether unattainable ... In order to defend ourselves from such partial judgements, we soon learn to set up in our own minds a judge between ourselves and those we live with. We conceive ourselves as acting in the presence of a person quite candid and equitable, of one who has no particular relation either to ourselves, or to those whose interests are affected by our conduct, who is neither father, nor brother, nor friend either to them or to us, but is merely a man in general, an impartial spectator who considers our conduct with the same indifference with which we regard that of other people.[21]

It may be asked, of course, to what degree of abstraction Smith believed such a process could be carried, and what form it could eventually take. But these are historical questions on the exact nature of Smith's argument and categories, and should not be confused with the question of whether we can be satisfied with his arguments. He certainly believed that it was possible for individuals to abstract a standard of judgment from the web of their own emotional and social relationships.

The second strategy Smith pursued was to draw as sharp a distinction as possible between moral judgments on the one hand and customs and manners on the other. In Part V of the *Theory* Smith set about distinguishing the general rules of morality, whose origins and functions had been defined and analysed in Part III, from those mainly morally neutral rules which were fashion, custom and the manners they engendered. Fashion was easily disposed of, the main point about it being Smith's liberal downgrading of styles of life to an ethically indifferent field. Manners were a more complex problem, and were split in two. They were either subsumed under general rules of morality (as particular cases in definite professions, and as adaptations to circumstances), or set against morality in the most direct way. Smith denied forcefully that custom could authorize anything against those rules; but the main point is that he denied custom could morally authorize anything. Custom could not be a principle of moral legitimation. He was of course alert to the fact that morality could be theorized as custom, and had to be careful lest the process of the moralization of mankind he had been describing should be mistaken as a process of the building up of custom. He had also to account for the many immoral customs on display in human history. There was tension in his theory between history and virtue, but there would not be a defeat of virtue. Smith isolated immoral custom from the general style of manners which had taken and was taking place in any nation and in any time. There were no cases of immoral general styles.

In this way Smith insulated a core of man's moral life from the several principles of conduct in which it was articulated through history. At this point in the development of Smith's argument, the core could be conceived of as protected from the encroachments both of man's corruptible self and of society's corrupting hierarchies by a double agency, the natural sentiment of sympathy on one side, and the general rules of morality on the other. Real protection, however, comes not from the two separately taken. The real agency is the process by which men move continuously back and forth between feeling for other beings and elaborating the feeling into abstract rules, trusting neither of the two separately. The process of feeling, abstracting, and re-sentimentalizing, which implies detachment in any phase, ensures that in the end we are responsible for the systems of rules we endorse.[22] This means that in Smith's philosophy these systems can be historicized without historicizing the moral sentiments at the same time, and that these systems are legitimately subjected to moral scrutiny. Therefore what was engendered in the complicated process by which Smith distanced himself from natural jurisprudence and the 'divine corporation' view of the moral world was a keen perception of the way the rules we live by are never naturally legitimated. His move was a Cartesian-like one. The very smallness of mankind's sympathy is meant to promote distance between the natural endowment and the systems historically built up by agents, so that no confusion is possible. We have to see here a basic discontinuity in the natural jurisprudence tradition, where the very inclusiveness of the natural law ensured confusion. Within the old framework we are enjoined by natural law to obey the rules that are governing us; but in Smith's moral philosophy we are enjoined to keep such a system of rules (or to change it to face unintended consequences) that we can legitimately obey. If we fail to see this difference we are likely to misunderstand the meaning, both of his historicizing moves and of the relation he is outlining between morals, politics, and economics on the one hand, and his meta-ethical discourse about the ground of morality on the other.

The situation of representative publicness which is described by Smith as the baseline of the moral and political human condition should be historically interpreted as the *problem* from which he started. To the implied question Smith answered that there were ways out of it. They were, of course, to be taken as always circumstantial, to be perpetually defeated, and perpetually sought for again. As is appropriate within the framework of a general theory of moral life, those ways are moral and not political in character. Moreover, they are most successfully achieved in the intercourse of private lives. But the moral device by which they are brought about consists in making them, in a way, public, in so far as they can be publicly argued about.[23] This public moral argumentation is not to be lost to further application. Here we reach the point where the impartial spectator must be shown as able to provide independent criteria in the field of political actions so as to justify them. It is clear that unless those criteria can be proved both autonomous and politically sound and effective, there will be no way of bridging the gap between the impartial spectator of private lives and the public actor.

The Impartial Actor and Political Innovation

I mentioned at the beginning that mankind's tendency to go along with the sentiments of the great may have a corrupting effect on moral judgment. There are at least two instances in which this may happen. The first has to do with the poor. Attitudes despising the poor epitomize the inability to establish a moralized relationship because there is a lack of sympathy. As lack of sympathy prevents the appearance of an impartial spectator, no moral relation can be constructed. It can hardly be doubted that, in the presence of enduring English public concern with the poor, and the continuous debate over it, which reached new prominence in the second half of the century, Smith could take that lack of sympathy as a natural attitude not to be overcome. Once again, he was identifying a problem, not proposing an unavoidable solution.

The second great instance we are given of a corruption of moral sentiments is the rage of party. The spirit of faction reveals a situation from which again the impartial spectator is missing.

In a nation distracted by faction, there are, no doubt, always a few, though commonly but a very few, who preserve their judgment untainted by the general contagion. They seldom amount to more than, here and there, a solitary individual, without any influence, excluded, by his own candour, from the confidence of either party, and who, though he may be one of the wisest, is necessarily, upon that very account, one of the most insignificant men in the society ... A true party-man hates and despises candour; and, in reality, there is no vice which could so effectually disqualify him for the trade of a party-man as that single virtue. The real, revered, and impartial spectator, therefore, is, upon no occasion, at a greater distance than admits the violence and rage of contending parties ... Of all the corrupters of moral sentiments, therefore, faction and fanaticism have always been by far the greatest.[24]

We are here in that time of dissensions which is a morally crucial situation in Smith's theory. As public spirit is directly contrasted by him with the spirit of party, we are likely to find here a clue to the formation of a public sphere, and we would do well to start by noticing that the spirit of party looks very much like being the corruption of a situation where the dominant principle of legitimation is the public interest described in the *Lectures on Jurisprudence* as one of the two principles of political allegiance. But its centrality is of a more general character. The two sets of virtues out of which man lives his moral life, the virtues of humanity and those of self-command, are founded on the very same principle, but the situations in which men exercise and learn them are incompatible. History provides no neutral field of practice. 'Under the boisterous and stormy sky of war and faction, of public tumult and confusion, the sturdy severity of self-command prospers the most, and can be most successfully cultivated. But, in such situations, the strongest suggestions of humanity must frequently be stifled or neglected; and every such neglect necessarily tends to weaken the principle of humanity.'[25] This situation therefore presents a problem for the balance of moral personality. But within a natural jurisprudential framework it is crucial in one more sense. It is the moment at which a law-centred vision has to face a discontinuity in the law. and has therefore possibly to resort to some other resource. It is very much a Machiavellian situation, and innovation is at the centre of it. Men divide into factions on a principle of conservation on the one side and innovation on the other. Faction ensues because the constitution, that is the balance of the state's different orders, for whatever reasons, has failed.

The love of our country seems, in ordinary cases, to involve in it two different principles; first a certain respect and reverence for that constitution or form of government which is actually established; and secondly, an earnest desire to render the condition of our fellow-citizens as safe, respectable, and happy as we can. He is not a citizen who is not disposed to respect the laws and to obey the civil magistrate; and he is certainly not a good citizen who does not wish to promote, by every means in his power, the welfare of the whole society of his fellow citizens.

In peaceable and quiet times, those two principles generally coincide and lead to the same conduct . . . But in times of public discontent, faction, and disorder, those two different principles may draw different ways, and even a wise man may be disposed to think some alteration necessary in that constitution or form of government, which, in its actual condition, appears plainly unable to maintain the public tranquillity. In such cases, however, it often requires, perhaps, the highest effort of political wisdom to determine when a real patriot ought to support and endeavour to re-establish the authority of the old system, and when he ought to give way to the more daring, but often dangerous spirit of innovation.[26]

When read against the background of Smith's distinction between the principle of authority and the principle of utility, and of Hume's historical and philosophical account of the British parties, both on the eve of the Civil War and after the Settlement, the situation described displays some interesting features. What is new in it is that the principle of conservation is linked to the defence of the particular interests which constitute the balance, the principle of innovation to the wish to promote the general welfare. Although there is no logical reason why, in the display of public spirit this situation brings forth, the two parties should be treated asymmetrically, in the following page they are; both the dangers and the glory belong to the party of innovation. We are advised in this way that we are entering here the field of an argument which is affected by a developmental perspective about particular circumstances, and before analysing them the general framework of a public spirit has to be rehearsed.

Public spirit is engendered by ambition, the beauty of utility, and a kind of generosity. Since none of them is considered spurious as a motive for 'exertions of public spirit', Smith has no reason for not allowing them to concur; but the principles on which each is founded are altogether different. Public spirit engendered by love of system, by 'regard to the beauty of order, of art and contrivance',[27] is grounded on admiration for the means, while discounting the ends. The men of public spirit moved by this principle can therefore lack sensitivity to the feelings of humanity. They lack sympathy. If these persons are innovators, they are dangerously so because they recognize no limits to their love of system. The imperial and royal reformers who appear in the last page of Part VI are of this character, and we can recognize in them the incompetent great of the beginning turned activists.[28]

Innovation, or reform, is a morally exacting policy because it implies interference with the interests, privileges, opinions and expectations of people, without leaving them the choice of the innumerable transactions that normally constitute the texture of human life. For this reason innovation cannot be pursued without a full comprehension of other people's autonomy through sympathy, and a full identification of the innovator with the impartial spectator. There is an unresolved contradiction in public spirit prompted by love of system. The love of system leads towards a desire for perfection in the machine of society and government, that is, towards innovation, but at the same time it does not provide the ground for that fully articulated moral attitude political innovation actually requires.

Political innovation requires enlarged generosity, that is the ability to weigh one's own choices against others' perceived situations, as the impartial spectator would do. It requires 'that public spirit which is founded upon the love of humanity, upon a real fellow-feeling with the inconveniences and distresses to which some of our fellow-citizens may be exposed'.[29] It requires that the legislator think not of himself, of the interests he is defending, or of the plans he is forwarding, so much as of the totality of the situation. It puts on the shoulder of the legislator the demanding task of exercising authority over others while recognizing moral equality with them. All in all, reform as a policy requires a particular moral environment. Its heavy demands have to do with the problems of morality, not with those of knowledge. Smith's cautious attitude to innovation and reform has less to do with a mistrust of systematic knowledge as against circumstantial knowledge than with a heightened sense of the moral fragility, which ever menaces the exercise of necessary power. At this point, the impartial spectator is both a moral structure and an effective dimension of political action, to the extent that moderation brought forth by sympathy for the other calls for responsive moderation from the other side. Far from being self-defeating, it may be a self-confirming policy.

The legislator is the leader of the successful party.[30] After he has won, he must enforce his own plans in the same way as an impartial spectator would dictate, refraining from 'great violence', or even force, applying 'reason and persuasion' instead. On this ground, the character of a legislator has to be understood as implying that a structured public life, as distinct from the legitimate exercise of power in civil society, is possible on two conditions. First, the legislator is capable of public virtue in that he is capable of a fully articulated moral life which has taught him how to deal morally with his fellow beings. There can be no public virtue unless full private humanity can be translated into it. The second condition is that a multiplicity of virtuous motivations (ambition, love of system, generosity, humanity) has to be available to the legislator. This condition overlaps with the first, but is by no means the same, since the multiplicity of motives is taken by Smith to be the normal condition of virtuous conduct. Nevertheless there are specific requirements here. The legislator first of all legislates morality to himself, and thereby states both a procedure and a standard which enables conflicting groups to reach agreement. There is ascendancy here, but it would be of no avail if the other could not be convinced. We have here a piece of the philosophy of liberal legislation, and we can also understand the historical process by which it was engendered within the field of moral philosophy, and not within the political discourse on sovereignty.

The crucial sentences I have quoted are taken from Part VI about the character of virtue, which was added to the 1790 edition. Two points have to be emphasized about it.[31] First, as philosophical speculations about the character of virtue have necessarily 'some influence upon our notions of right and wrong in many particular cases',[32] the question concerning the nature of virtue, which is a philosophical question about a matter of fact, has normative import and allows for normative discourse. In consequence, Smith's explanation of the legislator's action has to be read with a due regard for his intentions, and seen both as an account of factually possible events in the likely circumstamces and as a circumstantial imperative. Secondly, it seems that Smith's new elaboration of the character of virtue, showing the way men may be able to build up their moral personalities in history, enabled him to express in the most forceful way how our moral sentiments risk being corrupted in society. The strength of corruption and the strength of moral character can now be seen as balancing each other. Therefore, Smith's re-elaboration of the last chapter in Part I for the 1790 edition can be seen as closely connected to this new part.

The victorious leader possibly won by force. Although we need not conceive of force in any simple way—and we know Smith thought there were complex reasons for any kind of supremacy—nevertheless the unstated modes of the victory present a problem. While we should not make too much of the implications of this single point, it is certainly telling about the ways Smith could envisage a change in the constitution. The constitution being in his theory primarily the material distribution of power between the orders of the country, and only secondarily the formalized shape of the exercise of power, a sudden, perhaps a violent endeavour to adapt the second to slow changes in the first is a likely event. Anyway, a change in the constitution does not happen by innumerable obscure transactions hidden in prescription. It happens publicly and by deliberation after a period of crisis and breakdown. The relationship of innovation to continuity—the legislator both *re-establishes* and *improves* the constitution—is both exposed and debated.[33] We may ask at this point what the institutional setting of such a debate may be.

The Public Relevance of Private Lives

The extreme situation of a legislator after a time of crisis has given us the clue about how a world of public men can be envisaged. The criterion which is morally binding upon the legislator is of such a character that it applies in any station of life. Public men are those people who are responsive to it. The first political problem that is raised in this way is what ability for public spirit the sovereign has. The question itself is a reversal of the jurisprudential question about what political agency is left to individuals after they have contracted out of their natural sovereignty. The question is now rather what ability for moral agency is left to those who exercise sovereignty, that is, those for whom ascendancy makes it unduly difficult to feel sympathy, to recognize mankind's basic equality. And this question becomes urgent at the moment at which sovereignty is seen as vested in a parliament, as Robertson contends Smith was doing.[34] At this moment the ethos of the sovereign need not be left to the random distribution of goods of the mind among anointed monarchs; it may well be discussed in morals and politics. In the end, Smith thought that virtuous attitudes were common amongst the middle ranks in upwardly mobile societies. In the micropolitics of private lives in a stabilized world, *fortuna* was probabilistically the daughter of virtue, so that there could scarcely exist a confrontation between *fortuna* and virtue for the middling ranks. They merely had to learn not to worship their society. And for contemporary British society Smith was even able to find, in his economic discourse, a supporting mechanism for the virtues of the common labourer. It was more difficult to predict the limits to the continuous existence of such an upwardly mobile society that rendered independent virtue a social achievement. It was equally difficult to identify an ethos for the ruling classes that might be more than the worshipping of their own superiority, since they were an hereditary rather than a natural aristocracy. Public spirit was a problem precisely because the men to whom the public was entrusted were by their very nature torn between indifference towards their fellow men's problems and an arrogant zeal in scheming plans of perfection.

As we are shifting here to Smith's evaluation of British contemporary circumstances, a gap has to be expected between the baseline of the common condition of mankind and an historical late achievement. As is well known, Smith was none too sanguine about the general political course British governments were following, and had been following, since the Revolution Settlement. But neither was he pessimistic about the educational possibilities for the British ruling classes. After all, the idea he had formed of their public spirit implied the description of a suitable balance between their ascendancy and a sense of the equality of mankind. As against the 'pomp and splendour' that had been the code of the Roman nobility, the style of the British Senate's behaviour had at least the appearance of that of an impartial spectator. 'The behaviour which is reckoned polite in England is a calm, composed, unpassionate serenity ... We are not then to expect that any thing passionate or exagerated will be admitted in the house of Lords. Nothing will be receiv'd there which is not or at least appears not to be a plain, just and exact account.'[35]

A plain, just and exact account is an account that could be approved of by the impartial spectator. We reach here the point where we might say that virtue is the taking into account of what other people think their rights are, whatever the origin and the form of these rights. This acknowledgement is the public sphere of men's lives.

In conclusion, in Smith's theory the conceptualization of public and private is neither one of two spheres in which different goods are pursued, nor one authorizing different kinds of actions in the two spheres. If ethics is about human motives, then motives cross the boundaries between spheres of action, so that these cannot be distinguished on a moral ground.[36] The point is so important in Smith's account that even the jurisdictional dichotomy can be seen as problematical. If there is a dimension of virtue by which all men in a way can be public, then private virtue that constitutes the texture of social life is a public concern, and, as there is no equality of ruling and being ruled, this sets a problem for freedom. On the one hand, 'even the most ordinary degree of kindness or beneficence . . . cannot, among equals, be extorted by force'; on the other,

> the civil magistrate is entrusted with the power not only of preserving the public peace by restraining injustice, but of promoting the prosperity of the commonwealth, by establishing good discipline, and by discouraging every sort of vice and impropriety; he may prescribe rules, therefore, which not only prohibit mutual injuries among fellow-citizens, but command mutual good offices to a certain degree . . . Of all the duties of a law-giver, however, this, perhaps, is that which it requires the greatest delicacy and reserve to execute with propriety and judgment. To neglect it altogether exposes the commonwealth to many gross disorders and shocking enormities, and to push it too far is destructive of all liberty, security, and justice.[37]

This is a situation where the power of the magistrate is not only a relationship between himself and his fellow-citizens, but is defined by the relations between the citizens themselves. His power appears to be complementary to their ability to define freely and satisfactorily their own relationships. As could be expected of someone who had never acknowledged either the state of nature or an original contract, Smith was reiterating that the spheres of civil government and private freedom, justice and the good life, had always to be redefined in history. To the historian this means that, if we wish to inquire further into the relation between Smith's politics and his economics, we should start from the fact that private and public, as they are connected in his moral philosophy, posit a redrawing of what is to be the political.

Notes

1. I wish to thank Ed Hundert for the generosity with which he has spent his time in improving my text. Financial support from the MURST, the Italian Ministry of University and Scientific Research, is gratefully acknowledged.
2. R. Koselleck, *Kritik und Krise. Ein Beitrag zur Pathogenese der bürgerlichen Welt* (Freiburg und München, 1959) pp. 1 and 8.
3. See S. Benhabib, 'Models of Public Space: Hannah Arendt, the Liberal Tradition, and Jürgen Habermas' in C. Calhoun (ed.) *Habermas and the Public Sphere* (Cambridge, MA and London, 1992).
4. For a reappraisal and endorsement of the classical distinction see N. Bobbio, 'La grande dicotomia: pubblico/privato' in *Stato, governo, società* (Torino, 1985).

5. J.G.A. Pocock, *The Machiavellian Moment: Florentine Political Thought and the Atlantic Republican Tradition* (Princeton, 1975); J.G.A. Pocock, *Virtue, Commerce, and History: Essays on Political Thought and History, Chiefly in the Eighteenth Century* (Cambridge, 1985) pp. 43–45, 70–71, 114ff; 'The Myth of John Locke and the Obsession with Liberalism' in J.G.A. Pocock and R. Ashcraft, *John Locke* (Los Angeles, 1980) pp. 16–17. For a view of the Scottish Enlightenment, and Adam Smith within it, as an answer to the civic humanist perspective, see particularly N.T. Phillipson, 'Towards a Definition of the Scottish Enlightenment', in P. Fritz and D. Williams (eds) *City and Society in the Eighteenth Century* (Toronto, 1973) pp. 125–47; 'Culture and society in the 18th Century Province: the Case of Edinburgh and the Scottish Enlightenment' in L. Stone (ed.) *The University in Society* (Princeton, 1974) pp. 407–48; and J. Robertson, 'The Scottish Enlightenment at the Limits of the Civic Tradition' in I. Hont and M. Ignatieff (eds) *Wealth and Virtue: The Shaping of Political Economy in the Scottish Enlightenment* (Cambridge, 1983) pp. 137–178.
6. A. Smith, *The Theory of Moral Sentiments* ed. by D.D. Raphael and A.L. Macfie (Oxford, 1976) I.iii.2.5. Hereafter referred to as *Theory*.
7. *Theory* I.iii.2.3. Note the reduction to triviality of *vita beata*.
8. *Theory* I.iii.2.4, and I.iii.2.1.
9. J. Habermas, *The Structural Transformation of the Public Sphere: An Inquiry into a Category of Bourgeois society* (Cambridge, MA, 1989) pp. 7 and 12.
10. W. Moyle, *An Essay upon the Constitution of the Roman Government* in *Two English Republican Tracts*, ed. by C. Robbins, (Cambridge, 1969) p. 250. For Mandeville in the Scottish context see Th.A. Horne, 'Envy and Commercial Society: Mandeville and Smith on "Private Vices, Public Benefits" ' *Political Theory* 9 (1981) pp. 551–69; M.M. Goldsmith, 'Regulating Anew the Moral and Political Sentiments of Mankind: Bernard Mandeville and the Scottish Enlightenment' *Journal of the History of Ideas* 40 (1988) pp. 587–606. I was happy to find the same kind of *problematique* I am sketching here in two chapters of E.J. Hundert's *The Enlightenment's Fable: Bernard Mandeville and the Discovery of Society* (Cambridge, 1994), which the author kindly let me read before publication.
11. G.J. Schochet, *The Authoritarian Family and Political Attitudes in 17th-Century England: Patriarchalism in Political Thought* (Oxford, 1975; repr. New Brunswick and London, 1988) pp. 10–12.
12. A notable instance of reading Smith's text out of context is J.C.D. Clark, *English Society 1688-1832: Ideology, Social Structure and Political Practice during the Ancien Regime* (Cambridge, 1985) pp. 55–56.
13. My attention was drawn to Nicole's essay in the English context by David Wootton's identification of an anonymous pamphlet of 1675 as a translation from Nicole. My quotations are from this edition: *The Grounds of Sovereignty and Greatness* (London, 1675) pp. 8 and 11. The text does not seem to me to differ from the well-known translation in the *Moral Essays* of 1678. See D. Wootton, *Divine Right and Democracy: An Anthology*

of Political Writing in Stuart England (Harmondsworth, 1986) pp. 74–75. J. Viner, *The Role of Providence in the Social Order: An Essay in Intellectual History* (Princeton, 1972) pp. 56–57, while reviewing Nicole's views about the invisible hand, did not connect him directly to Smith's moral philosophy.

14. F. Hutcheson, *An Inquiry into the Original of our Ideas of Beauty and Virtue* (London, 1725) p. 213.

15. Since both are grounded in the need for recognition, which involves the actor in a zero-sum game, and are set within the context of a monarchical and aristocratic civil society, individual interests must be in competition and may be in conflict, with consequences for the way Smith conceived of the clash of social and economic interests. There are important implications for my argument in Q. Skinner, 'The Republican Ideal of Political Liberty' in G. Bock, Q. Skinner and M. Viroli (eds) *Machiavelli and Republicanism* (Cambridge, 1990) pp. 293–309, where a republican ideal of negative liberty is reconstructed.

16. What I describe as a shift from an ethics of ends to an ethics of motives can also be described as an exit from the ethical model of the 'Divine Corporation' as defined by J.B. Schneewind, 'The Divine Corporation and the History of Ethics' in R. Rorty, J.B. Schneewind and Q. Skinner (eds) *Philosophy in History: Essays on the Historiography of Philosophy* (Cambridge, 1984) pp. 173–91. The case he makes about Kant's ambivalences seems to parallel Smith's case. I am not asserting that there are not in fact arguments in the *Theory* which are very much part of an ethics of ends; just that they are subordinated, however awkwardly, to a different framework. By Schneewind see also 'Natural Law, Skepticism, and Methods of Ethics' *Journal of the History of Ideas*, 102 (1991) pp. 289–308 (p. 302).

17. *Theory* I.iii.2.8.

18. *Theory* I.iii.3.1.

19. *Theory* I.iii.5. D. Gobetti, *Private and Public: Individuals, Households, and Body Politic in Locke and Hutcheson* (London and New York, 1992), shows how the models of the relations in the private sphere within the natural jurisprudence paradigm impinge on the conceptualization of political agency in the public sphere.

20. I take J. Dunn, 'From Applied Theology to Social Analysis: the Break between John Locke and the Scottish Enlightenment' in *Wealth and Virtue*, pp. 119-35, to be the best presentation of this line of argument. For the opposite view see K. Haakonssen, *The Science of a Legislator: The Natural Jurisprudence of David Hume and Adam Smith* (Cambridge, 1981) pp. 54ff.

21. *Theory* pp. 130 and 129, text from editions 2–5.

22. The case made by Smith in *Theory* III.6.13, is that of a 'bigoted Roman Catholic' who, during the massacre of St. Bartholomew, saves some Protestants out of compassion, but cannot be entirely approved because he does so against his sense of duty.

23. Since the road followed by Smith set him against some of the most celebrated moralists of his age we may well tell him apart from the most famous 'Spectator' of his century. The Addisonian impartial spectator can be an onlooker in that he behaves as if dumb, and he is prepared to resign speech because he does not want to be looked at. He exercises influence by hints and example. He lives 'in the world rather as a spectator of mankind, than as one of the species'. The Smithian spectator is a highly articulated member of the species who is ever in dialogue with other members; in a proper sense moral judgment can only be a debate in which disputants are equal.

24. *Theory* III.3.43.

25. *Theory* III.3.37.

26. *Theory* VI.ii.2.11–12.

27. *Theory* IV.1.11.

28. I agree that the *économistes* are a very important target of these remarks by Smith, as shown by I. Hont, 'The Political Economy of the "Unnatural and Retrograde" Order: Adam Smith and Natural Liberty' in *Französische Revolution und Politische Ökonomie: Schriften aus dem Karl-Marx-Haus* (Trier, 1989) pp. 122–49. But my interpretation of the general theoretical import of those passages is markedly different.

29. *Theory* VI.ii.2.15.

30. It is indirectly but very clearly implied in Smith's text that the successful party is the party of innovation. This accounts for the fact that all his warnings are for that party; but it leaves us wondering about the outcome of a conservative party of principle and system winning the hand. It leaves us speculating as well about a likely Smithian inclination to think of a conservative party as a non-principled party, as a party of traditional authority.

31. There had been enough political tension about reform in Britain during the late 1780s to provide a realistically specific background to the re-thematization of civil dissensions, re-establishment and innovation.

32. *Theory* VII.iii.intro.3.

33. One consequence is that Smith's lesson in moderation is of a different kind from Hume's. Hume's moderation is very much a matter of right judgment, when not of exposing private interests concealed 'under pretence of public good'. Smith's explanation implies more troubled situations and less settled minds; it is more responsive to the varieties of situations in history, and more keenly aware of the dangers to which the achieved peace, freedom and politeness are likely to expose men's characters.

34. J. Robertson, 'The Legacy of Adam Smith: Government and Economic Development in the *Wealth of Nations*' in R. Bellamy (ed.) *Victorian Liberalism: Nineteenth Century Political Thought and Practice* (London and New York, 1990) pp. 15–41.

35. A. Smith, *Lectures on Rhetoric and Belles Lettres* ed. by J. C. Bryce (Oxford, 1983) ii.249–250, and 251.

36. For this reason I think there is a basic misunderstanding of Smith's views in R. Nieli, 'Spheres of Intimacy and the Adam Smith Problem' *Journal of the History of Ideas* 97 (1986) pp. 611–24.
37. *Theory* II.ii.1.8.

Eleven

William Godwin and the Idea of Historical Commemoration: History as Public Memory and Private Sentiment

Mark Salber Phillips

> ... strangers, when they visit France, will hasten with impatience
> to the Champs de Mars, filled with that enthusiasm which is
> awakened by the view of a place where any great scene has been
> acted. I think I hear them exclaim, 'here the Federation was held!'
> ... I see them pointing out the spot on which the altar of the
> country stood. I see them eagerly searching for the place where
> they have heard it recorded, that the National Assembly were
> seated! I think of these things, and then repeat to myself with
> transport, 'I, was a spectator of the Federation'.
>   Helen Maria Williams, *Letters from France* (1790)

Helen Maria Williams's sense of historical pilgrimage is rooted in some
of the oldest habits of western culture, but it also points to a perception
of history that has been increasingly cultivated since her time.[1] The
idea of public commemoration by marking 'historic sites' is a pervasive
feature of contemporary societies. For us, history is not only a story to
be narrated; it is an experience to be evoked, and no form of evocation
is more widespread than the practice of erecting commemorative plaques
and monuments. History, traditionally regarded as a book to be read,
has become a scene to be revisited.[2]

This intermingling of the associations of past and place has become
so pervasive that we take it for granted. But apparently this was not

yet so in Britain at the end of the eighteenth century. Nearly twenty years after Williams published the first volume of her history, another English friend of the Revolution, William Godwin, outlined a proposal for evoking England's own past by raising a subscription to mark in the simplest possible manner the burial places of notable men. It is striking, however, that Godwin advanced his *Essay on Sepulchres* (1809) as a kind of visionary experiment—a 'speculation and solemn reverie' —whose feasibility even he could not really credit. Indeed the work, which Godwin published at his own expense, seems to have attracted very little notice, then or since.[3]

The interest of Godwin's essay, however, is not simply its anticipation of later commemorative programmes. Godwin's essay proves to be one of a number of contemporary texts that explore the emotional resonances of historic places by calling on the psychological doctrine of association. Taken together, these texts show the power of associationalism—joined with other aspects of the culture of sensibility—to cultivate a response to the scenes of history that is essentially inward. The consequence of this intensified interest in private and subjective experience was to undermine a hitherto unquestioned identification of history with public life and public lessons.

In the classical tradition that has dominated the writing of history in the West, history was regarded as a narrative of public acts by public men—a definition that excludes forms of experience as well as classes of people that seem to lie outside of this focus on public agency. Similarly, the prime audience for history was thought to consist of those who might benefit from the kinds of public lessons history offers. In short, 'publicness' was universally regarded as a key marker of historical writing, setting it off from competitive genres whose audiences—men without public standing or classical education, as well as women of all classes—would be attracted to more private pathways offered in biographies, memoirs, and novels.[4]

Godwin's proposal would alter history's traditional face with respect to both public and private memory. The simple grave-markers he wanted to see erected could not determine the contents or lessons of the past in the ways that are possible in more elaborate forms of com-memoration and especially in narrative. Thus a systematic programme of historical markers would create a more open theatre for remembrance, adding a new dimension to history's traditional public role.[5] But Godwin does not stop with the public meaning of past lives. His evocation of the historical associations of place aims to intensify the sense of inward engagement with historical experience as much as to mark a public space. Like Williams's historical pilgrims, visitors to

Godwin's commemorated sites would be invited to participate in a new relationship to history that is essentially inward and spectatorial. In this way, Godwin's 'reverie', along with other contemporary explorations of historical association, represents an historical sensibility undergoing a transformation brought about by the value given to private experience.

I

The central idea of Godwin's *Sepulchres* is stated in its subtitle—'a proposal for erecting some memorial of the illustrious dead in all ages on the spot where their remain has been interred'. Characteristically, he begins his essay on historical memory with the personal experience of bereavement, founding his sense of the value of public commemoration on sentiments of affection and loss that are both universal and private. The loss of a friend, he writes, is the greatest of all the losses we can sustain; to us 'his person was a little world'—and though Godwin keeps to the masculine pronoun, we inevitably think of his account of the death of Mary Wollstonecraft, which readers found so affecting.[6] When a friend dies, it is impossible to separate our sense of him from reminders of his physical person. As a result, 'every thing which practically has been *associated* with my friend acquires a value from that consideration; his ring, his watch, his books, and his habitation. The value of these as having been his, is not merely fictitious; they have an empire over my mind; they can make me happy or unhappy; they can torture, and they can tranquillise; they can purify my sentiments, and make me similar to the man I love . . .'[7]

The extraordinary power Godwin attributes to these objects has nothing to do with their ordinary physical qualities or functions; their value lies in the fact that they are the survivors of the 'little world' we have lost. Thus their 'empire' lies entirely—and arbitrarily—in their biographical associations. Public memories, too, are governed by the same associationalist principle. But in this public context, the place of burial takes on the function of provoking recollection. For this reason, Godwin urges the importance of marking the very spot where the illustrious dead lie buried. This insistent literalness may come as a surprise to the modern reader, for whom 'association' is a weaker, more metaphoric concept:

> Man is a creature who depends for his feelings upon the operations of sense . . . When I have visited the monuments of our English kings, I study their transactions in a graver spirit than before.

Portraits may be imaginary; the scenes where great events have occurred are the scenes of these events no longer; but the dust that is covered by his tomb, is simply and literally *the great man himself*.[8]

These sentiments underline the difference between Godwin's proposal and contemporary programmes of memorial statuary blossoming in the patriotic atmosphere of the struggle with France.[9] In contrast to the classically-draped statues of British naval heroes that were beginning to fill St. Paul's, Godwin's plan asks only for the simplest of markers to fix the place of burial. Though he does not say so, this plainness suited the contemporary psychological doctrine of associationalism, which argued that the power of association would be greatest where the linkages between ideas were least subject to distracting interruption. A horizontal stone, a tablet on a wall, in rural areas a plain wooden cross—these simple memorials would offer no images of the hero. Nor would the tribute be removed from the landscape to enhance a national pantheon or decorate the monuments to civic pride springing up in provincial centres. On the contrary, in Godwin's vision, everything would be left to the power of association and to the sense of place. In consequence, unlike the monuments that found official favour and changed the urban landscapes of London or Birmingham, Godwin's speculative programme of commemoration finds its home in the private life of the individual mind. Sumptuousness and decoration are not required by his plan, Godwin writes, 'the object is to mark the place where the great and the excellent of the earth repose, and to leave the rest to the mind of the spectator.'[10]

At the heart of *Sepulchres* stands Godwin's own emotional response to the places of history. Among the 'accidents' that led him to his proposal was a visit to Westminster, where he found that most of the great figures he looked for had been missed out. Pilgrimage to another abbey—Thetford in Norfolk —brought out the elegiac strain in his romance of place:

As I wandered through the limits of the enclosure, I trod upon the remains of the Bigods, the Mowbrays, and the Howards, men who in their day had exhibited vast magnificence, and upheld the pride of chivalry, who in their passions had shaken states, and in their untamed fierceness had bid defiance to the resentments of kings. Ponderous monuments graced with sculptures and diversi- fied with copious sepulchral inscriptions, once marked the place where they lay; and marble clamped with iron, and defended with balustrades, protected it from invasion. All now was speechless, and the grass grew as freely where their bones reposed, as over a peasant's grave.[11]

The politics of this elegy differ markedly from the radicalism of *Political Justice* (1793). But as he demonstrates in historical works as well as his novels, the romantic associations of the Middle Ages hold a strong attraction to Godwin. In *Sepulchres*, however, the main point is to demonstrate his own susceptibility to the historical associations that attach themselves to the landscape of old England—to offer himself, in short, as an example of the power of place at work. The Tower, the House of Commons, the scenes of battle in the Civil War: such places have a power to 'call up'—to use his earlier phrase—the life of the nation:

> I never understood the annals of chivalry so well, as when I walked among the ruins of Kenilworth Castle. I no longer trusted to the tale of the historian, the cold and uncertain record of words formed upon paper, I beheld the queen, 'of lion-port,
>> Girt with many a baron bold,
>> And gorgeous dames,
> uprear her starry front.' The subtle, the audacious and murder-dealing Leicester stood before me. I heard the trampling of horses, and the clangour of trumpets.[12]

In imagination, Godwin has become a direct witness of the scenes of history. In this place of historical pilgrimage, he can *see* and *hear* the life of medieval England with an immediacy no narrative could match—or could only match, as Godwin does here, by a strategy that calls attention to the inadequacy of the 'old and uncertain record of words'.

At other times, another voice speaks out, one not less romantic, but prophetic rather than nostalgic in its intonations:

> I would say with Ezekiel, the Hebrew, in his Vision, 'Let these dry bones live! Not let them live merely in cold generalities and idle homilies of morality; but let them live, as my friends, my philosophers, my instructors, and my guides!
>
> The men that have lived, are they less important than the men of the present day? Had their thoughts less of sinew and substance; were their passions less earnest, their conceptions less vigorous, their speech less fervent, or their deeds less lofty and less real, than ours? ... To him who is of a mind rightly framed, the world is a thousand times more populous, than to the man, to whom everything that is not flesh and blood, is nothing ... They are not

dead. They are still with us in their stories, in their words, in their writings, in the consequences that do not cease to flow fresh from what they did: they still have their place, where we may visit them, and where, if we dwell in a composed and a quiet spirit, we shall not fail to be conscious of their presence.

What I plead for in the present proposal, is that by a simple and perhaps infallible means, we should paralyse the hand of Oblivion.[13]

In these places, Godwin seems to anticipate Thomas Carlyle, and like Carlyle in *Heroes and Hero Worship*, he has heroes of the spirit uppermost in his mind. He argues for a generous and inclusive programme of commemoration, but he worries that ordinary people will be drawn to military and naval figures, rather than the writers and thinkers that populate his own imagination. Great military figures like Scipio have 'dwindled into a name', he insists, while the ancient poets and philosophers have come down to us entire. They 'appear' before us in all their wholeness and individuality, and still have the power to illuminate our souls.[14]

Another kind of difficulty is posed by the literalness of his belief in finding the exact place of burial. There must be no room to suspect that the marker is simply a convenient fiction; such scepticism would muffle the evocative power of the actual grave. Fortunately, Godwin writes, it happens that a 'spirit of antiquarian research' is one of the characteristics of the present age, and he ends the essay with a proposal that nicely combines his antiquarian and sentimentalist interests. An atlas should be created which would ensure permanence and exact knowledge of burial sites, even in times of unrest—a proviso that says much about the wider context in which his project for commemoration was conceived. In addition, there must be a catalogue. This document 'might be despicable to the literal man and the calculator; but it would be a precious relic to the man of sentiment, and prove to be a Traveller's Guide, of a very different measure of utility, from the "Catalogue of Gentlemen's Seats", which is now appended to the "Book of Post Roads through Every Part of Gt. Britain".'[15]

II

As I have indicated, Godwin presents his essay as a kind of visionary proposal, one without precedent and quite probably without practicality. Even so, his tacit use of associationalist doctrines indicates an essential background to his ideas. Here Archibald Alison's *Essays on the Nature and Principles of Taste* (1790) is a key text.

Neither Alison's sermons nor his *Essays* show him to be a man for whom history is a central interest; nonetheless, in developing his psychology of aesthetic emotions, Alison gives attention to history as a rich source of associational images. This exploration of the power of historical association opens up possibilities for a new reading of history—one which might undercut history's traditional emphasis on public instruction in favour of its newly articulated powers of evocation.[16]

Alison brings together two influential themes in eighteenth-century thought. Writers on art and aesthetics hoped to give their judgments a sounder philosophical basis by shifting attention from the qualities of objects to the processes of perception. Concurrently, Hume, Hartley, and others thought that the 'association of ideas' might explain how the mind could build complex ideas out of simple perceptions. Alison systematically applied the principle of the association of ideas to the question of taste so as to give the fullest play to the powers of association in determining the way in which we experience beauty. In his hands, the association of ideas becomes so flexible a conductor of emotional currents that parts of life until now little touched by the contemporary tendency to aestheticize experience can flow with new feeling.

The essence of Alison's general argument is that, 'Matter is not beautiful in itself, but derives its beauty from the Expression of Mind.'[17] When a beautiful object is presented to the mind, we are conscious of a 'train of thought' awakened in the imagination. This imaginative response is richer than anything the object alone could produce and may even have little ostensible relation to the object itself—a gap that is made up by the principle of the association of ideas.[18] Alison believes that the associative process is automatic, and he emphasizes that it is quickest and most intense where the the imagination is most free and spontaneous. 'It is, then, indeed, in this powerless state of reverie,' he writes, 'when we are carried on by our conceptions, not guiding them, that the deepest emotions of beauty or sublimity are felt, that our hearts swell with feelings which language is too weak to express, and that in the depth of silence and astonishment we pay to the charm that enthrals us, the most flattering mark of our applause.'[19]

I have already indicated that Godwin tacitly endorsed this doctrine in his choice of simple, undecorated grave-markers. From the standpoint of classical historiography, on the other hand, cultivating the 'powerless state of reverie' undermines fundamental principles that give history its ethical value. It is a long way from Alison's dreamy spectatorialism to the humanist's claim that history instructs the active will. The suspended animation in which associationalist currents move most powerfully is a deeply private state of mind, far removed from the alertness to public lessons inculcated by exemplary history.[20]

When Alison turns from the general mechanism of association to the more specific question of its sources and influences, private experience remains prominent. The 'interesting recollections of childhood' bring special meaning to particular scenes or books, or perhaps to a favourite piece of music. 'The view of the house where one was born', Alison writes, 'or of the school where one was educated and the gay years of infancy were passed, are indifferent to no man.'[21] But biographical associations of a less personal kind can also have the same effect. Places linked to people we admire possess an emotional resonance, even when the landscape itself has little attraction. Memories of the dead mingle with the scenery to produce a kind of sanctity in the place. 'There are scenes, undoubtedly, more beautiful than Runnymede,' he writes, 'yet to those who recollect the great event which passed there, there is no scene, perhaps, which so strongly seizes upon the imagination.'

The emotions excited by historical recollection are very different from any that natural scenery by itself could produce, but they 'unite themseves' with the inferior emotions in such a way that the scene itself seems charmed.[22] The Vaucluse is made more beautiful by the memory of Petrarch; the Alps become still more majestic by association with Hannibal's crossing; 'and who is there, that could stand on the banks of the Rubicon without feeling his imagination kindle, and his heart beat high?'[23] Similarly, the field of any celebrated battle becomes sublime through association. 'No man, acquainted with English history, can behold the field of Agincourt, without some emotion of this kind. The additional conceptions which this association produces, and which fill the mind of the spectator on the prospect of that memorable field, diffuse themselves in some measure over the scene, and give it a sublimity which does not naturally belong to it.'

At Agincourt, as envisioned by Alison, history and landscape blend into each other. All parts of the scene come together in a single experience that is both vivid and curiously indistinct. The mind, in consequence, is filled with a new emotion, an historical sublime, in which the associations of time and place run together. The resulting view of the actual field of battle is deliberately hazy, leaving the spectator free to pursue his own inward vision of history.

But Alison, whose theory is universal, does not limit himself to such exalted scenes. Association springs from experience in all its forms. It is shaped by nationality, by social station, by habits of work—all of which add up to bodies of shared knowledge. The more we know of any subject, he writes, the more meaning it has for us and the richer may be its effects. Thus the peasant has no sense of the beauty of a mathematical theory, nor does the habitual townsman respond to the pleasures of the countryside. Professional knowledge, similarly, endows the painter with a greater delight in the technical triumphs of a colleague than the layman can understand. For the same reasons, educated men will enjoy everything reminiscent of classical times—and for those most immersed in antiquities, the effect is most powerful:

> The antiquarian in his cabinet, surrounded by the relics of former ages, seems to himself to be removed to periods that are long since past . . . All that is venerable or laudable in the history of these times present themselves to his memory. The gallantry, the heroism, the patriotism of antiquity, rise again before his view, softened by the obscurity in which they are involved, and rendered more seducing to the imagination by that obscurity itself, which, while it mingles a sentiment of regret amid his pursuits, serves at the same time to stimulate his fancy to fill up by its own creation those long intervals of time of whch history has preserved no record. The relics he contemplates seem to approach him still nearer to the ages of his regard. The dress, the furniture, the arms of the times, are so many assistances to his imagination, in guiding or directing its exercise, and offering him a thousand sources of imagery, provide him with an almost inexhaustible field in which his memory and his fancy may expatiate.[24]

On this view, the emotions of history are essentially a possession of men of the political class, who share the reading and travel that give resonance to historical events and places. This is particularly true for the classical past, and Alison comments on the 'emotion of sublime delight, which every man of common sensibility feels upon the first prospect of Rome'. Present-day Rome, he says, echoing Gibbon, is no more than a scene of destruction and triumphant superstition.[25] Yet this is not what the onlooker feels. 'It is ancient Rome which fills his imagination. It is the country of Caesar, and Cicero, and Virgil, which is before him.' Years of study have populated his imagination with images of this world. 'Take from him these associations, conceal from him that it is Rome that he sees, and how different would be his emotion!'

In this image of the historical spectator in the wreckage of ancient Rome, Alison finds the ideal illustration of his general thesis. What better example could there be to show that objects in themselves are powerless to create the 'emotions' of beauty or sublimity evoked by such sights? Even so, Alison himself shows no interest in exploring the implications of such a scene for historical studies. History is for him no more than an illustration of a principle which, in its universality, is at work in all areas of emotional/aesthetic response. In this regard he treats history as a close cousin to the picturesque, which is the subject of the next section of the *Essay*. The view of Rome, like the picturesque landscape, involves the viewer with a rich trove of associations and provides the theorist with a ready laboratory of aesthetic emotions.

Within these limits, Alison's associationalism seems to point towards the sort of fusion of place and memory which Godwin later proposed. Moreover, by showing how easily the associationalist principle could be extended to history, he provides an opening to an analysis of historical writing that is passional and essentially private. Such a view would focus on the emotional responses of the reader, rather than—as traditionally—on maxims of conduct or explanations of events. When read in an associationalist frame, history might loosen its ancient tie to public action, setting the reader free to become a sort of sentimental traveller in past times.

III

The fusion of historical association and place which Alison theorized and Godwin would have liked to promote left traces in other contemporary texts, especially those concerned with travel, topography, and literary history. In writings of this sort, there is evidence that the intensification of national sentiment in the struggles with revolutionary France may have contributed to the desire to explore, and exploit, the possibility of historical commemoration.

Though its high culture remained officially cosmopolitan, the eighteenth century showed a growing interest in ideas of patriotism and 'local attachment'.[26] For much of the century, the idea of intense loyalty to place was primarily associated with harsh climates and unsophisticated peoples. A favourite example, popularized by Rousseau, is the 'mal du pays' of the Swiss soldier who, on hearing the particular song of his homeland—is overcome with nostalgia and loses all his famous military virtues. And the homesick mercenary was sometimes joined by the Hottentot and the Highlander in this unshakable attachment to uncomfortable places.

On this level, the idea of local attachment serves to reinforce, rather than contradict, the predominant cosmopolitanism of the

Enlightenment, since it is clear that 'mal du pays' is thought of as a condition encountered in countries shaped by nature more than by history. Even so, these discussions of nostalgia gave form to the idea that, as Boswell wrote in his journals, 'There are ideas attached to particular places which it is almost impossible to express.'[27]

Associationalism, too, provided an opening to the recognition of the power of national sentiment. Though it was Alison's view that associationalism provides support for the universal norms of neo-classicism, it is clear that his ideas could be called upon to explain the diversity of national taste. As Alison himself pointed out, national associations provide their own particular stock of images, thus intensifying a Roman's response to Virgil, for example, in ways that moderns cannot possibly share.

National sentiment and local association enter into Samuel Rogers' popular long poem, 'The Pleasures of Memory' (1792). 'The Poem begins,' he explains in his introductory gloss, 'with the description of an obscure village, and of the pleasing melancholy which it excites on being revisited after a long absence. This mixed sensation is an effect of the Memory.' Rogers' explanation for this 'mixed sensation' is a brief restatement of the psychology of association as it is active in producing feelings of patriotism and reverence for antiquity: 'When ideas have any relation whatever, they are attractive of each other in the mind; and the perception of any object naturally leads to the idea of another, which was connected with it either in time or place, or which can be compared or contrasted with it. Hence arises our attachment to inanimate objects; hence also, in some degree, the love of our country, and the emotion with which we contemplate the celebrated scenes of antiquity.'[28]

In the body of the poem the link between patriotism, individual memory, and the association of ideas is developed a little further; here, too, a larger framework of historical memory is invoked, making it clear that for Rogers, as for Alison, history gives rise to some of the richest examples of the associative power of memory:

> Thus kindred objects kindred thoughts inspire,
> As summer-clouds flash forth electric fire.
> And hence this spot gives back the joys of youth,
> Warm as the life, and with the mirror's truth.
> Hence home-felt pleasure prompts the Patriot's sigh
> This makes him wish to live, and dare to die.
> ... And hence the charm historic scenes impart;
> Hence the Tiber awes, and Avon melts the heart.
> Aerial forms in Tempe's classic vale

Glance thro' the gloom and whisper in the gale;
In wild Vaucluse with love and Laura dwell,
And watch and weep in Eloisa's cell.[29]

Rogers' invocation of Laura and Eloisa suggests the importance of literary history—and of the female—to the associationalist programme. At the same time, Tempe and Tiber draw our attention again to the prominence of images of the classical world in these evocations of history and memory. It seems clear that the fusion of place and past times came most easily, almost naturally, to Englishmen when the scene was classical; after all, the classical world was not simply more ancient than anything English, it also presented itself in texts which modern readers had long been accustomed to regarding as indistinguishably literary and historical.

Rogers' fusion of literary landscape and cultivated memory had a kind of precedent in the work of mid-century 'gardenists', who marked their creations with urns, inscriptions, and classical temples. Such emblematic devices turned the garden into a place of contemplation, inviting the visitor to connect each place or vista to specific moral themes. These gardens, then, were associationalist experiments, just as Godwin hoped all England might one day become. But despite Stowe's celebration of British worthies, neo-classical taste ensured that the language of cultural memory remained idealized and Roman. For all its celebrated Englishness, the garden was a reminder of journeys elsewhere. It took some time for Englishmen, schooled in Italian travels and views of Rome, to feel the power of historical association in more ordinary settings. In this sense, the most visionary part of Godwin's proposal may have been that he took Britain herself as a landscape of history.[30]

IV

Contemporary travel literature offers some valuable hints about the possibilities—and also the limits—of this extension of historical feeling to the British landscape. William Gilpin's well-known explorations of Britain in search of the picturesque illustrate this point. Gilpin's affective approach to landscape has affinities to Alison's exploration of association. It would not be hard to imagine Gilpin's travels as providing an occasion for a wider appreciation of the aesthetics of place in which history, joined to the picturesque, would add her own colours to the pictorial imagination.

In fact, Gilpin frequently mentions significant historical events connected to the places he describes, but his historical descriptions suggest something more traditional. History does not become a part of his aesthetic; rather it remains—with few exceptions—a separate category of interest to the traveller. 'Few towns offer a fairer field to an antiquary, than Carlisle', Gilpin writes in his tour of Cumberland and Westmoreland (1786). 'Its origin and history, are remote, curious and obscure . . .' Two pages later, however, he declares: 'But I mean not to enter into the history of Carlisle: it concerns me only as an object of beauty.'[31] So, too, when Gilpin pauses to mention the death of Edward I, an entertainment presented for Queen Elizabeth, an incident connected to Cromwell, or an anecdote of the '45, each historical reference arises in connection with a specific place, but there is no desire to fuse historical memory and visual impression to evoke the unique experience of place.[32]

In short, picturesque beauty and historical interest remain separate categories. 'The country around Newberry furnished little amusement', he reports in the *Observations on the River Wye* (1782), 'but if it is not picturesque, it is very historical.' But this particular passage continues with a tantalizing look towards another possibility:

> In every historical country there are a set of ideas which peculiarly belong to it. Hastings and Tewksbury; Runnemede [sic] and Clarendon, have all their associate ideas. The ruins of abbeys and castles have another set: and it is a soothing amusement in travelling, to assimulate [sic] the mind to the ideas of the country. The ground we now trod, has many historical ideas associated with it; two great battles, a long siege, and the death of the gallant Lord Falkland.[33]

This seems an intriguing anticipation of Alison's associationalism, but there is no follow-up to the passage, which falls at the very end of the book. We are left with no more than a tantalizing suggestion that certain kinds of places—ruined abbeys and castles, scenes of battle or of sieges—retain a special power over the mind, which accommodates itself in some way to the strong impressions formed in their presence.

Ruins, of course, are the obvious collecting points for historical sentiment. In his tour of Cumberland and Westmoreland, Gilpin writes a brief, unremarkable history of Warwick Castle, but concludes on a note of romantic nostalgia: 'Such is the present state of a structure, which two hundred years ago was second to none in England . . . But now in Ossian's plaintive language, "Its walls are desolate: the grey moss whitens the stone: the fox looks out from the window; and rank grass waves round its head." '34

Gilpin championed the Gothic style in architecture, and it is clear that the remains of medieval England had special power for him.35 But his feeling is less for the memorials of human life than for the works of nature. The more, in fact, a ruin becomes a part of nature, the more it can be seen simply as a physical object removed from human time, the freer he is to respond on his favourite aesthetic grounds. Nor is there the gap, which for Alison is so significant, between the physical object and its imaginative associations. 'Nature has now made it her own', Gilpin writes at Tintern. 'Time has worn off all the traces of the rule . . .'36 In another place, he declares that the proprietor who 'owns' a ruin is really no more than the guardian of a sacred trust because in truth, if not strictly in law, the ruin stands outside of the human world: 'A ruin is a sacred thing. Rooted for ages in the soil; assimilated to it; and become, as it were a part of it; we consider it as a work of nature, rather than of art.'37

Where, on the other hand, medieval remains call human history rather than nature to mind, another, more guarded response prevails. Contemplating the vast ruins of Glastonbury, Gilpin recognizes the power of this 'amazing combination of various buildings . . . perhaps the largest society under one government, and the most extensive foundation that ever appeared in England'. Nonetheless, his description moves on inevitably to a severe dismissal of everything un-enlightened in monastic life,38 and he completes his extensive review of Glaston-bury's history with a perfectly conventional anecdote of the death of its last abbot, an innocent and bewildered victim of Henry VIII's brutality.39

V

It is instructive to compare Gilpin's responses to the human landscape of England with those of a slightly later traveller writing in the patriotic atmosphere produced by war with France. Samuel Jackson Pratt was a prolific man of letters whose works are something of a barometer of contemporary moods.40 Contemporaries knew Pratt best for his books of travel, which he entitled *Gleanings*. The first volumes (1795) ranged over Wales, Holland, and Westphalia, but at the end of the decade Pratt turned to scenes closer to home with his *Gleanings in England; Descriptive of the Countenance, Mind, and Character of the Country* (1799).

As the subtitle suggests, Pratt's purpose is different from Gilpin's and his scope wider. He writes about inns and the commercial exports of Lynn, the superiority of English roads and the coldness of the English character. He talks about taste, the picturesque, and the failings of Methodism. As regards politics and literature, Pratt shows clearly which way the winds were blowing in this anti-revolutionary decade. He praises the reactionary review, the *Anti-Jacobin*, and satirizes the excesses of sentimentalism—this in a long novelistic segment portraying the devastation of the countryside that results from the unwise benevolence of an eccentric landlord.

'The point proposed,' writes Pratt, 'is an amusing, interesting, and true idea of England, and of Englishmen in their various classes.'[41] Manners and travels are frequently paired in this way, but as a domestic traveller, Pratt is addressing an audience already largely familiar with local custom. His real purpose is celebratory. England, he says fondly, is only a little place, like an ant hill, 'but which, like the ant hill, is populated by the most industrious, ingenious, and wonder working creatures in the universe'.[42]

The later chapters in particular are soaked in a patriotic spirit stirred by naval battles and threats of invasion. 'War must for ever be a scourge,' he writes on the news of Nelson's victories, 'but the love of country, my friend, is an inborn emotion; and to preserve our birth place from invasion is a sacred principle that uplifts the filial arm throughout the globe.'[43] Pratt is no mindless jingo, and there is room in his patriotic fervour to recognize doubts and legitimate dissension.[44] But patriotism casts its glow on his view of England—especially when the 'Gleaner' looks out to sea. Witness the rubrics introducing Chapter 22:

> Cromer—Beeston Priory—Cromer Beach—Views of the ocean in different parts of the day and evening—The Author gleaneth the Sea—Also the five late victories upon it—A retrospect of Naval Glory of England —Borrows some golden ears from living English Bards, to make his sheath-offering presented to English heroes more worthy of their acceptance.

Here, as the chapter headings clearly indicate, a conventional description of picturesque landscape becomes associated with English naval traditions and recent triumphs over the French. In short, at Cromer Beach, Pratt re-imagines the sea as a specifically English 'place', resonant with patriotic associations, and he completes his description with a long praise-poem to the naval heroes of England.

Away from sea and battle, Pratt offers another kind of patriotic description in his picture of Houghton, the house of Robert Walpole. It requires a lengthy excerpt:

> The first impression made on the mind of a classic traveller upon a first view of plantations which have been cultured, and mansions that have been erected by illustrious persons, more particularly if their celebrity has been derived from the splendour of intellectual or moral qualities, is that, my friend, which will impress yours, long before the doors of this noble edifice shall be opened to you by the servant permitted to shew them. With the rapidity of thought, your mind will go back to all you ever heard or read of the celebrated founder, and those distinguished relatives who have successively possessed and ennobled it. The inanimate objects first looked at, within and without, will soon become secondary. The simple circumstance of knowing that many of the trees in the magnificent woods were planted by Sir Robert Walpole, will carry your reflections from the plantation to the planter, and all which refers solely to vegetation, however delicious its charms at other times to the senses, will give place to more profound reflections. You will take a retrospective view of the the extraordinary man who continued first British Minister of State from the time that the structure was begun in 1722 to its complete finishing inside and out, in 1735. The whole compass of your mind will fill with the events, characters and deep public concerns which marked the epoch of his administration. The history of this little island, and of the vast continent, as connected with, and suffer me to say, in many respects, dependent on its politicks and its commerce, will croud [sic] upon you: for awhile, woods which have long been the admiration of travellers, will shrink diminished before you, or be so subordinate to the governing idea, that you will be able to afford them no distinct notice; and the very first portrait you are shewn of this Minister, or of Horace Walpole, will engross your attention, though the keeper of the house lions, who has little time to spare for contemplative visitors, will be impatient to draw you off from Statesmen and from Bards, to her Derbyshire marble, bronze Gladiators . . .[45]

Though connected in obvious ways to the patriotic themes of this book, this passage is by no means typical of *Gleanings*. Nonetheless, despite its exceptionality, the description of Houghton is worth calling attention to. Pratt gives us much more here than a conventional traveller's picture of a great house. His description has less to do with physical images than with echoes of Walpole's work as builder, planter, and Minister. These echoes in turn become part of a more general account of the way in which historical associations of place work their way through the mind of the spectator. In fact, since his work is topographical, rather than theoretical, Pratt's tracing of the process of historical association is fuller and more specific than anything Alison himself has to offer. And Houghton, as a native English site, neither ruinous nor romantic—a place, in fact, with very little sense of the heroic—nicely illustrates the breadth of possibilities awaiting anyone proposing to trace the associations of history across the map of modern Britain.

VI

I would like to end with John Aikin and his sister, Anna Laetitia Barbauld—two writers close to Godwin in background and politics who nonetheless arrived at an assessment of the associations of place in English history quite different from the one promoted in the *Essay on Sepulchres*.

In his *Letters from a Father to his Son* (1793 and 1800), John Aikin acknowledges the power of association in general terms, only to dismiss the particular associations of the English past. Aikin begins with a sceptical look at the century's passion for ruins, which he is inclined to see as indulgent and self-deceiving.[46] Ruins might have some beauty as 'objects of sight', but for a ruin to be worth preserving, it must be the relic of a building originally of some beauty and importance. 'With respect to the *sentimental* effects of ruins,' he goes on to say, 'they are all referable to that principle of association which connects animate with inanimate things, and past with present, by the relation of place.' These associations have a powerful appeal to the imagination, says Aikin, and he illustrates the thought—as it had been illustrated so often before—with reference to battlefields, 'ruined palaces', and abandoned cities. Scenes like these have the power to move every susceptible breast.[47]

Aikin's view of the psychological effect of ruins seems no different from Godwin's, and he goes on to speak of their effect of 'elevated melancholy' and to quote Dyer's *Ruins of Rome*. But while conceding the evocative power of such places, Aikin refuses to give in to indiscriminate sentimentalism. It is necessary, he argues, that the place and its relics 'refer to somewhat really interesting'. In other words, Aikin refuses to accord any sentimental value to ruinousness itself. With the same literalness, he insists that 'the emotions inspired by the recollected scene be of a kind not incongruous with those we are likely to bring with us to the spot'. But this is hardly the usual situation: the 'gay party' approaching the 'awful pile of religious ruins' would soon lose its spirit if they really felt 'the force of its associations'. In fact, he concludes, this incongruity of emotions is proof of how little the ruin-hunters are truly affected by the scenes they visit.

Aikin's insistence that ruins not be sentimentalized, that they be taken seriously as reminders of the past as it really was, results in a conclusion that turns Godwin's proposal upside down: 'Upon the principle of association it will, however, appear, that the great part of the relics of antiquity in this country can produce but trifling effects on the heart. The ideas they suggest are those of forms of life offering nothing dignified or pleasing to the mind.' The castle and the monastery remind us only of stern tyranny and brutal ignorance. 'We are rejoiced that their date is past; and we can have little inducement to recal them from that oblivion into which they are deservedly sunk, and which best accords with their primitive insignificance.'[48]

Thus Aikin is prepared to turn his back on the dark associations of the past in the name of an enlightened present. But a decade later, his sister, Anna Laetitia Barbauld, could no longer subscribe to this hopeful view of England's progress. Her long narrative poem *Eighteen Hundred and Eleven* is a further essay on the melancholy spirit of ruins, but the broken landscape she contemplates is a relic not of the past, but of the present—a projection into the future of the wreck of contemporary Britain.

Mrs Barbauld personifies history as an erratic, unpredictable spirit: 'The Genius now forsakes the favoured shore,/And hates, capricious, what he loved before.' But in truth the movements of history seem to her all too predictable: 'Arts, arms, and wealth destroy the fruits they bring;/Commerce, like beauty, knows no second spring.'[49] Without its wealth or spirit of liberty, England would join other empires past their zenith and sink into a new (wholly un-romantic) dark age.[50] Still, there is consolation of a kind in the thought that the inheritance of English philosophy would live on in the New World, and some day a youth from 'the Blue Mountains or Ontario's lake', might make a pilgrimage to gaze on the ruins of London:

> Or of some crumbling turret mined by time,
> The broken stairs with perilous step shall climb,
> Thence stretch their view the wide horizon round,
> By scattered hamlets trace its ancient bound
> And choked no more with fleets, fair Thames survey
> Through reeds and sedge pursue his idle way.[51]

Not surprisingly, Mrs Barbauld's dark prophecy was widely attacked, notably by Southey—once a friend of the Aikins—in a vicious review in the *Quarterly*. The Napoleonic era demanded a simpler loyalty and a very different sort of vision of the British landscape. Yet thirty years later Macaulay would echo this poem in a famous passage in which he comfortably imagines a time in remote futurity when 'some traveller from New Zealand shall, in the midst of a vast solitude, take his stand on a broken arch of London Bridge to sketch the ruins of St Paul's'.[52] By then the war with Napoleon was a heroic memory and the vision of time's decay, taken so seriously by both the writer and her critics in 1811, was hardly more than a flourish.

VII

How Godwin read *Eighteen Hundred and Eleven* I do not know, but it is clear that he would have disagreed with both of the Aikins. In a striking passage in the *Essay on Sepulchres*, Godwin argues for the choice of living in an old country, with all its richness of association, against life in the New World, surrounded only by the bounty of nature. In older lands, Godwin writes, there is on every side 'some object connected with a heart moving tale' or a scene where 'the deepest interests of a nation . . . have been strenuously agitated'.[53] Even scenes and objects that are not truly historical can have this power: old traditions or novels, even though not strictly true, may still endow a place with a 'beautiful association'.

Generally we connect this embracing of the pleasures and burdens of living in the presence of history not with Godwin, but with his opponent in the Revolution debate, Edmund Burke. As a contemporary reviewer of the *Essay on Sepulchres* noted with some irony, 'this *Meditation among the tombs* . . . unlike other productions of Mr. Godwin's pen, is more in the style of *antient piety* than of *modern philosophy*.'[54] Perhaps so—but in light of the texts we have surveyed, it seems clear that the desire for an emotional engagement with history belonged to no one author and no single politics. And when we recall the role of associationalism in promoting the idea of historical evocation, we must conclude that 'modern philosophy' and 'antient piety' were not always such enemies to one another.

Notes

1. This essay was written before the appearance of Mark Philp's new edition of *The Political and Philosophical Writings of William Godwin* [London, 1993], volume 6 of which includes Godwin's *Essay on Sepulchres*. It may be some time before this invaluable, but rather expensive edition is widely available; for this reason, I have chosen to retain the references to the first edition (1809), but I have added new page references in square brackets. I am grateful to Mark Philp for sending me a copy of the text and prefatory material, which readers will wish to consult for further suggestions regarding the context of Godwin's *Essay*. I am also pleased to take this chance to thank the organizers of the Exeter Conference on the 'Public Sphere in Eighteenth-Century Europe'. I am especially grateful to Dario Castiglione for his warm welcome and encouragement. I am also pleased to acknowledge the helpful criticisms of Stefan Collini, Gus Heidemann, April London, and Ruth Phillips.

2. For a broad discussion of this theme, see D. Lowenthal, *The Past is a Foreign Country* (Cambridge, 1985); and P. Wright, *On Living in an Old Country* (London, 1985). For a history of one national tradition of commemoration in its institutional context, see C.J. Taylor, *Negotiating the Past. The Making of Canada's National Parks and Sites* (Montreal, 1990).

3. In his biography of Godwin, Don Locke quotes a letter from Mary Lamb as 'best' describing the work. She writes satirically that it is a 'great work which Godwin is going to publish to enlighten the world once more.' The biographer's own view is no more positive: 'In fact the great charm of this little pamphlet is the deadly seriousness with which Godwin approaches his modest, not to say silly, little suggestion. But no doubt he numbered himself among those former and future great dead men who could thus be remembered down all the ages. Once he had suggested men might be able to conquer death by reason alone, but now he preferred to put his trust in a cross of wood and a mark on a map.' D. Locke, *A Fantasy of Reason: The Life and Thought of William Godwin* (London, 1980) pp. 223–24.

4. I have elaborated these themes at greater length in a forthcoming essay entitled 'Adam Smith and the Narrative of Private Life', which will appear in a volume of studies on *The Historical Imagination in Early Modern Britain* ed. by D. Sacks and D. Kelley.

5. Wordsworth's reflections on epitaphs seem relevant here: 'But an epitaph is not a proud writing shut up for the studious: it is exposed to all—to the wise and the most ignorant; it is condescending, perspicuous, and lovingly solicits regard; its story and admonitions are brief, that the thoughtless, the busy, and indolent, may not be deterred, nor the impatient tired.' 'Essays Upon Epitaphs' in *Prose Works of William Wordsworth* ed. by W.J.B. Owen and J.W. Smyser (Oxford, 1974) p. 59.

6. Godwin provides some grounds for this association when he muses on the loss of support that would be involved if the lost friend were someone

with whom one had dwelled under the same roof—if she 'were the wife of my bosom.' W. Godwin, *Essay on Sepulchres* (London, 1809) pp. 12–13 [Philp: pp. 8-9].

7. This emphasis is added: Godwin, *Sepulchres* pp. 6–7 [Philp: p. 8].

8. Godwin, *Sepulchres* pp. 66–67 [Philp: p. 20].

9. On the idea in associationalist psychology that the force of association would be greatest where least impeded by distracting alternatives, see the discussion of Archibald Alison below. Regarding the monuments at St. Paul's and the civic uses of memorial statuary, see A. Yarrington, *The Commemoration of the Hero, 1800–1864* (New York, 1988).

10. Godwin, *Sepulchres* pp. 57-58 [Philp: p. 18].

11. Godwin, *Sepulchres* pp. 45 [Philp pp. 15–16].

12. Godwin, *Sepulchres* pp. 71-72 [Philp: p. 21].

13. Godwin, *Sepulchres* pp. 74-81 [Philp: pp. 22–23].

14. 'Military and naval achievements are of temporary operation: the victories of Cimon and Scipio are passed away; these great heroes have dwindled into a name; but the whole of Plato and Xenephon, and Virgil have desccended to us, undefaced, undismembered, and complete ... I am acquainted with their peculiarities; their inmost thoughts are familiar to me; they appear before me with all the attributes of individuality; I can ruminate upon their lessons and sentiments at leisure, till my whole soul is lighted up with the spirit of these authors.' *Sepulchres* pp. 109–10 [Philp: p. 28]. The formulation, needless to say, is once again spectatorial.

15. Godwin, *Sepulchres* pp. 112, 115–16 [Philp: pp. 29–30].

16. The second edition of Alison's essay, which appeared in 1811, was enthusiastically welcomed by Francis Jeffrey in the *Edinburgh Review*. This lengthy essay was reprinted in the *Encyclopaedia Britannica* as the article on 'Beauty' as well as in Jeffrey's popular collected essays. Jeffrey helped to give Alison a lasting influence, especially in Scotland, making his work, like Burke's, an important bridge to the next century.

17. A. Alison, *Essays on the Nature and Principles of Taste* (Edinburgh, 1790; repr. Hildesheim, 1968). See also S. Monk, *The Sublime. A Study of Critical Theories in XVIII-Century England* (Michigan, 1960).

18. 'Trains of pleasing or of solemn thought arise spontaneously within our minds, our hearts swell with emotions, of which the objects before us seem to afford no adequate cause.' Alison, *Taste* pp. 2–3. On the association of ideas and aesthetics, see M. Kallich, *The Association of Ideas and Critical Theory in 18th-Century England* (The Hague, 1970).

19. Alison, *Taste* pp. 14, 42.

20. This aesthetic stance of disengagement was a point of criticism for Coleridge, but Alison's 'bewitching reverie' seems very close to Kames' 'ideal presence'. These were not unusual critical doctrines in this time. See Kames, *Elements of Criticism* (Edinburgh, 1762).

21. The passage continues: 'They recall so many images of past happiness and past affections [*sic*], they are connected with so many strong or valued emotions, and lead altogether to so long a train of feelings and

recollections, that there is hardly any scene which one ever beholds with so much rapture.' Alison, *Taste* p. 15.

22. Alison, *Taste* p. 16.
23. Alison, *Taste* p. 18.
24. Alison, *Taste* pp. 27–28.
25. The echo of Gibbon seems deliberate: the Rome we picture 'is not the triumph of superstition over the wreck of human greatness, and its monuments erected upon the very spot where the first honours of humanity have been gained'. Alison, *Taste* p. 28.
26. On local attachment, see the helpful survey by A. McKillop, 'Local Attachment and Cosmopolitanism—The Eighteenth-Century Pattern,' in F.W. Hilles and H. Bloom (eds) *From Sensibility to Romanticism* (New York, 1965) pp. 191–218. On the growth of patriotic sentiment in this period, see G. Newman, *The Rise of English Nationalism* (New York, 1987) and L. Colley, *Britons* (New Haven, 1992).
27. Boswell, *The Ominous Years, 1774–1776*, Ryskamp and Pottle (eds) (New York, 1963); quoted in McKillop, 'Local Attachment' p. 205.
28. S. Rogers, 'The Pleasures of Memory' in *Poetical Works* (London, 1869) pp. 3–4.
29. Rogers, *Works* pp. 13–14.
30. On eighteenth-century gardens and their use of association, see: H. F. Clark, 'Eighteenth-Century Elysiums: The role of 'Association' in the Landscape Movement', *Journal of the Warburg and Courtauld Institutes* VI (1943) pp. 165–89; R. Paulson, *Emblem and Expression. Meaning in English Art of the Eighteenth Century* (London, 1975); J. D. Hunt and P. Willis, *The Genius of the Place: The English Landscape Garden 1620–1820* (Cambridge, MA, rev. ed. 1988).
31. W. Gilpin, *Observations relative Chiefly to Picturesque Beauty made in the Year 1772, On Several Parts of England; Particularly the Mountains and Lakes of Cumberland, and Westmoreland* (London, 1782) pp. 93, 95.
32. Gilpin, *Cumberland* I p. 45; II pp. 97–99, 112, 199–200.
33. *Observations on the River Wye and several parts of South Wales relative chiefly to Picturesque Beauty made in the summer of the year 1770* (London, 1782) p. 98.
34. Gilpin, *Cumberland* pp. 39–41, 43. On 'view hunting' and the literary interest in ruins, see I. Ousby, *The Englishman's England* (Cambridge, 1990) ; A. Janowitz, *England's Ruins; Poetic Purpose and the National Landcape* (Oxford, 1990).
35. Gilpin, *Observations on the Western Parts of England relative chiefly to Picturesque Beauty* . . . (London, 1798) pp. 63–64.
36. Gilpin, *River Wye* p. 33.
37. Gilpin, *Cumberland* II p. 188.
38. 'On the other hand, when we consider five hundred persons, bred up in indolence, and lost to the commonwealth; when we consider that these houses were the great nurseries of superstition, bigotry, and ignorance;

the stews of sloth, stupidity, and perhaps intemperance . . .' Gilpin, *Western Parts* pp. 137–38.

39. It is worth comparing these scenes to his encounter with Stonehenge, a pre-medieval structure which Gilpin found alien and—despite the advantage of its ruinous condition—un-picturesque. Nonetheless, he could not deny its power: 'But it is not the elegance of the work, but the grandeur of the idea that strikes us . . . To be immured, as it were, by such hideous walls of rock; and to see the landscape through such strange apertures must have thrown the imagination into a wonderful ferment. The Druid, though savage in his nature, had the sublimest ideas of the object of his worship, whatever it was.'

   The interest here is that the passage shows Gilpin feeling his way inside an alien landscape, trying to imagine the experiences it once held. But this was a kind of 'assimulation' he seldom looked for or achieved. See Gilpin, *Western Parts* p. 80.

40. According to a recent summary, his works are 'an accurate and energetic response to changing tastes in the writing and reading of late 18th century novels.' See A. London on Pratt, in the *Dictionary of Literary Biography*, v. 39 p. 362.

41. S. J. Pratt, *Gleanings in England; descriptive of the countenance, mind and character of the country* IV (London 1799) p. 6. Note that this is designated as volume IV as a continuation of the previous volumes on Wales, Holland, and Westphalia.

42. Pratt, *Gleanings* p. 1.

43. Pratt, *Gleanings* p. 489.

44. Pratt retained some worry about the dangers of war, especially for a commercial country like Britain: 'Every prospect that art, or nature can display . . . every scene which many may enjoy or his Maker bestow, is in a manner annihilated by war—and the very sight of a commercial, turned into a military, nation—as is now the case of Great Britain—while it reflects the image of public virtue, and of patriotism, mingles with it the idea of mutilated life, unnatural deaths, and groaning world.' (pp. 566–67, and 578). Nonetheless, he left no doubt that his heart was stirred by the threat of a French invasion: '. . . yet the view of a whole country putting on the Armour of Patriotism, on one great, pure, and pious principle, concerning which, even those who continue to lift up the dissenting voice against whatever else regards the origin and progress of the war, are unanimous—the preservation of their natal earth from an Invader.'

45. Pratt, *Gleanings* pp. 202ff.

46. J. Aikin, *Letters from a Father to his Son, on various Topics relative to Literature and the Conduct of Life* (New York, [1796–1800] 1971) pp. 262–73.

47. Aikin, *Letters* p. 268.

48. 'The castellated mansion of the ancient Baron, of which nothing is left but a shattered tower, frowning over the fruitful vale, reminds us only of the stern tyranny, brutal ignorance, and gross licentiousness, which

stained the times of feudal anarchy. And if we look back to the original state of our ordinary monastic remains, what shall we see but a set of beings engaged in a dull round of indolent pleasures, and superstitious practices, alike debasing to the heart and understanding.' Aikin, *Letters* p. 271.

Aikin's negative sense of English history stands close to harshly critical views Godwin expressed in a work of the same time. See his essay 'Of History and Romance,' written in 1797, first published as an Appendix to the Penguin edition of *Caleb Williams* ed. M. Hindle (London, 1988) pp. 366–67: 'What sort of an object is the history of England? Till the extinction of the wars of York and Lancaster, it is one scene of barbarism and cruelty . . .' The only exception he makes is the struggle for liberty in the time of the Stuarts, 'the only portion of our history interesting to the heart of man'.

49. A. L. Barbauld, *Works* (London, 1825) I pp. 232–50.

50. 'Night, Gothic night, again may shade the plains/Where Power is seated, and where Science reigns.'

51. Barbauld, *Works* I pp. 241–42.

52. See the opening pages of his essay on Ranke's *History of the Popes: Critical and Historical Essays* (London, 1907) II p. 39.

53. Godwin, *Sepulchres* p. 67 [Philp: p. 20]: The full passage reads: 'I love to dwell in a country, where, on whichever side I turn, I find some object connected with a heart-moving tale, or some scene where the deepest interests of a nation for ages to succeed, have been strenuously agitated, and emphatically decided. A tale of invention, or of idle tradition merely, is of great power in this respect.'

54. *Monthly Review* 61 (1810) p. 111.

Twelve

A Historical Postscript

Jonathan Barry

Throughout this volume the shifting boundaries of public and private, in language and in practice, in the eighteenth century and in modern scholarship, have become obvious. At the very least, we have learnt to see public and private as dialectic terms, whose interrelationships are perhaps more important than their boundaries. Indeed public and private, as given states, seem less helpful as concepts than the active words associated with them—publicity, publicness and publication, for example, set against privacy, privateness and even privatization! If we are dealing with spaces, they are ones that are constantly being signposted, invaded, redefined and debated, both then and now. To give but two examples, John Brewer has shown how the private both took its definition from the 'non-public' and how the 'public' had an extraordinary capacity to absorb and represent the private. In his sensitive analysis of how private lives, indeed the very self, were identified through public forms he develops Habermas's original observation that 'subjectivity, as the innermost core of the private, was always already oriented to an audience [*Publikum*]'.[1] Likewise Vivien Jones's consideration of the figure of the prostitute, violating the boundaries of public and private, offers an illuminating way of exploring the tension that Habermas noted, but did not develop, between the two dimensions of the private—namely its economic character as the domain of contractual transactions and its intimate character as the area of personal relationships defined by the patriarchal family. Prostitution forms the inverted image of marriage, where also, as Ursula Vogel explores, the patriarchal dimension of the private renders a purely contractual relationship unacceptable to 'the public'.[2]

In this respect the essays here, while taking Habermas's work into deeper and more complex areas, can be seen as working within the paradigm he established. In his introduction to the latest edition of his work Habermas himself recognized the validity of exploring these issues.[3] In complicating matters, however, they also insist on the need to view Habermas's model not just as one of 'structure' but equally, perhaps more, as one of 'transformation'. In line with most recent cultural history, the emphasis is less on the deterministic effect of 'a culture', in this case the 'bourgeois public sphere', than of the range of possibilities, strategies and changes that can be discovered within a particular 'field of force'.[4] As Jones in particular brings out, the whole issue of agency and responsibility must always be kept in mind; neither people nor even 'texts' were or are willing to 'lie down and die', in the face either of contemporary pressures or of historical models!

This emphasis on agency, however, sits rather uneasily with the basic spatial metaphor underlying both Habermas's 'Public Sphere' (at least in its English formulation) and this volume's 'boundaries'. Admittedly, several of the essays here succeed in bringing the spatial dimension to the fore and thus, by problematizing it, using it fruitfully. Brewer, Jones and Pesante, for example, all consider critically the notion of a 'spectatorial vision'. In Luisa Pesante's case, following Habermas, it is that of private individuals who, through their experience of judgment and morality in family relationships, are able to view the public with impartiality and sympathy. The other two reverse the direction, considering how far the public both identified itself and policed the nature of private relationships through publicity, publication and what one might call 'the humanitarian gaze'. Vogel further problematizes the link often made between 'private space' and women's space by reminding us that, within a patriarchal model, women were not defined as 'domestic', but rather defined by their relationship to men: provided they were suitably subject to male authority there were often good reasons—not least economic ones—for them to act outside the home. Mark Phillips also draws our attention to the complex nature of space by considering the associations which specific spaces could develop with both public and private histories. Here too the world of public and private intersect and are interdependent, whether it is in the 'representative publicness' of humanist history, where past examples of individual behaviour act as public models for future conduct, or in what Phillips considers to be the new form of association whereby history operates primarily by exciting the sympathy of each generation for the past, conceived as sharing human emotions and hopes.

Phillips's essay reminds us, however, that space is not the only dimension. It may be helpful to ask how well Habermasian paradigms of public and private stand up when subject to examination through the fourth dimension —that of time. In general, recent efforts to create a history of public and private life have devoted much less attention to the time dimension than to that of space. There have been few efforts, for example, to relate such work to the (much less extensive) debate over the differentiation between leisure and work and the emergence of measured time.[5] At a different level, as Phillips explores, different public and private worlds could operate on different timescales— Christian, classical, linear, cyclical, seasonal and according to phases of life. The eighteenth century has been associated with revolutionary reconceptions of both childhood and old age, even death, in relation to adulthood, all of which have profound implications for our sense of how private and public might intersect.[6] I shall return to this theme at the end.

The question of time is also at stake in another sense. Both in Habermas' work and in this collection the 'eighteenth century' has a curiously timeless quality. It stands less for a precise chronological period than for a 'stage', one which can be reached or instantiated at different moments, for example, in different countries.[7] As Dario Castiglione's remarks suggest, we can situate the 'eighteenth century' under discussion here only by placing it in intellectual context, but we can also test any model against the effects of 'real time' conjunctures. The chronologies of most of the essays here tend to reinforce Habermas's original schema, within which the baton of 'eighteenth-centuriness' passed across boundaries from England to France to Germany, before collapsing in the face of the French Revolution, which redefines time as much as space, redrawing Europe's cultural boundaries and establishing a new 'modernity'.[8] Yet throughout the eighteenth century, not just after 1789, the countries considered here, plus those unjustly neglected, such as the United Provinces, the Italian states and Switzerland (all, interestingly, deviants from the pattern of monarchy and/or nationhood), were in close cultural contact within the 'Republic of Letters' as well as through the balance of state power. This point is made with great force in Christian Laursen's essay, where he draws our attention to the crucial role played by the Netherlands and by the divided jurisdictions, both of Europe as a whole and of Germany in particular, in generating a de facto 'Republic of Letters' which undermined efforts at censorship and enabled a 'comparative' approach to politics and culture which tended to precede, rather than follow from, any intellectual models for such 'freedom of the press'.

Once we begin to question the standard Enlightenment model of time and space, moreover, we may begin to question the primacy of the eighteenth century itself in many of the developments being analysed. If we begin with late eighteenth-century moments, whether they be Kant's moment of Enlightenment or the French Revolution, then we tend, naturally, to look back into the eighteenth century to find either contrasts by which to sketch out modernity or new developments by which to explain its growth. Yet if we abandon this perspective (with its implications of history as linear) and prepare to range more freely over the past for transformations of public and private, then we can begin to postulate other chronologies. In the English case, for example, although Habermas privileges the age of the *Spectator*, the more obvious candidate for a cultural revolution is provided by the Civil War and its aftermath. One does not need to adopt a Marxian view of the 1640s as a 'bourgeois revolution' (though one can, with some plausibility) to see that it had profound effects in most of the spheres with which Habermas is concerned. To give a few obvious examples, it saw a parliamentary and ultimately a republican challenge both to the notion of a person embodying the state and to the vision of government as a personal and private affair. The court ceased to be the focus of power and never regained this position, despite the Restoration. Both sides in the war and after found themselves obliged to seek legitimacy in the eyes of public opinion, notably through the burgeoning press. There was an extraordinary efflorescence of schemes and societies devoted to advancing the public good, many of them associated with the figure of Samuel Hartlib: outcomes included the coffee house and the Royal Society. At the same time the whole world of the private was rocked, both by the execution of the nation's 'father' and by the political, religious and social challenges to family and gender roles created by revolution. Most of these forces were expressed in a religious form, notably in the emergence of the radical sects. The claim to freedom of conscience—divorcing public from private belief—was made and never fully silenced thereafter.[9]

The point of drawing attention, very crudely of course, to this earlier period is not to suggest that we should merely rediscover the 'bourgeois public sphere' in mid-seventeenth-century England. Many of the developments of that period were temporary and almost all of them were contested. In particular, the unsettled state of the public encouraged private interests to seek to reshape the public in their exclusive image. Most obviously, those groups who can plausibly be described as seeking to separate public and private in religion were both encouraged and required to establish a 'godly state', partly to protect their own freedom to worship but also from a millenial vision in which the 'saints' could transform the world. It was out of their disillusion with the failure of such schemes of transformation, matched by the subsequent disillusion of 'conservatives' when they found they could not 'restore' the previous conditions, that there emerged the precarious compromise which characterized early eighteenth-century England. Behind its conventions for decorous public debate lay alarm at party passions and extreme shifts of state power. It was less a case of a public awakening to discover its potential than of a public, or specific parts of it, struggling to re-establish boundaries. It was less the liberation than the reduction, perhaps one might say the domestication, of the public sphere.

Habermas's failure to recognize this dimension, except in the occasional aside, is reflected both in the chronological confusions of his presentation and in his refusal to recognize the role of partisanship in England's cultural developments, for example in Addison's and Steele's aims for the *Spectator*. At a number of points, for example in discussing the first reference to public opinion, the rise of coffee houses and so on, he notes mid-seventeenth century developments, while in other areas he either ignores or drastically postdates changes, for example the rise of concerts and of epistolary novels. His insistence on viewing 1688 as the transformative moment leads him to a number of problems, not least because he is committed to associating this with a particular Marxist timetable for transformation. Thus we learn that 1688 marked the end of the struggle between land and money and the start of that between commercial and industrial capitalism, an analysis that would surprise most historians of the period. For Habermas, Great Britain's importance lies in its priority in reaching the stage of 'mercantile capitalism', which rendered it the model for developments on the continent as this same system took root elsewhere.[10]

In challenging this economic model and emphasizing the political roots of English developments, one can, far from giving 'priority' to the English case, instead see the English experience as one in a series of European crises, arising from the destabilizing forces of Renaissance and Reformation. The progressive collapse of existing states, or rather of existing regimes which had subsequently to be re-established as 'states', from fifteenth-century Italy across Europe to seventeenth-century Britain, had already created many of the circumstances faced by Civil War Britain in other places—hence the dependence of the British on Continental intellectuals (like Hartlib) and ideas (civic republicanism, natural law and rights theories, millenarian and pietist religious ideas) to help make sense of, and move forward from, their specific crisis.[11] In each conjuncture the circumstances were different, not least because of the ability to think about its relationship to the earlier experiences, but many of the basic ingredients were repeated. Amongst others we might point to the struggle to control and exploit the press, the choice between religious toleration and religious uniformity in the face of pluralism, the consequent need to identify a source of public morality and legitimacy outside the religious sphere, the need to re-establish the relationship between the personal and dynastic continuity of a sovereign line and the common good of the 'state'. In so far as an *ancien régime* emerged from such struggles—and it did so only in *some* parts of Europe—it was not as a timeless and 'natural' entity, however much it sought to present itself as such, but as a contingent outcome, surrounded by reminders, practical and intellectual, of alternative possibilities.

In this respect, of course, I am restating many of the emphases of Reinhart Koselleck, whose *Critique and Crisis* may be seen as both the starting-point but also the target of Habermas's work.[12] Habermas's debt to Koselleck is visible, for example in those moments when he does concede the ideological roots of change, where he refers in Koselleckian terms to 'the religious civil war' as a catalyst of change.[13] But in general, Habermas suppresses Koselleck's account in favour of his own gradualist economic explanation. Hence his failure to explore how far, as the German essays in this collection suggest, the growth of a public sphere was often encouraged by (and policed by) a growing state apparatus. Hence too Habermas's decision to emphasize the similarities, rather than the differences, between British and Franco-German experience. For Koselleck Britain constitutes the exception, where the failure of absolutism and the continuation of partisan dispute kept alive the link between politics and morality, public and private responsibility, which had been fatally severed in absolutist states where religious civil war had been overcome through the growth of a state which instituted amoral politics as the necessary price for overcoming religious differences.[14]

A number of the essays here seem to point in a Koselleckian rather than a Habermasian direction, while also suggesting some refinements in Koselleck's account. Laursen, as noted, presents an account of press developments that emphasizes the impact of religio-political divides, although he tempers Koselleck's contrast between British freedom and Continental absolutism by reminding us of the varieties of Continental experience. Both Castiglione and Pesante offer us accounts of the English and Scottish Enlightenments in which the control of both religious enthusiasm and partisan bitterness remain a priority and in which, Pesante suggests, Smith's fundamental problem is still the Machiavellian (and hence Koselleckian?) one of how to be a moral legislator when recreating a state after crisis. In both accounts the need to establish the appropriate moderation and impartiality, while retaining a link between private morality and public life, is critical. Likewise both Edoardo Tortarolo and Laursen bring out the extent to which German debates and practices regarding the role of the press and censorship took for granted the priority of serving public order, which set (often implicit) limits to what could be printed, while allowing room for debate about how far the play of ideas might not serve to strengthen the state, at least if limited to the exchange of expertise between professional groups. Here again, the contrast between Britain and the Continent seems less sharp than Koselleck postulated, for, as Castiglione brings out, those who sought to 'theorize' the role of public opinion (or a free press) in Britain were profoundly ambivalent about the desirability and likely consequences of pluralism and of politics as the clash of interests, decided by the uncertain consequences of representative government. While such freedom was regarded as a feature of civilization and commercial advance, it was also distrusted, not least because it left open the threat that enthusiasm and ideological division might sweep away disinterested statesmanship. Furthermore, the complex debates these essays uncover cast doubt on Koselleck's (somewhat contradictory) contention that Enlightenment thinking was both 'hypocritical', in its refusal to recognize its own political status and, simultaneously, ignorant of the rationale of the state system which it criticized, because it had 'forgotten' the origins of absolutism in the overcoming of 'religious civil war'.[15] Instead, we are presented with an Enlightenment all too conscious both of the political implications of its actions and of the ultimate threat of the breakdown of public order, but also able to imagine diverse strategies to meet such circumstances, not least by comparing the different European routes that had been taken out of 'crisis'.

So far I have emphasized the politico-religious setting, but it is equally important to associate this 'eighteenth century' with that which has been emerging from the recent flurry of work on 'the birth of a consumer society'. Of course, this interpretative framework, itself drawing on the Enlightenment self-image of its age as 'polite and commercial' (to quote a recent title), contains within it a number of divergent, if not contradictory, perspectives.[16] For some historians this consumer society (like our own) enjoyed the beneficent effects of market forces in satisfying both private and public goods—allowing competing claims to be resolved by consumer choices, whether in religion, publishing or lifestyle. Furthermore, rather than undermining the political establishment by bolstering the power of a new 'bourgeoisie', many now see the consumer society as underwriting the position of the existing aristocracy, establishing them as the cultural arbiters and thus legitimating their positions of power. By shifting the focus from production to consumption, historians can make the greatest consumers (the 'notables') not the greatest producers into the vanguard of commercial modernization. Ironically, given his emphasis on mercantile capitalism as the underlying 'structure' of this period, Habermas's picture has proved easy to adapt to this kind of account. Not only does he himself see both absolutist states and England as still aristocratic, but in his story even the bourgeoisie participates as consumers, not as producers, of the public sphere.[17] As Laursen notes regarding the press, Habermas is curiously silent about the role of capitalist production and its effects on the provision of a public sphere. He drastically postdates the commodification of culture, and is reluctant to highlight an aspect that would call into question his claim that, at this period unlike later, the 'bourgeois public sphere' could operate in relative freedom from market pressures towards 'mass culture'.[18] In this respect Habermas's implicit model is remarkably similar to that of many conservative (and, perhaps, Frankfurt School) critics of 'mass culture', for whom the eighteenth century forms a golden age in which aristocratic taste and bourgeois consumerism could be combined, prior to the vulgarization produced by industrial mass production.

Other historians have challenged this version of the story. Quite apart from the explanatory problems of privileging demand over supply, the 'beneficent hand' of consumerism threw up quite as many paradoxes and problems for the eighteenth century as it does today. The debates over 'luxury' and over the compatibility of commercial advance with civic or religious virtue (the latter unduly neglected in recent scholarship in comparison with the former) brought to the surface acute anxieties. In these debates the plasticity of the notion of commerce allowed all kinds of interest groups, such as landed gentry, merchants, manufacturers, artisans and professionals, to proffer their own models of how the market and the public good could be correlated with private interests. There was a profound unwillingness to allow the market or consumer choice to determine the nature of the public—an unwillingness articulated in the perpetual contrasts drawn between public good and private interests and encapsulated in the relentless satirical caricature of the period. Here, in contrast to Habermas's postulation of an innocently commercialized public sphere to be corrupted by the forces of the nineteenth-century mass market, we find an eighteenth century deeply troubled that such a mass market was already in play and thus constructing many of its institutions precisely to avoid the effects of that market, or at least to avoid the impression that it was the market that dominated. Hence the characteristic eighteenth-century models of patronage and association, whereby the dependence of public good on private choice was made more acceptable, because such choices were made collectively in the name of such common virtues as charity, sociability, patriotism, liberty and the like. It is a tribute to the immense effort put into such activity that its outcome can so easily be seen as an effortless, nay inevitable, spirit of the age, not as the fragile work of art that it seemed at the time.[19]

As suggested, association formed a vital element in this effort to forge a dimension between public and private. Once again Habermas's work re-inforces other historiographical traditions in seeing this as an age of sociability, in particular of voluntary associations, purged of their corporatist links with guilds, churches or councils and now recreated on the basis of liberty, equality and fraternity: associations amongst whom Freemasons are often given prominence. There has long been an intense debate about how to understand such associations and how far to accept their self-image as models of Enlightenment. As several essays here suggest, many of these groupings were much less divorced from state or professional authority than they appeared to be. Membership of such bodies might be useful to personal careers (including those of the entrepreneurs who serviced them), while in their jockeying for prestige or members or publicity these groups often sought the support of the state or other bodies of authority, as Goodman shows. Moreover, many of these bodies operated not in public but in private and more through exclusivity than openness. Again, the classic example is that of the Freemasons (although it is important to note that the obsessive secrecy often associated with them was not a major characteristic of eighteenth-century English Freemasonry). Following Koselleck, Habermas was well aware of this paradox, and thus postulated that the Freemasons be seen as a preliminary stage in the emergence of a public sphere, a stage that was itself to 'fall prey to its own ideology', losing the lead to other, more genuinely open associations, which 'no longer needed affirmation by means of demonstrative fraternization cere-monies'.[20] The chronology postulated here is not verified, and would certainly not work in the English case, but it draws attention to the need to explore the role of secrecy (as of censorship) in defining the public. The mention of fraternization also reminds us, as Dena Goodman emphasizes, that one of the crucial boundaries in such associations was between men and women. To maintain their public respectability whilst meeting in private, Masons had to exclude women from their meetings. Or was it perhaps the other way round: to justify an all-male fraternity now required forms of private meetings from which women could be excluded, without the old political or occupational grounds for doing so? (This last issue raises the relationship between gender and the public-private distinction, to which we must return.)

Before leaving associations, it is worth dwelling a little longer on the model of new, voluntary association, which is so important to the Habermasian public sphere. As with previous forms of 'novelty' we may well ask, how novel and by what effort? To take the Freemasonry example again, should we regard this as a 'new' eighteenth-century phenomenon or recall what this movement owes to its guild origins and to its Scottish development during the late sixteenth and seventeenth centuries? Are the many parallels between the organizational and ritual forms of this and other associations, on the one hand, and older public bodies—guilds, churches, councils and so on—to be understood as merely coincidental or historic, or did they still help to shape the meaning of eighteenth-century sociability? My own work suggests that the boundaries between 'voluntary' and 'corporatist', old and new, public and private association in this period were far more fluid than the Habermasian model implies. In particular, many of the strategies —rhetorical, ceremonial and so on—by which associations of private people claimed a place on the public stage depended crucially on the appropriation of older forms of legitimacy: the use of times, places, languages, activities, which were still redolent with traditional authority. One might note, for example, how keen these 'novel' associations were to identify themselves with honour and antiquity, in their proliferation of orders, hierarchies, genealogies and mythical pasts.[21] In short, as Pesante stresses, and as Habermas recognizes in his 1989 essay, the dimension of 'representative publicness' was still very much alive and kicking in eighteenth-century associational life and it is only by the device of discarding such elements as part of a 'residual culture' that one can present such associations as resolutely 'modern'.[22]

Arguably, the growth of 'new' associations reflected less the emergence of a new model of association than the seriousness of the problems facing older forms—guild, church, council and the like—as they became tainted with political and religious divisions. This factionalization of the existing public sphere seemed to require the forging of new associations, but at the same time the new were constantly threatened by the rivalries that plagued the old, not least because, in seeking to appropriate the 'representative publicness' of the older forms, they could not avoid becoming entangled with the divisive, as well as the unifying, forces that such publicness entailed. Here again we need to find a halfway position between Habermasian optimism and Koselleckian despair, in exploring how far the rhetoric and practices of these associations were shaped by their, often highly self-conscious, efforts to establish their legitimate place in society.

Alongside associations the press has characteristically been given pride of place in the establishment of the public sphere, and this importance is rightly reflected in many of the essays here. However, as we have come to expect, it is not an all-conquering press with an obvious task of enlightenment that emerges, but rather one of great variety, with readers, writers and editors all carefully and self-consciously negotiating the slippery paths between public interest and private interests (commercial, cultural, emotional) and between publication and privacy. Several of the essays here stress the importance in such matters, not only of the audience or readership, but also of whether the writer or editor can be confident of the nature and reactions of that audience. As Tortarolo argues, when the press can be neatly segmented into a variety of markets, each catering for a specific type of reader, then varying levels of openness and censorship could be imagined, allowing for the free play of ideas for the public good in certain spheres, but limiting them in others. It was when a single 'public' erased such distinctions that a crisis emerged, one he dates to the 1780s (predating, one notes, the effects of 1789). In the English case, one would have to date such a crisis back to the 1640s at least, but it may be more fruitful to replace a notion of 'before and after' with a sense of the constant tension within a commercialized press between the exploitation of niche markets and their erasure in favour of mass penetration, a choice of strategies often dictated by the effects of ideological crises both on reader demand and on the (often highly ideologically-charged) aims of producers.[23]

Likewise, Malcolm Cook explores the ways in which the presentation of fiction was heavily influenced by the degree of uncertainty in identifying the audience and the very 'public' and self-conscious way in which the various parties took on 'roles' in negotiating this tricky situation. Crucial here was the anonymity of the reader, which both challenged the writer or editor to establish a relationship with the reader which was simultaneously public (and hence both regulated and reproducible, not least commercially) and at the same time, at least in the fictional domain, 'private', not to say intimate, in its claims. When this relationship involved a male writer and many (if not a majority of) female readers, this process became particularly delicate. But anonymity was also, of course, both a problem and an opportunity for writers.

Lesley Sharpe's account of Hippel's text on women's rights lays stress on the liberating effect of both anonymity and irony in allowing a respectable state servant to make a radical case, but in such an allusive way as to preserve (can one suggest?) the arcana of knowledge from too broad a public. Thus in the press, as in association, secrecy was a crucial resource. Yet it was not possible to police the impact of the press, unlike association, with any assurance, since one could not impose rules of membership (though the practice of book subscription and reading clubs had similar effects, perhaps). Rather, control of the press often had to be sought indirectly, through such matters as the price of publications or the availability of the education and leisure to read their products. The politics of knowledge involved in these areas is not explored in the essays here, though one might note that, for England at least, Habermas's assumption that the reading public excluded a 'plebeian' public is now highly debatable.[24] Equally, the assumption that women were largely excluded from a reading public is increasingly doubtful, just as, in England at least, their crucial role as producers, at least of fiction, has become increasingly apparent. As Jones's essay demonstrates, backing up a point made forcefully by both Ludmilla Jordanova and Ros Ballaster at the symposia from which this collection arose, women were by no means merely the 'passive objects' of male observation and writing in this period, but often intervened in the public sphere, taking advantage where they could of those aspects of the press and its conventions that enabled them to put their case. As Goodman has shown, here and elsewhere, the salons of eighteenth-century France provide another crucial example of (some) women's ability to establish a public sphere for themselves, in competition with other public spheres in which male dominance was more assured.[25]

It has often been suggested that Habermas was guilty of gender-blindness in his account of the public sphere. Although he himself admits that he failed to explore the position of women within the model he established, such an accusation ignores the gender division which Habermas places at the core of his account. As already noted in relation to Jones's essay, Habermas himself divides the 'private sphere' into two parts, namely the world of commercial transactions and that of 'the patriarchal conjugal family'. Habermas postulates a direct relationship between the two, as regards the male head of household, since 'to the autonomy of property owners in the market corresponded a self-presentation of human beings in the family', in the form of 'a private autonomy denying its economic origins', with the three crucial elements of 'voluntariness, community of love and cultivation'. But he stressed the internal contradictions of this model, including 'the dependence of the wife and children on the male head of the family; private autonomy in the former realm was transferred into authority in the latter and made any pretended freedom of individuals illusory'.[26] It is from this contradiction that Vogel begins her incisive account of how the framers of the *Code Napoléon* rationalized their exemption of marriage relations from the logic of universal rights and contractual relationships, using, as she shows, a complex mixture of appeals to nature and to the demands of public order. Sharpe's presentation of Hippel shows him grappling with the same question, but apparently reaching a rather different conclusion, namely that it was in the interests of both nature and public order that women's talents be welcomed into the public sphere. Given the 'playful' nature of Hippel's text it is hard at times to tell whether women's greater freedom is intended to make them better mothers or rather to produce a 'structural transformation of the public sphere', since Hippel clearly hopes that the removal of false consciousness and anxiety, which male subjection of women supposedly generates in male public figures, will assist in recreating a public sphere of true enlightenment. One suspects that women feature in this bachelor's account more as a device with which to expose male failings than out of a genuine desire to liberate women. At any rate, Hippel's case does something to vindicate Vogel's rather Habermasian conclusion that the problem with the liberal project is not that it was inherently anti-female but that it failed to stick to its own logic as applied to marriage. As such her view contrasts with the rather darker perspective on liberal humanitarianism offered by Jones, who is more inclined to a Foucauldian model within which liberal ideology requires for its own operation an 'other', be it of gender, race or class, who can be subject to the paternalistic observation and control of the liberals themselves.[27] What both accounts have in common, however, is their recognition that such issues are constantly being contested and 'remade'. Given the focus of her study, Vogel is bound to regard the French Revolution as a decisive moment, generating a crisis of patriarchy out of which a new settlement had to be made. But this was hardly the first such crisis (as historians of the French Revolution might usefully remind themselves) —witness the fascinating work recently done on both the German Reformation and the English Revolution.[28]

As Vogel reminds us, during such efforts to re-produce gender roles and boundaries, a (if not the) central issue was always that of family (and in particular women) in the reproduction of the social order, both at the level of the individual family and of society as a whole. Habermas was well aware of this, and of the contradictions that this generated between the family as a place of autonomy and the family as the key player in 'the reproduction of capital' and in ensuring the training of the next generation in 'strict conformity with societally necessary requirements'.[29] As these observations suggest, 'private' life had never been a purely private matter, since it had always been taken for granted that the survival of society depended on the proper carrying out of this process. Here, once again, Habermas's chronology is distorted by his belief that public concern for the inner workings of the 'bourgeois family' was the specific product of a new phase of 'mercantile capitalism', in which, for the first time, the household became subject to state intervention, thereby generating, in turn, the intervention of the bourgeois head of household into the public sphere.[30] As no flesh is put on these interesting suggestions, it is hard to know what weight to give them, but one should certainly observe that local, if not national, governments had long been interfering in this fashion and that, certainly in the case of urban society, the nature of bourgeois politics had long been shaped by an interaction between the needs of society to regulate households and use them to reproduce good citizens, on the one hand, and the needs of each household to ensure its survival (in a danger-filled world) by taking advantage of various regulatory and welfare mechanisms that society could offer.

As I have argued elsewhere, it was within such a complex world of interdependency that we can understand the 'civilizing process', at both family and societal level, building on the insights of Norbert Elias.[31] Elias has not featured in this collection, but arguably his work has as much to offer our understanding of private and public as that of his German counterparts, particularly if we follow his general agenda rather than being too impressed by his specific working out of the process in the case of 'the court society', whose focus on Louis XIV's Versailles reinforces the profoundly misleading impression that 'civilizing' trickled down to bourgeois society from a courtly aristocracy.[32] As we have seen, aspects of Habermas's account follow the same assumption, with its privileging of French national absolutism as the model of European development leading to 1789. If instead we pay equal attention to the complex politics of city-states and representative governments across western Europe, then we can draw up a very different trajectory for the civilizing process and hence for the interplay of public and private, one which respects variety and looks for cyclical as well as linear tendencies.

Thus far this 'historical postscript' has perhaps conformed all too predictably to type, preferring to look for what Tortarolo calls 'multifarious historical phenomena', rather than the simplified ideal type of historical sociology. Having laid such emphasis, however, on continuity and variety and on the need to see eighteenth-century Europe in relation to its past, rather than its future, I wish to end with one speculation regarding a change which may, indeed, have had profound effects on the public-private relationship within the bourgeois public sphere and which does appear to gather force during the eighteenth century. In one sense it is a very practical and specific change, regarding the role of the household in the reproduction of bourgeois society, but in its ramifications it may be said to affect all the issues touched upon here and indeed the whole notion of an 'Enlightenment' project or 'modernity'.

Despite challenging Habermas's account of the role of the bourgeois family in social reproduction, I would like to suggest that he put his finger on a crucial issue in drawing attention to the tension between the cultivation of freedom and the development of social conformity within the household.[33] During the eighteenth century, one might argue, both the nature and the balance of this tension changed, although the tension remained, as it still does. At the level of bourgeois society (and perhaps above), there are signs of a re-evaluation, both of the balance within the family between the conjugal and the parental, laying greater emphasis on the former, and, within the parental relationship, towards an emphasis on freedom. The classic expression of this, though only one of many and by no means the first, is, of course, the work of Locke. These changes are related to two further changes. The first is the decline of the 'artificial family', above all that of apprentice or servant and master, as a means of reproducing bourgeois society (as opposed to its role as a means of training the lower class and obtaining labour). This in turn had profound implications for the shift from certain types of corporatism and bourgeois association, such as guilds, towards others, such as professional associations and friendly societies, as well as the sociable associations discussed here. The second is a gradual decline in anxiety about the sheer survival of the family into the next generation, or at least a decline in the importance of socio-political measures to ensure such survival. This in turn reflects the gradual improvement in the demographic chances of the bourgeois family from the early eighteenth century onwards, plus the emergence of new methods of insuring against disaster and providing 'capital' (educational and social as well as financial) both for the survivors in this generation (for example, widows) and for the next generation.

If, as suggested above, the politics of bourgeois society had long been dominated by the notion of a community of patriarchal households, headship of which both entitled and required participation in political life, this was shifting to a different conception of political possibilities, in which other priorities and rules of involvement could be imagined. This, in turn, altered attitudes towards customs and traditions, reflected, for example, in the decline in interest in 'freedoms' as historical and legal entitlements, towards 'freedom' as an abstract notion derived from 'nature' rather than nurture. Put at its crudest, it freed the bourgeois male to think more about his own interests and happiness and less about securing his and his family's future. Paradoxically, this made him less inclined to respect the past and the values of collective survival and more inclined to trust the new and and that which he could identify as the outcome of his own voluntary choice. Of course, this liberation brought its own discontents and anxieties, and it rested, in many ways, on an illusion of freedom and on the dependence of others. But out of it arose the ideology of bourgeois individualism.[34] For that reason alone, given the uses made of that particular ideology in manipulating the languages of public and private in our own age, we need critical studies of its development.

Notes

1. J. Habermas, *The Structural Transformation of the Public Sphere* (Cambridge, MA, 1989) p. 49.
2. Habermas, *Structural Transformation* pp. 46–48.
3. J. Habermas, 'Further Reflections on the Public Sphere' in C. Calhoun (ed.) *Habermas and the Public Sphere* (Cambridge, MA, 1992) pp. 425–30.
4. See, for example, J. Barry and J. Melling, 'The Problem of Culture: an Introduction' in J. Melling and J. Barry (eds) *Culture in History* (Exeter, 1992) pp. 3–27.
5. See my review of R. Chartier (ed.) *A History of Private Life* III: *Passions of the Renaissance* (Cambridge, MA, 1989) in *French History* 4 (1990) 394–96.
6. For an introduction to this material see L. Jordanova, 'The Representation of the Family in the Eighteenth Century', in J. H. Pittock and A. Wear (eds) *Interpretation and Cultural History* (Basingstoke, 1991) pp. 109–34.
7. Habermas, *Structural Transformation*, preface; Habermas, 'Further Reflections' pp. 422–23.
8. In Habermas, 'Further Reflections' pp. 423–24, the French Revolution is still privileged as the trigger for 'politicization'.
9. C. Webster, *The Great Instauration* (London, 1975) is the classic study. See also the works of Christopher Hill, distilled in his *The Intellectual Consequences of the English Revolution* (Madison, 1980). Habermas, *Structural Transformation*, p. 266 n. 62 does recognize the role of religious toleration in the growth of a 'public sphere', but, quite apart from relegating this to a footnote, he misleadingly identifies it as a product of Reformation

theology as such (as opposed to religious pluralism) and once again seeks to identify it as a manifestation of 'capitalism'.

10. Habermas, *Structural Transformation* pp. 26, 32–33, 37–39, 43, 49–50, 57–59, 62.
11. This has been a major theme of the 'Cambridge' school of the history of political thought, e.g. J.G.A. Pocock, *The Machiavellian Moment* (Princeton, 1975); Q. Skinner, *The Foundations of Modern Political Thought* 2 vols (Cambridge, 1978); R. Tuck, *Philosophy and Government 1572–1651* (Cambridge, 1993).
12. R. Koselleck, *Critique and Crisis* (Oxford, 1988). A most helpful discussion of the relationship between Koselleck and Habermas, with a splendid critique of both in light of recent scholarship, is provided by A.J. La Vopa, 'Conceiving a Public: Ideas and Society in Eighteenth-Century Europe' *Journal of Modern History* 64 (1992) pp. 79–116.
13. Habermas, *Structural Transformation* pp. 62, 64, 90.
14. Koselleck, *Critique* pp. 2, 15, 47, 58–59. England does provide a 'model' theory for the Continent in the works of Locke, composed in the face of the final phase of 'Stuart absolutism' (p. 53), but its subsequent practice is unique.
15. Koselleck, *Critique* pp. 16, 38–39.
16. See P. Langford, *A Polite and Commercial People: England 1727–1783* (Oxford, 1989); J. Brewer and R. Porter (eds) *Consumption and the World of Goods* (London, 1992); J. Barry, 'Consumers' Passions: The Middle Class in Eighteenth-Century England' *Historical Journal* 34 (1991) pp. 207–16.
17. Habermas, *Structural Transformation* pp. 37, 62.
18. Habermas, *Structural Transformation* p. 36.
19. I have explored some of these issues in 'Publicity and the Public Good: Presenting Medicine in Eighteenth-Century Bristol' in W. Bynum and R. Porter (eds) *Medical Fringe and Medical Orthodoxy 1750–1850* (Beckenham, 1987) pp. 29–39; 'Provincial Town Culture 1640–1780: Urbane or Civic?' in Pittock and Wear (eds) *Interpretation and Cultural History* pp. 198–234; 'Cultural Patronage and the Anglican Crisis: Bristol c.1689–1775' in J. Walsh, C. Haydon and S. Taylor (eds) *The Church of England c.1689–c.1833: From Toleration to Tractarianism* (Cambridge, 1993) pp. 191–208.
20. Habermas, *Structural Transformation* p. 35.
21. D. Stevenson, *The Origins of Freemasonry: Scotland's Century 1598–1710* (Cambridge, 1988); J. Barry, 'Urban Identity and the Middling Sort in Early Modern England' *Annales: E.S.C.* 18 (1993) pp. 853–84; J. Barry, 'Bourgeois Collectivism: Urban Association and the Middling Sort' in J. Barry and C. Brooks (eds) *The Middling Sort of People: Culture, Society and Politics in England 1550–1800* (Basingstoke, 1994) pp. 84–112, 242–49. La Vopa, 'Conceiving the Public,' brings together research on Continental associations, e.g. German freemasonry, that reaches similar conclusions.
22. Habermas, 'Further Reflections' pp. 426–7.
23. J. Barry, 'The Press and the Politics of Culture in Bristol, 1660–1775',

in J. Black and J. Gregory (eds) *Culture, Politics and Society in Britain 1660–1800* (Manchester, 1991) pp. 49–81.

24. J. Barry, 'Literacy and Literature in Popular Culture', in T. Harris (ed.) *Popular Culture in England c.1500–1850* (Basingstoke, 1995) pp. 69–94, 232–41.
25. For a review of this material see the section on the public sphere in the eighteenth century in *French Historical Studies* 17 (1992) no. 4 Fall Issue.
26. Habermas, *Structural Transformation* pp. 46–47.
27. For a Foucauldian analysis of humanitarianism see R. McGowen, 'Power and Humanity, or Foucault among the Historians' in C. Jones and R. Porter (eds) *Reassessing Foucault: Power, Medicine and the Body* (London, 1994) pp. 91–112.
28. Compare L. Hunt, *The Family Romance of the French Revolution* (Berkeley and Los Angeles, 1992), with, for example, L. Roper, *Oedipus and the Devil* (London, 1994), M. Ezell, *The Patriarch's Wife* (Chapel Hill, 1987), P. Mack, *Visionary Women* (London, 1993).
29. Habermas, *Structural Transformation* pp. 47–8.
30. Habermas, *Structural Transformation* pp. 19–24.
31. Barry, 'Bourgeois Collectivism'.
32. N. Elias, *The Civilizing Process* 2 vols (Oxford, 1979–82); S. Mennell, *Norbert Elias* (Oxford, 1989).
33. Habermas, *Structural Transformation*, p.48.
34. J. Barry, 'Introduction' in Barry and Brooks (eds) *The Middling Sort of People* pp. 1–27, 217–27; J. Barry, 'The Making of the Middle Classes' *Past and Present* 145 (1994) pp. 194–208.

Index